RETIRE
&
THRIVE

OTHER KIPLINGER BOOKS

Kiplinger's Practical Guide to Your Money
Kiplinger's Guide to Investing Success
But Which Mutual Funds?
Buying & Selling a Home
Making Money in Real Estate
Financing College
Retire Worry-Free
Dollars & Sense for Kids
Next Step: The Real World
Home•ology
Taming the Paper Tiger at Home
The Consumer's Guide to Experts
Know Your Legal Rights
Switching Careers

KIPLINGER'S BUSINESS-MANAGEMENT LIBRARY

Practical Tech for Your Business
Business 2010
Customer Once, Client Forever
Raising Capital
Taming the Paper Tiger at Work
Cash Rules
Hunting Heads
Parting Company
You Can't Fire Me, I'm Your Father
Fast-Track Business Growth

For tables of contents and excerpts for our books, visit: www.kiplinger.com.

For information about volume discounts, contact: Cindy Greene, Kiplinger Books, 1729 H Street, N.W., Washington, DC 20006; 202-887-6431; cgreene@kiplinger.com.

RETIRE & THRIVE

REMARKABLE PEOPLE, AGE 50-PLUS,

SHARE THEIR CREATIVE, PRODUCTIVE &

PROFITABLE RETIREMENT STRATEGIES

BY ROBERT K. OTTERBOURG

KIPLINGER BOOKS, Washington, D.C.

Published by
The Kiplinger Washington Editors, Inc.
1729 H Street, N.W.
Washington, DC 20006
www.kiplinger.com

Library of Congress Cataloging-in-Publication Data

Otterbourg, Robert K.
    Retire & Thrive: remarkable people, age 50 plus, share their creative,
productive & profitable retirement strategies / by Robert K. Otterbourg.
        p. cm.
    "Unlike the other editions...the third edition lowers the entry age...to
anyone over 50"—P. .
    Includes index.
    ISBN 0-938721-37-2 (pbk.)
    1. Retirement—United States—Planning. 2. Retirement—United
States—Case studies. 3. Retirees—United States—Attitudes—Case
Studies. I. Title: Retire and thrive. II. Title.

HQ1063.2.U6077   2003
646.7'9--dc21   2003054645

This publication is intended to provide guidance in regard to the subject matter
covered. It is sold with the understanding that the author and publisher are not herein
engaged in rendering legal, accounting, tax or other professional services. If such services
are required, professional assistance should be sought.

Third edition. Printed in the United States of America.

9 8 7 6 5 4 3 2 1

Dedication

TO MY FAMILY: Susan, Laura, Katherine, Kenneth and Sam. Thanks for putting up with my endless stories and what is often called my offbeat sense of humor. Each of you, in your own way and collectively, give me unlimited joy.

Table of Contents

Introduction

RETIREMENT, LIKE THE OL' GRAY MARE IN THE FOLK song, "ain't what it used to be." As a matter of fact, retirement today bears so little resemblance to its old self that we should probably retire the word "retire." Years ago, retirement was short and not-so-sweet. The typical retiree lived about a decade in modest circumstances, sedentary activities and declining health. Private and public pensions were not so generous, if one had them at all. Old age correlated inevitably with frailty and ill health, which is blessedly not the case today.

We're living today in an era of the 20-year retirement. What we call retirement is actually one-quarter of our lives, maybe more—and it is far from sedentary. Financial planning and improving health have made possible a full, satisfying and highly active two decades of retirement.

Recently, these trends have intersected with dramatic changes in the American workplace...downsizing of large corporations, more-frequent changing of jobs and whole careers, and a surge in entrepreneurship among people of all ages.

What this means is that more and more men and women who are age 50 plus are giving a lot of thought to their futures:

- They are retiring from one career only to launch a new one.
- They are starting businesses of their own.
- They are going back to college to learn new skills, either for fun or profit.
- They are becoming paid consultants or volunteer advisers.
- They are lending their knowledge to small businesses and nonprofits.
- They are turning hobbies into businesses.
- They are turning their businesses over to the younger generation, while staying involved via mentor or emeritus roles.

Whether officially "working" or "retired," they are leading full, satisfying lives.

In this wonderful book by Bob Otterbourg—himself a dynamic retiree—you'll meet dozens of creative, highly energetic men and women who caught their second wind. They retired and thrived, and their stories will show you how you can do it, too. Full of practical lessons you can apply to your own experience, *Retire & Thrive* provides countless ideas to make your retirement decades of living every bit as exciting as the middle years.

On behalf of all of us at the Kiplinger organization, my best wishes to you, as you begin the next stage of an exciting journey.

KNIGHT A. KIPLINGER
Editor, *The Kiplinger Letters*
Editor in Chief, *Kiplinger's Personal Finance Magazine*
Washington, D.C.

What's Next?

WHEN I RECEIVE *THE SCENE,* COLGATE University's alumni newspaper, I first turn to the class note section. I've always enjoyed reading about the professional and personal achievements of classmates. That's how it went for nearly 35 years. Then something happened. Those same dynamic classmates switched the subject of their correspondence—from career to retirement. One sold his business, packed up and moved to Florida. Another opted for early retirement and reported that he was golfing every day. Still others chatted about activities that I couldn't imagine including as part of my lifestyle. What they were doing seemed—to me—about as enjoyable as a month of Sundays. How, I wondered, do they fill the 2,000 to 2,500 hours or more annually that they once devoted to their careers? Why would anyone even want to retire? Retirement was something that I had never considered, not even when I exited the public relations field to become a writer.

With those musings, the die was cast. The result is *Retire & Thrive,* a source of ideas, reassurance and inspiration for those who want to catch a second wind in "retirement," however and whenever it comes. For some, retirement, or whatever you want to call it, comes in their early to mid fifties and for others in their sixties, but for a growing number of people, retirement in the usual sense never becomes part of their lifestyle.

Early, Late or Never

The first edition of this book was published in 1995. The initial intention was to focus on people 55- to 65-years-old, including those who became victims of corporate downsizing and its close kin, early retirement, as well as those who elected to work indefinitely and not retire.

I soon found that I was limiting my editorial horizons by excluding people in their fifties, many of whom were losing their jobs or prematurely retiring. As a result, I packaged everyone from ages 50 to 65 into what I called the 50-plus set. By using age 50 as the starting point, I deliberately set a trap for the older members of the baby-boomer generation, who would begin to turn 50 in 1996. I thought that they, too, should be asking, "What's next?"

In February, 2003, broadcaster Jane Pauley asked herself the same question and announced that she was leaving NBC after 27 years with the TV network. Her comments in *The New York Times* caught my attention: "I kept walking by bookstores and seeing titles talking about second acts of life." She said that at age 52 she still found herself wondering "what's next, or even, what is it I really want to do?...I think women think a lot about cycles. This year another cycle came around: My contract was up. It seemed an opportunity to take a life audit."

A generation ago, an out-of-work, 52-year-old executive would most likely have found an equivalent or even better new job. Early retirement in the face of layoffs and downsizing were not common occurrences. The message now, however, is loud and clear for those severed from the workplace: To survive, they need to adopt different career and lifestyle objectives. Chances are they will not be able to duplicate the job that they just lost. Furthermore, in the employment marketplace there is little discernible difference between a 52-year-old and someone who is ten years older. The future is bright for job-seekers 50-plus who are resourceful, inventive and willing to do things differently. Others have less reason to be cheery.

The declining stock market of the past several years chilled retirement and retirement prospects for millions of Americans, a topic to be discussed further in Chapter 1. Simply put, retirement income from investments and other financial instruments was reduced to the point that some prospective early retirees delayed their retirement. Even as the stock market rebounds, prospective and current retirees will still be looking for ways to offset the losses their portfolios suffered.

NEED A BETTER CRYSTAL BALL. The third edition reflects the mood of the 21st century. I'm amazed how fast the world has moved in the past few years. I should have used a better brand of tea leaves to help me forecast many of the trends noted in the first and second editions. As such, this edition recognizes both the ongoing events and the trends that presently or will soon affect the 50-plus set:

As a starter, computers and data communications have really come of age. In the mid 1990s, comparatively few consumers, other than business users, were routinely corresponding by e-mail or browsing the Web in search of information. Nowadays, electronic transmission has become nearly ritualistic. Friends and business associates exchange e-mail addresses as readily—and sometimes more readily—than a telephone number.

The statistics tell the story. When the Census Bureau began collecting data on Internet use in 1997, fewer than half of the households with computers reported having anyone who used the Internet. By 2000, more than 80% of households with computers had at least one member using the Internet at home. In recognition of this change and the way that readers most likely retrieve information, I have used Websites rather than street addresses and telephone numbers for the cited organizations.

BABY BOOMERS GROW GRAY WHISKERS. Baby boomers, once cute little kids in diapers and later young adults who vowed never to "trust anyone over 30," are already turning 50 and even nearing 60. Men and women in this "never-going-to-get-old" age group are actively considering future workplace and lifestyle alternatives. AARP noted this trend several years ago by creating two demographic editions of its magazines—*My Generation*, directed toward readers age 50 to 60, and *Modern Maturity*, to its older readers. In early 2003, AARP consolidated both magazines under one title, *AARP: The Magazine,* although it is published in three discrete editions appealing to readers in their 50s, 60s and 70s. More than a ploy to attract advertisers, this strategy shows that the retirement years affect a broad spectrum of ages—and interests.

Along with the graying of the baby boomers is a parallel phenomenon, aptly called the Sandwich Generation. As Americans live longer, the 50-year-old as well as the 65-year-old are helpmates to one or both living parents. In addition to paying college tuition and wedding expenses for their children, a typical 50-year-old might be attending to an 80-year-old mother or father—or both parents.

What Lies Ahead

The first chapter sets the stage by exploring attitudes about retirement and describing 50-plus-set trends. Chapter 2 discusses how to plan for these life events. The next three chapters concentrate on what I find are the three most vibrant nonwork activities: becoming a student, working as a volunteer and pursuing a hobby. The concluding chapters focus on the dynamics in the workplace: staying on, though very likely with a change of pace or focus; changing careers or becoming self-employed; or escaping from retirement and returning to the workplace.

The editorial guideline for *Retire & Thrive* is clear-cut. The introductory part of each chapter highlights societal and demographic information, and relevant how-to information; the balance of the chapter is given to human-interest profiles. This book isn't intended to be encyclopedic. Rather, the groups and activities cited were selected because they would have particular appeal to a diverse 50-plus-set audience. Simply put, *Retire & Thrive* is intended for anyone age 50 to 65, in or out of the workplace.

The anecdotal profiles support the theme of each chapter. They are organized so that you learn what 50-plus set people are presently doing and, just as important, the different routes they took to reach their present lifestyle. A number of the men and women portrayed are in their late 60s and 70s, but in nearly every instance they adopted their present lifestyle formula

before they reached retirement age. I've included 30 new profiles in this edition and retired a similar number that appeared
in the first and second editions. Read the profiles carefully.
They reveal why it was hardly a slam dunk for these people to
achieve a different lifestyle. Along the way, they experienced
indecision and frustration before each of them found a comfortable yet challenging fit.

You'll note that while half of the profiled folks presently reside
in North Carolina, that's a somewhat deceptive statistic because
most of them lived and worked in other parts of the nation
before they relocated to North Carolina to take a new job or
retire. Whenever I consider reaching out to more candidates for
profiles from other parts of the U.S., I hear of someone within
50 miles of my home who has a wonderful story to tell.

Do not for a moment think that this book profiles the afflu-
ent. Only a few interviewees are wealthy. Nearly all of the others, even those who have secure pensions and sound investments, are living on smaller incomes, exacerbated to some
extent by the decline in value of their investments, than when
they were in the workforce. While financial issues stand front
and center as retirement looms, dealing with them is not the primary thrust of this book. Finding ways to make the most of your
time and energy is the goal.

Nearly all of the women interviewed for this book deferred
careers for a decade or two to raise their children. Their lives and
careers typically followed this chronology: a year or so after graduating from college they married; they had children and stayed
home until the children were at least in elementary school; they
went to graduate or professional school; and then they entered
the workplace. The question many such women face is: Why
become a full or part-time retiree at age 65 when you only just
started your career at age 35 or 40?

Few newsmakers are profiled. I found no need to interview
the rich and famous when I could profile people, just like you,
who have produced real-life solutions to retirement in their
50-plus years.

A few of the people I interviewed agreed to share their stories,
but asked that I preserve their privacy by giving them pseudo-

nyms or using an abbreviated form of their names. I honored their requests.

No Formulas

The editorial placement of many of the profiles provided a particular challenge. Those profiled could have easily been featured in several different chapters since their range of interests typifies the diversity that underscores the 50-plus set.

It would be much simpler if we could fit everyone in the 50-plus set into neat little boxes, but real people defy that type of classification. Rather they are discovering and implementing different lifestyle plans. Some of the solutions might lead you to think that 50-plus-set members are dabblers. Hardly the case. A retiree might work as a part-time professional three days a week, serve as a volunteer two mornings and then spend an equal amount of time with a hobby. More often than not, the people profiled selected a lifestyle that includes a combination of interests described so wonderfully as "portfolio careers" by futurist Charles Handy (profiled in Chapter 2) in his book, *The Age of Unreason*.

Though they would deride such a description, the people in *Retire & Thrive* are, in a special sense, adventurers. The people you are about to meet, regardless of their interests, are all active and energetic. None are "couch potatoes." They have created a 50-plus lifestyle uniquely their own, with no intention to retire but the flexibility to see themselves in a new role. By doing so, they reinvented themselves. Some developed new skills, but most took existing talents and reshaped them to meet new objectives.

The only certainty for the 50-plus set is that one size doesn't fit all. Unlike many other cycles in one's life, in this one there's no grading system to indicate whether you are excelling or failing in retirement. Simply put, there are no rules on what's right and what's wrong. You can try a hobby or part-time job, and if you don't like it, you can drop it and try something new. Thus, with differing views on retirement, the people profiled in *Retire & Thrive* adhere to the sentiments that Frank Sinatra lyrically depicted in "My Way":

And more, much more than this, I did it my way.

Acknowledgments

WRITING AN ACKNOWLEDGMENT FOR A BOOK seems akin to preparing an acceptance speech to deliver at an Academy Awards ceremony. You want to thank everyone starting with your first grade teacher.

After nearly 18 years of running my own public relations firm, I decided in the late 1980s to change careers or, better yet, return to writing, my initial occupational port of entry. In 1995, Kiplinger Books published the first edition of *Retire & Thrive*, and this is the third edition. This edition is in many ways the most inclusive. Unlike the other editions, which were written primarily for folks age 60 plus, the third edition lowers the entry age so that *Retire & Thrive* also appeals to anyone over age 50.

I would like to thank just a few people who were my invaluable partners in producing this book. My literary agent since 1991, Edward Knappman, of the New England Publishing Associates, continues to provide thoughtful insight and perspective in the publishing world. I am especially grateful to the reference librarians at Durham County Public Library, who, on numerous occasions, showed me ways to reduce what might have been hours of endless research. At times, I find that researching the old-fashioned way is a pleasant break from the computer screen.

My special thanks once again go to David Harrison, director of Kiplinger Books; Pat Mertz Esswein, its managing editor; and Cindy Greene, the book division's administrator, for making the third edition of this book possible and for making our ten-year relationship professionally rewarding and personally delightful.

My wife, Susan, receives double recognition, first in the dedication and here again. As usual, she was an invaluable and much-needed sounding board.

RETIRE
&
THRIVE

What's All the Fuss About Retirement?

I **F YOU'VE BEEN COASTING ALONG CONTENTEDLY** toward midlife, AARP (www.aarp.org), formerly the American Association of Retired Persons, knows how to elevate your blood pressure: A membership invitation arrives on your 50th birthday. So much for immortality. For a $12.50 membership fee, you're entered into AARP's expanding database of 35 million members, and you have taken the first step as a participant in the great retirement game.

When we become 50 we are understandably ambivalent, if not indifferent, about retirement. Youth, we rightfully maintain, is still on our side. Retirement seems like an event in the distant future. But sooner than we anticipated, retirement is on our doorstep. It may even be accelerated by the twin effects of downsizing and early-retirement buyout plans. Retirement-related questions begin to surface, and at best, we have entered into uncharted waters.

As the many profiles in this book will make clear, it's difficult to define "retirement." We've euphemistically called retirement the "golden age" and the "leisure years." The French call it "The Third Age" or the age of living (which follows the ages of learning and working), possibly the most accurate of these descriptions. Contrary to the dictionary definition, retirement need not be a "withdrawal from one's position or occupation, or from active working life."

A TAKE ON RETIREMENT

"Retirement is a bad word in this society, particularly, as it turns out, for those who have not yet retired. There is no doubt that it represents a major turning point in life. It is also a major opportunity. Common belief is that those who retire either shrivel up on park benches or fritter away the rest of their lives playing bingo and shuffleboard in senior-citizen centers."

From *Growing Old*
by Christopher Hallowell

In fact, looking at the current environment of corporate restructuring and those affected by it, the AARP found that "those nearing retirement no longer seek it as a sharp break with the past." Rather, today's "preretired" seek continuity. Many anticipate "retiring" from their lifelong career only to continue working, either in a new job in the field they've been in or in an unrelated area.

Much depends on how you feel about your career. As much as some people enjoy their work, they might be emotionally burned out and physically exhausted after 30 to 40 years; they're ready to take a break or do something different. Countering those emotions may be a feeling of guilt, especially among "Depression-age babies" who were born in the 1930s. They were inoculated with a self-perpetuating work ethic that makes it difficult to accept retirement of any sort.

When counseling retirees, Boston gerontologist and sociology professor David Karp finds that "some feel that there are important things left unfinished in their work lives. As would be expected, people with unfinished agendas were relatively more engaged in work and least likely to look on retirement favorably."

No so with Gary Johnson, At age 53, Gary doesn't consider himself retired. "I just don't work," he says. Gary decided to call it quits in 1999 at age 50, a year after his employer, Scudder Stevens & Clark, the financial management firm, was acquired by Zurich Insurance.

Gary had held a series of jobs after graduating from Colgate University in 1971. He worked for Seafirst Bank in Seattle and Mellon Bank in Pittsburgh and earned his MBA from the University of Rochester when he was in his early 30s. After Gary joined Scudder Stevens in the late 1980s, his career had zoomed. When he left, he was a senior partner and manager of Scudder's fixed-income research.

Gary and his wife, Luana, sold their suburban Boston home and moved to a summer place they had bought years earlier in Mattaspoisett, Massachusetts, midway between Providence, Rhode Island, and Cape Cod. Their child was already grown and living in New York. Gary's goal was to get a doctorate in applied mathematics at Brown University and to join a college faculty. Two years later, he left Brown with a master's degree and taught math for one year at a charter school. "I left when I found that I wasn't comfortable teaching kids who were disinterested in learning."

Unlike the financial distress experienced during this period by some of Gary's contemporaries who had been downsized and were eagerly seeking employment, Gary's financial problems were minimized thanks to a favorable Zurich severance buyout and a personal investment portfolio that Gary had assembled during his Scudder years.

No longer pursuing an additional graduate degree or an academic career, Gary returned to public service, with which he had had experience while planting trees in Washington State in the 1970s (work that was subsequently destroyed when Mt. St. Helens erupted). "I'm now a full-time volunteer. Besides working with the Coalition for Buzzards Bay [a nonprofit organization dedicated to the restoration, protection and sustainable use of the bay and its watershed], I'm president of the

HOW DO YOU FEEL ABOUT RETIREMENT?

- Do you see retirement as a reward for a lifetime of hard work or as a punishment for growing old?

- Is it an opportunity to learn and do things you've always longed to pursue?

- Is retirement like a banishment from a way of life that you've cultivated over the years?

- Is retirement something you've determined never to do, based on someone else's experience?

- Are you looking forward to it, planning and dreaming over it?

Mattapoisett Land Trust. We already own 380 acres and our goal is to increase the acreage."

Where's the Equal Opportunity?

Of course, feelings and decisions about retirement may be complicated by a husband or wife's attitude toward it. Many husbands are ready to leave corporate America and perhaps enjoy some leisure time with their wives. Not so with their wives. Oftentimes, the women are in their fifties and sixties, but not ready to retire, having only entered the workplace in their early to mid forties, once their children were in high school or college. "They are too busy making a mark," says gerontologist David Karp. "In their fifties, many men feel an urgency to do things that their occupational lives had made difficult, whereas many women feel an urgency to do occupational things their family lives have made difficult." He notes, not surprisingly, that men and women of the same chronological age often talk very differently about their work. "Many women are 'turning on' at

WHICH ONE ARE YOU?

Lydia Brönte, in her book, *The Longevity Factor,* describes retirees as follows:

- **Homesteaders,** who stay in the same field all their lives and remain endlessly fascinated by the work they chose;

- **Transformers,** who find their dream job only after a major career shift;

- **Explorers,** who, in the pursuit of opportunity and growth, make periodic career changes throughout their lives;

- **Long growth curver and late bloomers,** who reach the highest peak later in life;

- **Retirees and returnees,** who thought they were leaving work permanently but returned to work having missed the activity and challenges.

the same age that their male counterparts are 'turning off.'" The good news for many male retirees, whatever their reason for retiring, is that their wives are providing a financial safety net. As many of the profiles in this book show, a wife's income and benefits package give her spouse flexibility in decision making that he might not otherwise have.

MEDIAN RETIREMENT AGE		
Years Including	Men	Women
1950–55	66.9	67.7
1955–60	65.8	66.2
1960–65	65.2	64.6
1965–70	64.2	64.2
1970–75	63.4	63.0
1975–80	63.0	63.2
1980–85	62.8	62.7
1985–90	62.6	62.8
1990–95[1]	62.7	62.6
1995–2000[2]	62.3	62.0
2000–2005[2]	61.7	61.2

[1]Based on 1990 actual and 1995 projected data.
[2]Based on projected data.
Source: *Monthly Labor Review*, U.S. Department of Labor

A working wife also gives her retired mate a breather in making the transition from the workplace to a new lifestyle. She avoids the homebound wife's cliché, "I married you for better or worse but not for lunch." In this changeover period, perhaps it is best that each spouse has some space. Bill Stanley (profiled in Chapter 6) works several days a week from his Ridgewood, New Jersey, home office as a career-coaching consultant. His wife, Viola, in her mid 50s and 13 years younger than Bill, is a full-time teacher who expects to teach until she's 65. Their separate day-time schedules pose few problems. Bill shops for food, and enjoys cooking and attending to household chores.

The Generation Gap

Our closest role models may not be much help in thinking about retirement. Growing up, I knew very few people who had retired. My parents and their friends were self-employed professionals or owners of small businesses who worked, as was the custom a generation ago, until they died or were physically unable to work. Since my father had virtually no retirement savings or benefits, retirement was not a part of the household vocabulary.

The formula was rather simplistic for our parents' generation. People worked longer and died earlier. In 1900, people who survived to age 65 could expect to live another 12 years,

A TAKE ON RETIREMENT

"Some men can retire with dignity and security as early as 50, others as late as 70. Within this range, the age at which a man retires from formal employment, and especially from a position of direct authority over others, should reflect his own needs, capabilities and life circumstances."

From *The Seasons of a Man's Life*
by Daniel Levinson

and 80% of men 65 or older were still working. Compare that with more recent figures (provided by the Center for Disease Control's Institute for Health Statistics): In 2000, life expectancy at age 65 increased to 17.9 years for the 35 million people over age 65 (men and women who live to age 65 can expect to live another 16 years and 19 years respectively), and nearly 18% of men and 10% of women who are age 65 or older were still working.

The Bureau of Labor Statistics (www.bls.gov) confirms that Americans are retiring earlier. In the early 1950s, the median retirement age of Americans was 67; in the early '90s, it was 62; and over the next several years it is expected to be age 61.

So we're living longer and leaving the workforce sooner. Simple arithmetic proves that most retirees need to find ways to redirect the 2,000 to 2,500 hours or more a year that were once spent at work.

A Financial Change of Fortune

A generation or two ago, a retirement package, if one existed, consisted of a testimonial gift together with a relatively small pension and equally small social security benefits. A pension was not always an inherent right. Less than 60 years ago, the average American worker, unless handicapped or ill, never considered retirement—or could afford to. The Social Security Act was passed in 1935 in response to the financial hardships caused by the Great Depression and to provide workers with the type of social benefits many Europeans had been enjoying for 50 years before.

For most Americans in the mid 1930s, retirement with an assured pension was limited to the wealthy and to a few long-term corporate and government employees. In an era when life expectancy was around 63 years, Congress set 65 as the age of eligibility to collect $30 a month in benefits. Over the next 55 years, social security coverage was broadened to include nearly all wage earners. New features were added in stages—in 1965, medicare insurance coverage and in 1974, the pegging of retirement benefits to the consumer price index. Even with these enhancements to the social security system, the average retiree in 1973 received a $166 monthly check, compared with approximately $846 in 2001. Nowadays, says AARP, 60% of workers take social security benefits beginning at age 62, the earliest age of eligibility, compared with 40% of workers in 1980 and 28% in 1970.

> ## A TAKE ON RETIREMENT
>
> "The self-employed live longer than those who work for others, and the reason most often given is that they are free to plan their own work. This independence seems to be the reason that farmers live almost as long as professional men in spite of the physical hazards of farming....The power to determine the course of one's career affects longevity more than the actual job description."
>
> From *The Good Years*
> by Caroline Bird

Not only have government-mandated benefits improved, but so has discretionary income. Marketers have discovered that the golden years for Americans between 55 and 64 are indeed bright in terms of discretionary income. While their incomes on average are slightly lower than that of the older baby boomers, these folks over 55 often have a financial advantage since their children have completed college and are self-supporting. Starting at age 65, income begins to decline.

How High Is Up?

How much money do I need to retire and live comfortably? That's the question that clouds much thinking about the otherwise fulfilling possibilities of retirement. While hardly of retirement age, Sherman McCoy in Thomas Wolfe's book, *The Bonfire of the Vanities,* pointed out that he was "going broke on a million dollars a year." Paul Terhorst, a renegade from corporate accounting, advises readers in *Cashing In on the American Dream—How to Retire at 35* on a variety of ways to live comfort-

A TAKE ON RETIREMENT

"I've seen a lot of old bulls retire, and I've watched what happens to them after they get out of harness," says Ivar Thorsen [a ranking New York City police officer, to Edward Delaney, a retired policeman]. "A few of them can handle it but not many....You'd be surprised how many drop dead a year or two after putting in their papers. Heart attack or stroke, cancer or bleeding ulcers. I don't know the medical or psychological reasons for it, but studies show it's a phenomenon that exists. When the pressure is suddenly removed, and stress vanishes, and there are no problems to solve, and drive and ambition disappear, the body just collapses....Or other things happen. They can't handle the freedom. No office to go to. No beat to pound. No shop talk. Their lives revolved around the Department and now suddenly they're out. It's like they were excommunicated."

From *The Third Deadly Sin*
by Lawrence Sanders

ably on $50 a day (in late 1980s dollars). You'll probably want to be nestled somewhere between these two extremes.

But it is critical that you develop some form of game plan, one tailored by you to meet your specific needs and interests. You should be comfortable with this plan. Above all, remember you're a newcomer to retirement and you don't know how you might feel about it in six months' time. It makes little sense to write any game plan in indelible ink. Chapter 2 gives you an opportunity to realistically assess your financial needs and resources for retirement. But in the meantime, as you're adjusting your attitude toward retirement, keep these key points in mind:

Learn how to live on a new budget. You'll discover a different pattern of expenses—a shift in wardrobe from suits to less costly casual sports clothes, less expensive midday lunches and the elimination of commuting costs, to name a few. These new guidelines may remain constant even if you return to the workplace or become a consultant depending on the new work environment you choose.

Keep debt low. Until you know your expenses, it makes little sense to pick up additional financial burdens, such as a boat or second home.

Don't use money as your sole excuse for not doing something. Instead, be creative. If you want to go on a two-week trip to Greece, you can spend $12,000 a person on a luxury tour or less than $4,200 through Elderhostel (see page 75). Being creative means looking for alternatives that complement your pocketbook.

Above all, be kind to yourself. Before you decide on a more permanent course of action, don't feel guilty if you linger over a second cup of morning coffee and the crossword puzzle. Chances are you're not down to your last dollar, so when something nice happens to you, celebrate appropriately. It's okay to be conservative, but there's no need to start squealing when you spend.

My Own Story

Unlike my father and his peers, I've already come to grips with certain aspects of retirement. Without labeling it as such, I innocently took my first step in the late 1980s in executing my version of retirement. Nearly 20 years of running my own public relations firm was enough. After a number of excellent years, I lost several accounts. Such setbacks in the past were usually only temporary. I would recharge my batteries and replace the lost business. But at 58, I was no longer as resilient or as patient. "If this is a problem at this age, what will happen when I am 65 or older?" I asked. Up to then, I had never considered retraining for another career or retiring.

The first step was to phase out of public relations. I discharged my secretary and embarked on a new career as a freelance writer. Two years later, my office lease ended, and I moved a truncated business into a spare room at home. Without much fanfare, I had created a new business lifestyle, bordering on semi-retirement.

The transition was easier than I anticipated. A few factors were in my favor: I knew what it was like to be self-employed, and I enjoyed being a writer. I was also a hobbyist as well as an officer and trustee of several not-for-profit groups. My daytime calendar was usually full. I anticipated few problems in my career and lifestyle switch.

As part of my changeover, I gave myself a 60th birthday present which I have renewed at five-year intervals: I set a goal to work as a full-time writer for the duration. In looking back over the past ten years and, more importantly, looking ahead, I'm pleased with my decision. I've blended writing, hobbies, volunteerism and family life into a rewarding lifestyle. Fortunately, my wife and I share similar lifestyle goals and views toward retirement.

Baby Boomers Come of Age

The demographers are having a field day interpreting what will happen to the baby-boomer generation. Many boomers are already in their late fifties, and they might have already retired or it may be just around the corner. For other boomers, retirement means only shifting gears, an opportunity to change careers or start a business.

Still other boomers have had retirement forced upon them. As downsizing victims, many have found it difficult to get another job that matches the one they lost. Some—especially those who walked away with generous severance packages—don't care. They want to work only part-time or find a less pressured job.

Others are deeply concerned that the stock-market decline over the early 2000s drastically reduced their net worth, and they may have had to reconsider their plans. A late 2002 AARP survey of 1,013 investors between ages 50 and 70 found that 77% of them had lost money in the stock market over the previous two years; one in four of them had lost between 25% and 50% in the value of their investments. As a result, 20% of those with declining portfolios postponed their retirement.

Kay Gresham, a vice president of Salomon Smith Barney, noted that some of her older clients who are living in retirement communities found that their personal expenses went up at least 5% a year, even as their dividend income declined. For the first time as retirees, they were spending principal. Her younger clients, however, faced a different dilemma. A number of them who are in their fifties had planned to retire in 2001 or 2002 but delayed their decision due to a plunge in the value of their portfolios. Kay said that clients whose portfolios suffered a loss of 75% found it difficult to retire from a well-paying job. Remember that the baby boomers are not yet eligible for social security or medicare benefits. Similarly, some would-be retirees cannot draw upon their pensions, and in some instances those accounts, too, were affected by the stock-market slump. Certainly many 401(k) accounts lost significant value.

Boomers can also read the longevity charts. At age 52, they expect to live another 30 or more years. They know that they represent about 45% of the workforce and they're the biggest consumer-spending age group. Unlike their parents and their older siblings, they don't intend to cease being workers and consumers once they retire.

Even for many who continue to have plenty of money in their retirement nest egg, work is an important part in their retirement planning. Boomers, says another AARP report, are not about to become an idle generation. Here's how boomers react to workplace and retirement issues: 80% expect to work at least part-time during their retirement; only 16% have no interest in any type of job. Of those interested in staying in the workforce, nearly one-third plan to work part-time primarily for the interest and enjoyment it brings, compared with 23% who would like to work part-time for the money. Slightly less than 20% are considering buying their own business.

Why are boomers so job oriented? The AARP says their generation needs more money than their parents' generation to live comfortably and they are more self-indulgent. It adds up to this: A retirement income based on pension, social security and personal investments will not pay the bills for consumer-oriented boomers.

Workplace Realities

Not everyone gets to pick the date when they'll retire, as Robert McCord discovered. He'll never forget the day the *Arkansas Gazette,* the oldest daily newspaper west of the Mississippi, was sold to the *Democrat,* its Little Rock rival. With its sale, Bob lost his job and could have ended his journalism career. Since the mid-1950s, Bob had held nearly every editorial position on the *Gazette* and *Democrat.* When Gannett, the *Gazette's* owner, sold the paper, Bob's career nearly ended at age 62.

Many of the other older *Gazette* reporters and editors retired

ARE YOU IN FOR A SURPRISE?

It's dangerous to assume that you can retire according to your own schedule. Your employer may have other ideas. If you're telling yourself any of the following, you may have become a pampered corporate chicken, one who may suffer the ax without a clue:

- I'm 55 and expect to retire from my job at age 65.

- We've never downsized before, or we've already had staff reductions. Why do I need an updated résumé?

- They wouldn't touch me after being here 30 years.

- I always do well in my annual job review.

You're ready for anything if you can say the following:

- I play "what if" games.

- I have a game plan tucked away in my drawer just in case.

- I'm going to school at night to upgrade my skills.

- I'm continually updating my computer skills and résumé.

- Job fairs and business shows keep me alert to new trends.

- I have a special emergency fund to cover a job loss.

before the sale because the *Democrat* was not interested in hiring the *Gazette's* senior and better-paid staff members. Bob was fortunate. His financial stresses were few. His expenses were fixed. The mortgage was paid, and the three McCord children were self-supporting. His wife, Muriel, did not work. What Bob really needed was a professional challenge.

Among the local media, Bob was well known and regarded, so it was not surprising when he got a call from one of the local television stations asking him to write and broadcast three editorials a week. Next, the *Arkansas Times* asked him to write a weekly political column. "I don't go downtown to work anymore," says Bob, "but I'm better off than a lot of other guys who lost their jobs and careers when the *Gazette* folded."

Will You Be Cut?

The result of the continuing round of corporate purges is a labor force of more than 20 million Americans between ages 50 and 65 who face the distinct possibility of working fewer hours, being laid off or pushed into some form of early retirement, and most likely never finding as good a job as the one they just lost.

In its 2001 survey, the American Management Association (www.amanet.org) said that nearly 60% of the major U.S. companies reported layoffs, the most reported since the survey began 15 years earlier. Production cutbacks targeted hourly wage workers, while staffing changes focused on supervisory and middle management.

Because early-retirement buyout packages proved to be more popular than their corporate designers had imagined, often stripping companies of too many high achievers, companies that once offered these packages have scaled them back or eliminated them. There is a sound reason why buyout packages are so popular, as Marilyn Mellis Longman (profiled in Chapter 2) and Jay Feldman (who you'll read about in Chapter 3), will attest: Managers anticipate what will happen to employees who remain with the company and choose to escape the corporate fallout of downsizing. Those who remain with the company gamble on doing equally well on a subsequent round of buyouts. Too often, they discover their strategy does not pay off.

After You're Out

The employment picture for the 50-plus set used to be a bleak one. Most unemployed workers over age 50 in nearly all job categories could not expect to find a new job commensurate with their abilities. And the older the workers got, the gloomier the employment opportunities became. When they did find work, chances were they'd be working for less money than in their previous job.

Companies driven by the need to cut costs tended to exhibit a negative attitude toward older workers, and large companies—

TIPS FOR DOWNSIZING

New York outplacement consultant Anita Lands provides these tips which are particularly applicable to those in their fifties who may be downsized:

- **Try the raise the hand approach:** "Take me and give me a package." This way you feel that you're master of your own fate. It avoids the feeling that you've been pinkslipped.

- **Some people feel liberated when they're downsized.** Get a good severance package and then get out.

- **Gray—as in gray hair—**is no longer as good as it was a few years ago; EEOC rulings aside, corporate America prefers younger personnel when they can get it.

- **Keep active.** Instead of sitting at home, become a volunteer. You might find some job possibilities with a nonprofit. There's less money but corporate skills are often transferable.

- **Uncertain times call for proactive career planning.** Do some defensive driving to prepare for the future. Take a certificate to provide new job skills before being downsized.

those with 1,000 or more employees—were often the most negative. This strategy might have made corporate sense, but it threatened workers, particularly those with a desire to work again.

How times have changed. As America ages, businesses are discovering they will continue to need older workers. Writing in the Conference Board's *Across the Board* magazine, Harvard psychologist Douglas Powell reported that companies will find fewer managers and professionals in the 24-to-44 age group to replace retiring workers. The alternative is to encourage the 50-plus set to defer retirement. Powell suggests that companies conduct career-strategy workshops for employees, starting in their early fifties, to help them decide if they want to stay on full-time, continue working an alternative schedule or retire. In short, he says companies need to retain a portion of the aging boomers in the organization.

In tracking workplace trends, the Conference Board (www .conference-board.org) also notes that while companies may need and want the services of experienced workers, "many employers still appear more interested in getting people of retirement age off their books and rehiring them as contingent workers." Even at the managerial and professional level, the trend is to shift the workload to independent consultants or temporaries because different work rules apply and management no longer has to offer health care, retirement and other benefit programs.

Setting the Work Rules

If you survive cutbacks and ignore the inducements of early-retirement payouts, you can, in theory, work indefinitely. The Federal Age Discrimination in Employment Act of 1967 made it illegal to discharge or fail to promote a worker between ages 40 and 65 due to age. Ten years later, the age was raised to 70, and in 1987 the age ceiling was eliminated.

Although corporate officers and partners in professional service firms usually sign employment contracts that specify their date of retirement, even here there are some admonitions. Federal regulations stipulate that employment may be terminated at age 65 only if the executive has been in a high policy-making position considered critical to the mission of the organization for the past two years and has earned a pension that will pay at least $44,000 a year. The act also addresses the issue of age discrimination as it relates to benefits: If it's more expensive for an employer to provide benefits for older employees, it may reduce the level of benefits, but it can't charge older employees more for them.

Some workers in hazardous jobs are governed by mandatory retirement. The Federal Aviation Administration (www.faa.gov) requires that pilots on the larger regional and all national airlines retire at age 60. The Age Discrimination Employment Act permits cities to retire police and firefighters at age 55. But even when retirement was voluntary, most police and firefighters retired in their fifties after 20 to 30 years of service, frequently due to job burnout or work-related health problems.

The Equal Employment Opportunity Commission (www.eeoc.gov), the custodian of the 1967 Act, monitors workplace conditions, including those that pressure employees to accept retirement as a way to reduce the workforce. In 2002, the EEOC received nearly 20,000 age discrimination filings, a jump of 14% from three years earlier. Baby boomers, age 40 to 59, made approximately two-thirds of those complaints, while the balance were made by people age 60 and older. As the economy soured, companies eliminated higher-paid jobs, often held by older workers.

The Social Security Penalty

Recipients of social security who are age 62 through full retirement age (age 65 and 2 months) and elect to work need to be aware of the penalties on excess work-related income. In 2003, for example, the government deducted $1 of benefits for each $2 received in salary or commissions (not including investment income) that exceeded $11,520. Thanks to the Senior Citizen's Freedom Act of 2000 the situation has become more favorable for people once they reach full-retirement age. Their social security benefits are no longer reduced by work-related income.

Collecting social security while continuing to work is still an issue that fuels passions, particularly when you're a double, and in some instances, a triple dipper who collects salary, pension and social security. The purists argue that if you work, you should not collect social security. But multiple pensioners have their supporters. "I paid into the system all these years, why not collect?" is a typical response from blue-collar workers as well as corporate executives.

Jackie Wooten, 55 (profiled in Chapter 8), is too young to collect social security, but is nonetheless collecting a pension as a retired school teacher. Within six months of her retirement, Jackie was back in the classroom, receiving both a state pension, based on 35 years' service, and a full-time teacher's salary.

Even for people who are affected by it, the penalty on earned income isn't as onerous as most people think. See the discussion beginning on page 267, which examines this issue in more detail.

What's Happening in the Professions?

Even here, the term "retirement" is difficult to define, and in some cases, expectations are changing. In accounting, architecture, law and medicine, for example, the practitioner who satisfies state licensing requirements and meets other professional obligations, such as continuing education, is still considered a member of the profession regardless of age and hours spent in active practice. However, there are practical limits:

When I had an annual medical examination a while back, I asked my doctor what retirement rules applied to physicians. "None whatsoever," said Dr. Bruce Tapper. Normally the type of medical specialty dictates to some extent when a physician retires, as do the amount and nature of physical activity required. As Bruce asked, "Would you use a 74-year-old doctor for complex surgery?"

The median retirement age for all but a few medical specialists is 65. Emergency-room doctors retire from that demanding environment somewhat earlier, while psychiatrists often work well into their seventies. Psychiatrists might even enjoy age as a possible ally. Somewhat like older judges, artists and musicians, their wisdom seems to grow with age in the public's eye, often allowing them to take on the persona of sage.

From a practical standpoint, partnership agreements often help winnow out older partners. Less productive partners are forced to leave firms whose partners are required to work a specific number of hours a year or bring in a sufficient volume of new business consistent with the terms of their partnership agreements. The paternalistic, "clubby" relationships, once the hallmark of many midsize to large partnerships, have nearly vanished, along with laissez-faire arrangements that once permitted older partners to work indefinitely, often on a reduced basis. Smaller firms have fewer rules and, of course, solo practitioners can operate indefinitely.

Thomas Evans, who until his recent retirement was a New York corporate attorney, notes that a lawyer's professional career life cycle has changed at most firms. "Until recently, the law-firm associate was young, underpaid and overworked. It

SUGGESTED READING

The Age of Unreason, by Charles Handy (Harvard Business School Press, 1998). A futurist speaks his mind on how we'll be working in the future.

Aging Well: Surprising Guideposts to a Happier Life From the Landmark Harvard Study of Adult Development, by George Vaillant (Little Brown & Co., 2003). A Harvard Medical School professor shows how we can change our lifestyle and live more fulfillingly.

Don't Retire, Rewire: 5 Steps to Fulfilling Work that Fuels Your Passion, Suits Your Personality, or Fills Your Pocket, by Jeri Sedlar, Rick Miners and Howard Fillit (Alpha Books, 2002). This is more than a feel-good book. Provides questions and tools for creating a framework for life in retirement.

The Fountain of Age, by Betty Friedan (Touchstone Books, 1994). Lively reading about retirees.

Gray Dawn, by Peter Peterson (Times Books, 2000). Discusses the aging of the population in the developed nations and the social and economic trends that will result.

The Longevity Factor, by Lydia Brönte (HarperCollins, 1993). How some well-known Americans view retirement.

A Map to the End of Time: Wayfarings With Friends and Philosophers, by Ronald Manheimer (W.W. Norton, 1999). Written by the director of the North Carolina Center for Creative Retirement. Stories from Manheimer's experience of teaching older students.

Rewired, Rehired or Retired? A Global Guide for the Experienced Worker, by Robert Critchley (Jossey-Bass, 2002). What direction are you taking in your career? This book delves into these issues.

was a form of apprenticeship. The next step was promotion to a junior partner. The pay was better, yet the partner was still required to work long hours. Eventually a lawyer age 50-plus moved to senior partner status. Lifestyle changed once again. The older lawyer worked fewer hours but was very well paid. It was a rite of passage to pay one's dues for 20 to 25 years and then reap the rewards in later life." But the partner's life tenure in all but a few midsize to large firms has virtually disappeared, and bloodletting has become more widespread. At one of Chicago's larger law firms, 20 of its 180 partners were dismissed on the same day, a situation that was explained to the *Wall Street Journal* this way by the head partner: "In today's economy, everybody has to pull his or her own weight. Everybody has to make a sustained contribution."

The news is better for the nation's 313,000 tenured college and university professors. Beginning in 1994, the federal government eliminated the mandatory retirement age of 70 for college faculty members. More professors are delaying their retirement, reports the Teachers Insurance and Annuity Association/College Retirement Equities Fund (www. tiaa/cref.org), the nation's largest provider of pensions to educators. In 1987, the proportion under age 70 was 89%, and the proportion age 70 or older was 11%. Ten years later, in 1997, 84% of TIAA-CREF participants receiving annuity income that year were under age 70 and 16% were age 70 or older.

While TIAF-CREF has not updated those figures in recent years, *The New York Times* noted in a 2002 article that "the great majority of faculty members are still retiring by their mid 60s...older faculty members are increasingly being offered retirement incentives." Colleges and universities, the Chronicle of High Education (www.chronicle.com) reports, are trying various incentives, such as financial bonuses or the opportunity to shift to part-time teaching, to encourage older faculty to retire. This approach to retirement must be working. A study by Linda Ghent of Eastern Illinois University and Steven Allen and Robert Clark of North Carolina State University, found that 35% of universities offered phased retirement to faculty members, while only 5% to 10% of employers in industry offer it.

The Corporate Lions

The attitudes of senior corporate executives toward retirement have attracted a number of observers, including author Jeffrey Sonnenfeld, now a Yale University School of Management administrator. Sonnenfeld was smitten with the topic when he was teaching at the Harvard Business School in the 1980s. He tracked how 50 CEOs, all running billion-dollar companies, were able to handle the transfer of power and their departure from active corporate life.

POINTS TO REMEMBER

- **So-called retirement age** comes faster than anyone thinks it will—and faster yet for those who are ousted by downsizing or offered early retirement.

- **There's no one definition** of retirement. How you view it is strictly a personal thing.

- **Longer life expectancy** means more years to spend in retirement.

- **Your role models** may not provide much help in preparing for retirement.

- **Fifty-plus-set managers** will find it increasingly difficult though not impossible to find another good job.

- **Women** view retirement differently than men.

- **The age of retirement** differs among professions and vocations.

- **CEOs**—believe it or not—have retirement problems much like your own.

In his book, *The Hero's Farewell* (Oxford University Press), Sonnenfeld categorizes how CEOs retire—if at all. He divides executives and their attitudes toward retirement into four groups:

- **The monarchs** leave involuntarily or die, in the best tradition of a Hollywood saga, with their boots on.
- **The generals** also leave involuntarily, but during their retirement years they plot a return. The General enjoys playing the role of the returning savior, and hopes to remain around long enough to take the firm and himself toward even greater glory.
- **The ambassadors,** by contrast, quit gracefully and frequently serve as post-retirement mentors. They often remain on the company's board of directors, do not try to sabotage their successor, and provide continuity and counsel.
- **The governors,** who serve a limited term, depart for other

interests and maintain very little ongoing ties with their company once they leave.

"When the time comes to step aside for newer and almost always younger leaders, many high corporate officers are beset with fears....Leaving office means a loss of heroic stature, a plunge into the abyss of insignificance, a kind of mortality," says Sonnenfeld.

Senior executives innately resist stepping down. "Violinists in retirement," says Sonnenfeld, "can still offer solo performances or play with small ensembles. A conductor, however, needs the full orchestra to be employed, and thus a conductor's skills are not usually portable in retirement. The lack of portability of their skills makes retirement threatening to chief executives....the transition for leaders means finding new, involving and challenging tasks."

Don't dismiss the problems facing CEOs as totally different from your own. While on the surface they may appear dissimilar, most 50-plus managers and professionals view stepping down much the same way as Sonnenfeld's monarchs, generals, ambassadors and governors.

ONE OF THE LIONS

Al Kronick
DEPARTMENT STORE CEO TURNED CONSULTANT

As spectacular as the corporate career of Albert Kronick had been, the announcement of his retirement was totally unexpected. Al retired voluntarily when he turned 50. He was chairman and CEO of Abraham & Straus, then the leading retail group within the Federated Department Store chain. Other than the several years that he spent as president of another Federated store in Dallas, Al's entire career since graduating from Harvard Business School had been spent at A&S. The Lazarus family, which then controlled Federated, was known for its strong leadership, and Al was one of its highest achievers. Al left at an age when most executives are just hitting full stride.

> **"The secret of Al's success? Learn when it's over, and don't look back and second-guess."**

"When I resigned from A&S, people wondered whether I was crazy or was actually fired. Considering these questions, I let them believe in the latter. They could not understand how I could step down at the height of my career while I was in excellent health and had a bright future.

"I had no plans to retire but I decided I would like to leave A&S on my terms while I was still a top performer. I liked my work and I enjoyed running one of New York's largest stores." There were other factors in Al's favor. He had saved enough money over the years, his two children were completing college and he had an excellent financial package, including stock in Federated and a vested pension plan. "I also felt that if I earned only another $30,000 a year, Joan (my wife) and I could live very well.

"I was also fortunate in other ways. As CEOs go, my ego was rather small. I had spent 25 years in retailing, but my life was never tied to the job. Friends were in other business fields or were professionals."

Though he had discussed his plans with Joan, Al had not developed a detailed, step-by-step plan for his retirement. "At first I thought I'd like to use my business skills in the nonprofit world, perhaps as a provost of a university. When I looked into these opportunities, I found that the lifestyle was actually very much like the business world that I had just left."

Throughout his career, Al had a reputation as a highly effective corporate manager working in a high-pressure field for a demanding employer. That combination attracted interest from a number of prospective employers. "I was offered other retail jobs but turned them down. The opportunity to continue working came when several companies asked me to be a paid consultant."

Now more than two decades later, Al has reduced the pace of his consulting assignments and concentrates his duties as a director of three companies and as the volunteer treasurer of the Brooklyn Botanic Gardens.

As we've seen throughout this chapter, circumstances have changed since Al Kronick left Federated and chose consulting as his retirement-career alternative. But one thing has remained constant, for Al and for anyone considering retirement: "The secret of Al's success," Joan says, "is to learn when it's over, and not look back and start to second-guess."

Planning for Retirement

MANY OF US SPEND MORE TIME PLANNING OUR next vacation than we do formulating a retirement strategy. That's no great surprise. You've been busy living your life. Who has the time to schedule every nuance of life far into the future? Then one day you get the wake-up call, maybe an early-retirement buyout offer or an invitation to attend a retirement-planning session. You're confronted with retirement head-on, especially the questions: What will I do next? How can I afford to do it?

Nearly two-thirds of preretirees, according to a Merrill Lynch survey, feel that they, rather than their employers or the government, have the prime responsibility for producing their retirement income. Still, other than emphasizing the need for a sound level of savings, some career counselors warn about the potential for retirement-planning overkill. "Unless the person has retired or is on the verge of doing so," notes Chicago-based outplacement consultants Challenger, Gray & Christmas (www.challengergray.com), "retirement-oriented considerations will necessarily prove theoretical. It takes an extremely well-organized person to really plan a retirement that is still in the future."

Don't take it for granted that your employer will provide

retirement planning. Only a handful of larger companies offer a comprehensive retirement-planning program, and then only to their high-echelon employees. What seems like disinterest in corporate-sponsored retirement planning parallels these other trends.

- **Companies are now providing fewer support services to their terminating employees,** according to a late 1990s survey of corporate severance practices by Coopers & Lybrand (now PricewaterhouseCoopers). These services, says the auditing firm, are being axed as companies look for ways to cut the costs of decreasing their workforce. When offered, outplacement services are more often provided to executives than nonexecutives.
- **Some companies are purposely limiting the scope of their financial planning workshops,** to some extent out of fear of liability from employees if investment advice turns sour.
- **The Conference Board noted a decline in corporate paternalism,** including a shift toward making employees more responsible for financial self-management.

You will have to depend on yourself to solve the twin dilemmas—or opportunities—of managing time and your money in retirement.

Almost everyone has been feeling the effects of these corporate cutbacks. Until its reorganization in the 1990s, IBM offered a retirement-education assistance program to all of its employees. This popular benefit program, which was eliminated to cut corporate expenses, reimbursed employees up to $2,500 for coursework they took in nearly any subject, ranging from computer training to golf lessons.

Simply put, you need to explore all avenues for retirement planning that are available through your employer, recognizing that as corporate cutbacks continue, these benefits will likely be reduced in many companies. That means you will have to depend on yourself to solve the twin dilemmas—or opportunities—of managing time and your money in retirement.

This chapter will help you change mental gears and show how to take charge of your upcoming retirement life.

Going Plural: A Model for Your Future?

Call it what you may, many in the 50-plus set believe that a portfolio, or patchwork, work-and-lifestyle formula represents smorgasbord living at its best. British consultant and author Charles Handy champions this cause in his book, *The Age of Unreason,* by showing how to combine various work and non-work interests into "portfolio" careers. (See his profile later in this chapter.)

It is only natural that professionals and the self-employed put into play all types of flexible work and lifestyle game plans in preparation for living in retirement. They have the option to reduce their work schedule yet stay put in the workplace. Corporate managers, by contrast, are guided by more rigid employment practices in the workplace. But once they leave their jobs they are free to create new lifestyles and structure different career patterns.

Going plural aptly describes the lifestyle approach taken by New York City's ex-mayor Edward Koch. "I never thought I would have a third career. To be honest, I never counted on a second, but there it was," he wrote in *Citizen Koch.* "And now, here I am, nearly three years into my new life as an attorney, radio talk-show host, newspaper columnist, television news commentator, syndicated movie reviewer, public speaker, university lecturer, commercial spokesperson and author (of mystery books). That's nine jobs by my count, which suits an old workaholic like me just fine." Though he did not reveal his income, he said it surpassed his former pay as mayor and member of Congress.

Ron Rich launched his version of a patchwork career when he lost his job as an elementary school teacher and principal. Ron decided to pursue a career in children's literature by starting a newsletter for librarians, teachers and parents. For the second leg in his program, he created "Let's Read a Book," in which he visits elementary schools and acts out his favorite books for children. He was then hired as a salesperson at a local bookstore. After six months, Ron was promoted to children's book specialist. Though not by choice, Ron traded in his old career for a work portfolio with three paid assignments.

Whatever route you take to get there, you can be sure that

your new lifestyle will resemble the oft-used pie chart. How you apportion the different pieces of the pie is your choice.

Time to Say Goodbye to Computer Illiteracy

"**N**ot one of us has a PC in our home or in our office," said J. Richard Munro, a former co-chairman of Time Warner Inc., describing himself and his fellow directors when he resigned from IBM's 18-member board of directors in the early '90s. Munro's revelation of computer illiteracy is embarrassing enough considering IBM's product line, but unfortunately his personal plight applies to many other senior-level executives who might very well need computer skills to survive in their post-retirement lifestyle. Put Dick's situation aside because he has the resources to obtain administrative help, but what about you? Knowing how to operate a desktop computer is no longer an optional skill.

While computer use has become almost ubiquitous in the years since Munro retired, there are still some holdouts like one retired college professor I know who has a boxed computer sitting in his office. He prefers to write a six-page letter by hand.

Or take Tom R., a soon-to-be retired corporate executive who plans to become a self-employed financial consultant. Despite his financial expertise, Tom is handicapped because he is computer illiterate. But Tom appears unconcerned. His homemade solution is to have a former secretary, also retired, process his handwritten notes into reports and letters. With this alternative, he sees no reason to learn how to operate a computer. In principle, that may be true. But practically speaking, he'll have less flexibility in how he gets his work done, and his approach will increase his lag time in responding to clients' requests for reports and impair his ability to handle assignments. He'll miss out on software tools that would permit him to work more efficiently and to better serve his clients. Simply put, the computer-illiterate manager stands little chance of getting a new full- or part-time job. Bottom line, Tom runs the risk of looking like a dinosaur.

Be smart, and avoid following in Tom's footsteps. Like it or

THE SENIORNET CONNECTION

Does SeniorNet (www.seniornet.org) operate within your community? It could be the perfect place to learn computing. Like other adult education programs, SeniorNet caters to retirees who want to learn in a classroom with their peers. Its forte is teaching computer skills exclusively to older adults who have never used a computer and feel uncomfortable at a keyboard—and who would feel even more uncomfortable learning how to use a computer in a classroom filled with younger students.

SeniorNet has grown to more than 220 centers throughout the U.S., the District of Columbia and several other countries, with a membership, age 55 plus, exceeding 39,000. Since its founding, SeniorNet has trained nearly 110,000 retirees. Costs vary by location. Besides SeniorNet's $40 annual membership fee, the Chapel Hill Center charges a $25 course fee and usually provides 16 hours of classroom instruction, four hours a week for four weeks, with no more than nine students in a class. By the time they finish the introductory course, students know the basics: how to boot-up a computer, do basic word processing, use e-mail and access Websites.

Once they've learned the fundamentals, students can sign up for courses in genealogy, graphics, Webpage design and *Quicken* financial software. SeniorNet also sponsors online discussion groups in different areas, including cooking and recipes, gardening, home and auto repair, and current events.

not, chances are you'll be required to be proficient in basic computer skills in most postretirement careers. Computer know-how is the "open sesame" to reentering the job market, starting a business, changing careers or becoming a consultant.

Instead, take a lesson from former President George Bush. While in the White House, he learned to use a computer to write memos and personal correspondence. As a starter, at least learn the fundamentals of word processing. It's best to start your lessons before leaving the active workplace, where you can more easily learn programs within the context of your daily work and call on those in the know to help out in a pinch. You might even ask a co-worker or one of your company's programmers or systems managers to teach you the ABCs. As a last resort, chances are one of

SENIORNET USERS

A SeniorNet survey on Internet use revealed that 91% of its members, who range in age from 50 to over 85, own a computer, and another 6% have access to one at work, a friend's house or the library. Approximately 92% spend from five to 20 or more hours on the Internet each week. Staying in touch with friends and relatives and keeping up with current events are the most popular Internet interests, followed by researching or checking investments and playing games. More than 85% of SeniorNet members have been using the Internet for at least two years.

your children—nowadays even a seven-year-old grandchild—can teach the fundamentals. As with any new skill, becoming proficient takes practice. After taking a few lessons, just turn on the computer and go for it.

If you can't get help within your company or from your own family members, there are nearly unlimited opportunities available within your community. Start the search at your local community college, where you will find low-cost courses in word processing, spreadsheet analysis and database management. If you feel uncomfortable in a group setting, don't give up. Ask for a referral to someone who can work with you one-to-one. Three to four lessons should have you on your way.

Move or Stay Put?

When it comes to retirement migration, your guess is as good as mine on the number of people who retire and relocate. Sociologist Charles Longino of Wake Forest University finds that approximately 4.5% of the retirement-age population relocates out-of-state each year and about the same number move within their home state.

But there's more to relocation than statistical analysis. Even though most retirees might never buy a retirement home, chances are they'll shop the marketplace for a city or town that complements the lifestyle they seek.

Starting at age 50 and continuing for the next ten to 15 years, hordes of curious Americans are on the road searching for potential places to move. They tour the Sun Belt states, look at communities and homes, examine the lifestyle, and return home. Some buy and others decide to stay put.

Why Move?

Family, friends and nostalgic haunts glue them to home base. Yet home base need not be a four-bedroom home on a one-acre lot. The alternatives are plentiful. Some stay put in the same home town but buy or rent a smaller home or apartment. Others hedge their bets by remodeling an existing home. And there are those folks who maintain both a winter and a summer home, ranging from a plush apartment on New York's Park Avenue and a home in Nantucket to retirees with a modest home and a recreational vehicle or a small condo in Florida.

The change in the tax law is a boon for retirees who want to buy a home more suitable to retirement, and at the same time augment their nest egg and their monthly cash flow. Gone is the one-time $125,000 capital-gains exclusion on the sale of a home. The 1997 Taxpayer Relief Act increased the ante for homesellers regardless of age to $250,000 for a single taxpayer, and $500,000 for a couple filing jointly. The new rules offer a form of financial downsizing that is especially attractive to the 50-plus set. What better incentive than to sell a home, replace it with a less expensive apartment or home, and pocket the balance?

Book profilees Tom Sawyer, Iris Rose Ruffing, Art Lebo, Armando (Mickey) Henriquez, Tom Young, Marilyn Longman, Rita Spina, Zen Palkoski and Herbert Halbrecht moved to North Carolina for different reasons. Too young to retire at age 58, Tom, an ophthalmologist, came from Milwaukee to join a Pinehurst-based practice. Iris Rose retired as a Girl Scout director in Chicago. A native of North Carolina, she returned home. Art was in search of an area that offered good sports, educational and lifestyle features. Mickey took a different route. His son was on the Duke University faculty when Mickey relocated from the metropolitan New York area to Durham. Mickey wanted no part of a retirement community. Instead, he built a house in Durham surrounded by neighbors of all ages. Tom Young settled in Raleigh to be near one of his four daughters, while Marilyn Longman and her husband were both early retirees who moved from Chicago in search of a better climate. Rita Spina was looking for a change from her fast-paced, New York professional lifestyle, and Zen Palkoski wanted to enjoy the region's outdoors.

Herb Halbrecht moved from suburban New York to Durham. To gain the full flavor of his relocation, see what Herb has to say about his priorities: "We wanted to live on or adjacent to a golf course. Gayla [his wife] is obsessive about golf and after 30-years-plus of being married to me, it was payback time. I wanted to be close to a major university to provide access to intellectual ferment. And, as one reaches retirement age, close proximity to world-class medical facilities becomes increasingly relevant. I also wanted to be near inner-city schools so I could volunteer as a tutor." And finally, like other retirees who move south, Herb poses this question: "Who needs ice storms and blizzards? Then again, who needs the summer humidity? But that's bearable and avoidable. The airport is convenient and so are highways to cooler summer weather in the north."

Too often retirees rent a home or apartment on a part-time basis, often seasonally, to see if they like the community or region. In theory, this practice makes sense, but seasonal relocation hardly represents an accurate gauge of what life there is like year-round. To get that realistic point of view, the retiree must sever ties "back home" and make their rented or seasonal home their only home.

What About a Retirement Community?

Retirees face a dilemma when they ponder whether to move or stay put. If they do decide to relocate, what type of community will they select after they have lived in the same home for 30 or more years? Do they favor a balanced urban or suburban residential area with neighbors of all ages, or would they prefer to move to Sun City, Arizona, by far the nation's largest retirement community with its 46,000 older residents?

Del Webb (www.delwebb.com), developer of a number of large-scale retirement communities, surveyed baby boomers who were about to turn 50. Approximately 50% said that they planned to move to another state when they retired. Another 21% said they intended to move to another city in the same state, 18% expected to relocate in the same community where they'd been living, and the remaining 10% were undecided on where they'd live. (Another Del Webb survey showed that nearly half of retired boomers plan to return to work.) Given this variety of preferences, Del Webb, which already has built about 80,000 homes in 10 Sun Belt communities, is hedging its bets. It built a retirement community 20 miles northeast of Sacramento for the 55-plus set who prefer northern California to the Sun Belt. The average home there costs about $210,000.

About 70% of the homeowners previously lived in the San Francisco Bay area, and somewhere between 30% to 40% of the residents work full- or part-time. The same rationale prompted Del Webb to break ground for a community of nearly 5,000 homes a mere 45 miles from downtown Chicago.

To get an accurate gauge of what life in a new location is like year-round, the retiree must sever ties "back home" and make their rented or seasonal home their only home.

Kinds of Places

Before looking at home sites, it's best to do your homework. Start off by knowing the difference between retirement communities. A leisure-oriented retirement community such as Sun City or Leisure World appeals to retirees who relocate when they first retire, in their mid fifties and sixties. A country-club lifestyle is the theme. As retirees age, many move again to a managed-care facility. Here they live independently, yet take their meals in a central dining room. The facility also provides amenities such as shuttle bus service to shopping malls and evening concerts, and on-site health care professionals.

If you're considering a move, the site selection possibilities should include:

- **A large city.** Surprisingly, a number of suburbanites relocate to the city to be nearer the array of activities that a large city has to offer.
- **A college community.** There's lots to do in terms of sports, adult education and cultural activities. It's even better when you're an alumnus.
- **A summer community.** Retirees are taking summer cottages and remodeling them for year-round rather than seasonal usage. That might sound like a great idea but it's best to visit

these towns in the off season. The weather could be dismal and the community desolate. In short, it might be a wonderful summer lifestyle but an impractical one for 12 months.

- **Returning home.** When both husband and wife are from the same area, returning home is often rewarding even if the couple hasn't lived there for many years. This is particularly delightful when there are fond memories of hometown USA.
- **Moving outside the U.S.** Mexico and Costa Rica appeal to some retirees. Guadalajara, Mexico, is home to 30,000 Americans and Canadians. The living is definitely cheaper but be aware that medicare does not apply cross the border.
- **Take to the road in a recreational vehicle.** According to a University of Michigan study, nearly half of the RVs on the road are owned by people over age 55. The question is, do you want to live in an RV year-round or use it seasonally? Americans, reports the Recreational Vehicle Industry Association (www.rvia.org), own about 9 million vehicles with RV ownership increasing by 100,000 vehicles a year. Many RV folks are snowbirds. They live in the north from April to October. Come fall, they hop into their RV and travel south.
- **Rural America.** Lots of Americans are trying to escape from congested metro centers for the quieter, and usually less expensive, lifestyle of a smaller community. Be cautious about this type of move unless you know and understand how life in a small town works. Be prepared to find that there may be few, if any, coffee bars, ethnic restaurants or other amenities associated with suburbia and large cities.
- **An air park.** For the pilots in the pack, the U.S. has nearly 450 communities, referred to as air parks, where homes are built along a runway. Not surprisingly air parks are most popular in Sun Belt states like Florida, Texas, Georgia and California.

Factors to Consider

Now it's time to examine the merchandise. Take these factors into consideration as you consider possible places to relocate to:

- **Health care services.** What about the local hospital and the medical community in general? This should be a prime consideration for anyone over age 60. Rural America might be scenic, but traveling 150 miles once a week to see a medical specialist makes little sense—and could be dangerous. So think ahead.

- **The job market.** Retirees often want to work part- or full-time. Even if you think you might not want to work after you settle down, investigate whether there's a demand for your skills.
- **Taxes.** Check the state and the city income, property and nuisance taxes. Otherwise, you might be in for a shock when you prepare your first tax return after you've moved. *Kiplinger's Personal Finance* magazine reported in mid 2002 that the combined annual property and income tax bill for a retired couple was the highest in Pennsylvania ($7,531) and the lowest in Delaware ($543).
- **Weather.** Sections of the Sun Belt might be a great place in January, but what about the hot and humid summer days?
- **Sports.** Like to play tennis, golf, fish and take walks? Is there a good golf course nearby? If it is a private club, is it affordable?
- **Religion.** Are there churches or synagogues in the community you're considering? Would you feel comfortable there?
- **Transportation.** How many miles is it to the airport? This is an important feature for retirees who want to visit children or take frequent vacations.
- **General amenities.** Good restaurants, retail stores, libraries and other activities are often taken for granted back home. Check to see if the area you're considering has enough of a variety for your needs.
- **Security.** Crime exists in the smallest hamlets. It's not just exclusive to metro centers. If you're particularly concerned, move to a gated community.
- **The politics.** Don't go where the prevailing political sentiment goes strongly against your grain.
- **Adult education.** Is there a community or four-year college within easy reach?
- **The emotional factor.** You probably don't want to think about it, but is this the place where you'd like to live the rest of your life?

Sources of Ideas and Support

There's nothing proprietary in the way that some groups have approached retirement planning. Anyone can start a self-help group. One thing remains constant: You need to take the initiative and personally put the ball into play.

A Little Life Planning

If your employer doesn't offer a retirement-planning program—and if it does, chances are the program will be devoted exclusively to financial planning—you might be able to find one locally that's similar to one sponsored in the past by New York University's Center for Career, Education & Life Planning (www.scps.org).

At the "Over 50? What's Next?" course, outplacement consultant Anita Lands told participants to focus on ways to clarify goals, manage change and develop a personal plan based on self-assessment and exploration of realistic alternatives in both work and leisure areas. Information and inspiration similar to what Anita offers in her course is available through many other college-sponsored and independent counseling and self-help groups.

Anita's preamble at the first session set the tone for the seminar and is a realistic primer for most soon-to-be retirees. "Whether you're thinking about changing jobs, working part-time, retiring or simply remaining productive, you can make a better decision when you see where the road is heading. Ongoing life and career planning is a must if you want to create and sustain a desirable level of satisfaction from your job and life."

The participants at one workshop series included nine women and four men, all 50-plus, who had either recently retired or were considering it. Their objectives differed: to change jobs or careers, reenter the job market, return to school or start their own businesses. David, a building supply company's chief financial officer, said he felt "stuck in the mud trying to figure it out. I'd go into my own business, but I'm not sure I want to take the risk." Then there was Maureen, a just-retired bank officer, who said, "I'm bored out of my mind. What's the next step? Will I be 'bad' if I don't go back to work immediately?"

Don't retire. Instead, retread—or in current parlance, rewire. In guiding the class, Anita employed many of the tools that she uses with her corporate outplacement clients. She encouraged students to think creatively, to consider different career or retirement options, and above all to take a fresh look at themselves, evaluate their work and leisure skills, set goals and implement an action plan.

Potential couch potatoes squirmed as Anita spoke:

"We have to learn how to transfer skills and develop new ones. We get locked into old skills, things that we do too easily.

"Remember, the way expenses are increasing, we are all under some pressure to earn extra money. One secret is to take an avocation and perhaps turn it into a vocation.

"Please rid your vocabulary of such baggage as 'should have,' 'would have' and 'could have.' Why turn 84 and still have the attitude of I 'should have' done something else after I retired?

> **"Avoid being referred to as a former VP. You need a new identity and it only comes by acquiring new skills, activities, and life values."**

"Avoid being referred to as a former VP. You need a new identity and it only comes by acquiring new skills, activities, and life values.

"Whether you work part- or full-time, you're still part of the workforce. It is time to plan your life on your terms. Up till now there have been scripts for school, work and family. The old scripts no longer apply. It's up to you to write a new one.

"Above all, don't retire—rather, retread."

Physicians Look Ahead

The American Medical Association (www.ama-assn.org) until recently sponsored workshops for physicians who ranged in age from their mid fifties to mid sixties and expected to retire within five years. While the seminars were designed for physicians, their message applies to folks in other fields who were weighing their post-practice options. Its objective was to help physicians consider all facets of retirement, from new lifestyle to investment and portfolio management, retirement income, estate planning, and a new career.

The attendees wondered how they would deal with possible boredom after an exciting and useful professional life. Would they be able to find an equivalent new lifestyle? What about a loss of self-esteem when they are no longer actively practicing medicine? "Are you prepared to face possible boredom when you no longer work 70-hour weeks?" the workshop's moderator asked. "How will you replace the professional relationship with patients and colleagues, and the loss of self-esteem?"

No quick cure-alls were prescribed. The suggested antidote was for the attendees to plan and develop practical new strategies that dealt with the day when they would no longer be part of the workforce. Attendees were encouraged to prepare a checklist of what they plan to do and how they'll do it. For example, did they plan to leave medicine totally or would they like to continue to work in the health care field, perhaps on a pro bono basis or as a part-time worker? What about developing hobbies, making travel a part of their lives, or perhaps relocating to another part of the country?

Though the workshop was directed at physicians, 50-plus-set professionals and managers in other fields can still benefit from its message: You can enjoy a satisfying, active new career without a full-time practice, using your skills—or developing new ones—as a consultant, volunteer, speaker or hobbyist.

Small-Company CEOs Seek a New Paradigm

CEOs of small to midsize companies have a different set of options than their brethren from larger companies when planning their switch from business to a different lifestyle, and corporate-sponsored outplacement usually isn't one of them. One possible solution is to retain a specialist who is familiar with the problems facing owner-managers. Interestingly, what such specialists suggest applies to other managers and professionals.

Carl Samuel's gun is for hire. As founder in 1986 of Business Life Transition (bltinc99@aol.com) and a management consultant since 1972, Carl assists business owners in considering and adjusting to the possibilities of a life beyond winning in business, for the period of life he calls "the second half of life." "They have a need to find something to organize their life around. It's hardly an easy process for the president of a company, a guy who enjoys making decisions."Carl tries to help clients take a fresh look at themselves. "The first half of their lives, they lived from the outside in, and now they must discover how to live from the inside out." He describes this as a critical step toward a successful second half of life. Once retired from the workforce, most former CEOs have lost their corporate clout. This is a particularly difficult challenge for a person who is an achiever, motivated by money, recognition, success, status and power. The transition into retirement is hardly an overnight process, often taking a few years to accomplish. It takes time to realize that "business as usual" is being replaced by another lifestyle. "Ultimately," Carl says,

> **"The first half of their lives, they lived from the outside in, and now they must discover how to live from the inside out."**

"the second half of life involves a quest for wholeness. It's about taking roads that haven't been taken and developing aspects of yourself that didn't get much attention during the first half of life." During this period, Carl finds that CEOs have five primary concerns on their minds:

- **Aging.** How much time do I have; how do I want to spend it?
- **Security.** How do I know that I have enough money to maintain my standard of living?
- **Self-identity.** Who am I besides my business, and what will I do?
- **Dreams.** What will give me meaning, purpose, vitality and relevance in my life?
- **Relationships.** What do I want, and who do I want to be with? During the CEOs' transition into retirement, Samuel suggests that they find some things to do temporarily while they're looking for activities with more long-term value.

Dr. Joel Goldberg, in New Jersey, is another niche consultant who advises CEOs on retirement. As president of Career Consultants (www.careerconsultants.info), and a consultant for 25 years in the techniques of change management and organization development, Joel advises clients who are typically in their mid fifties to mid sixties, and, more often than not, are the founders and presidents of companies with less than $100 million

SUGGESTED READING

Kiplinger's Guide to Investing Success, by Theodore Miller (Kiplinger Books, 2003). A commonsense guide to investing that will help you grow your nest egg and make the most of what you have.

Prime Time: How Baby Boomers Will Revolutionize Retirement & Transform America, by Marc Freedman (Public Affairs, 2002). This book provides boomers with an opportunity to a look at different lifestyle options.

Retire Early—And Live the Life You Want Now, by Suzie Orman (Owl Books, 2001). Discusses the issues in a language readers will understand.

Retirement Migration in America, by Charles Longino (Vacation Publications, 1995). An academic expert explores relocation trends.

Retirement Places Rated, by David Savageau (Macmillan, 1999). Helps retirees weigh alternatives.

Retire Retire Worry-Free (Kiplinger Books, 2001). An easy-to-read primer, written by the staff of *Kiplinger's Personal Finance* magazine, that will help you determine your retirement needs and resources.

in sales. All of Joel's counseling is done one-to-one.

Joel has not reduced his counseling services to a short-term fix or an easy-to-use checklist. "It takes time and planning. There's a need to think the problem through, take a look at different options, and learn how to detach. Whatever the approach, the shock of retiring is enormous. Thus, sufficient advance planning is critical.

"In the first meeting," Joel notes, "I find many of them to be restless, bored and tired, but they would like to work forever. They must face a central issue in their lives—letting go."

Severing ties with one's business has an emotional impact that often affects family relationships. Some business owners divorce after 40 or more years of marriage. They discover differences of opinion brought about by the process of retiring that are irreconcilable.

Clients are naturally concerned with managerial succession. It is often the first time that they have openly discussed this problem with an outsider. The CEOs of closely held and family-owned businesses have strong emotional attachments after running the company for 30 or more years. They need to be presented with alternatives—selling the company or turning ownership over to a new generation of family or nonfamily managers.

"I show them how to invent a new scenario. Remember, these are high achievers. They have more than ample incomes, and they are emotionally tied to their business. Most are good in their corporate planning but have done little of it in their personal lives. I get them to start reflecting on their lives. What would they like to do if they could do it all over again? It's a process that takes several years; it's not something that can be done overnight. I personally abhor the idea of retirement. I get them to think of it as redirecting their experiences into other areas—whatever they find satisfying."

Some of Joel's clients are interested in becoming directors of other companies or nonprofit organizations. He helps them prepare a résumé for those purposes and introduces them to companies and organizations that might need their services.

> **"In the first meeting,"** Joel notes, **"I find many of them to be restless, bored and tired, but they would like to work forever. They must face a central issue in their lives—letting go."**

Letting go does not always produce a Cinderella ending. Joel tells about one CEO who was training his son to be his successor. But the CEO had no way to fairly evaluate his son's business skills. "We suggested that he establish an independent board to conduct the evaluation. They found that the son did not have sufficient management skills to run the business. As a result, the company was sold." A transition in management within the family was scuttled.

Sometimes, after evaluating the alternatives, the CEO decides not to retire. "It's their business and they can do what they want."

Say Hello to "Our Group"

When "Our Group" has lunch in a midtown New York City restaurant, they look like any other luncheon meeting of six midlife business and professional women. Their conversation varies from work to lifestyle issues. But the group actually has a different purpose. These former New York City teachers and administrators meet monthly as a postretirement support group.

Little did Mary R. and her friends realize that they were pathfinders when they started what they refer to as "Our Group," an organization that has no charter, official status, officers or dues. Ever since their first meeting more than 30 months ago, they have provided each other with informal and ongoing support that goes well beyond the assistance offered by many structured organizations.

The first lunch meeting after their retirement set the tone for future meetings. Little time was spent reminiscing—or as Mary puts it, "we have better things to discuss." They typically talk about part-time work, using free time and adjusting to a less hectic lifestyle that includes the freedom to have a leisurely breakfast, read the newspaper and not leave for work at 7 A.M. At one lunch, they chatted about a newspaper article they had read on Charles Handy's concept of "portfolio careers" and how his concept applies to them.

Our Group has found that six members is a practical number to meet and talk over lunch or dinner in a restaurant, or to meet in someone's living room. They see no need to expand beyond their present number.

Our Group has created a basic formula that could easily serve as a template for many other retirees:

- **The group shares a strong common thread**—for example, the same employer or similar professional training or jobs.
- **Its members know and generally respect each other.**
- **The group is small.**
- **The meetings are informal but directed.**
- **The group avoids letting one or two of the members dominate** it or its agenda, or letting the group become a stage for "show-and-tell" instead of mutual support and discussion.
- **The meetings, while informal,** depend for their continuity on the professional tone of the participants.
- **Above all, gossip is downplayed.**
- **Although this "birds of a feather" group has no officers,** it needs one or two active members to handle a few administrative

---

POINTS TO REMEMBER

- **Retirement planning** is an individual responsibility.

- **Corporate paternalism is diminishing,** and few employers offer help in retirement planning.

- **Retirement provides the chance** to juggle many interests— work and play—at once.

- **You can find plenty of opportunities** for ideas and support before and after retirement.

- **More than ever, this is the time** to think flexibly and creatively—and to become computer literate.

- **It's never too soon to take stock** of your financial needs and resources in retirement.

---

functions, such as sending out meeting notices or setting an agenda, informal as it may be.

Our Group started in the early '90s when the New York City Board of Education, as part of its downsizing plan, sweetened its retirement package to encourage teachers and administrators to retire ahead of schedule.

One of Mary's friends came to her soon after the board made its offer. She was uncertain about accepting the early-retirement package and asked Mary for her advice. The teachers' union had provided printed handouts digesting the key issues but offered little practical counseling. The union, too, seemed uneducated on the pros and cons of an early buyout. The future members of Our Group looked for advice from their peers. "I decided to lend an ear," Mary noted. "The word spread, and a few of us decided to get together informally and discuss the retirement package. We were not totally sold on early retirement or the advantages of the board's package. What it would mean? What would we do when we were no longer working? We were not mentally ready to retire."

Even with their reservations, they all accepted the board's

buyout plan. They were aware of current buyout trends in corporate America, and knew that, as in industry, the board's next buyout offer might not be as generous. Looking back, their decision was correct. Future buyouts were skimpier as the board of education attempted to control early-retirement costs.

"Since my retirement decision was made so hastily," Barbara, another group member, noted, "I needed the group as a support. Though we each have different family setups, the group has become a sort of extended family. As old friends, we're frank and honest with each other. That's what you need when you've just left a job after 25 years and you're looking for new things to do."

> **"We shared so many things over the years as colleagues and friends over cups of coffee or lunch in the teachers' room. As retirees we continue to share our experiences."**

Several in Our Group have already returned to work as part-timers or substitute teachers. Judith substitutes several days a month, Arlene teaches history at a community college, Mary is studying for a doctorate, Charlotte helps her husband in his business, and Frances is an artist. And Barbara, who discovered in retirement that she needed the discipline of a job, now works three days a week as a guidance counselor at a private school.

Our Group is "a continuation of a fulfilling work experience," says Charlotte. "We shared so many things over the years as colleagues and friends over cups of coffee or lunch in the teachers' room. As retirees we continue to share our experiences."

How They Planned Their Retirement

There are two types of retirees. Some switch from the active workforce on their own terms, often meticulously planning each step in advance. The others have a more abrupt transition. They report to work on Friday to learn that their job has either been eliminated or they have been asked to take early retirement.

The long-term planners do not necessarily have the advantage. Often they need to conduct their retirement planning in secrecy because a premature announcement might offend employers, co-workers or partners and could even put their current job in jeopardy.

The diverse group you will meet on the following pages includes the CEO of a small public company, a partner in a large law firm, a computer programmer with a large company, and two former corporate managers who use computers extensively.

DIVIDING HIS TIME

Charles Handy

PERSONNEL EXECUTIVE, ECONOMIST AND TEACHER TURNED PORTFOLIO CAREERIST

Charles Handy practices what he preaches in his book, *The Age of Unreason,* by living a portfolio career. His lifestyle has been one of discovering "how the different bits of work in our life fit together to form a balanced whole." Charles believes that more people of all ages, not just early retirees and the 50-plus set, will soon be living portfolio careers as a result of technological, societal and corporate organizational changes.

To define the portfolio career, Handy divides work into two groups: paid work, consisting of wage work and fee work; and free work, which includes home work (work around the house, including tending to children), gift work (volunteerism) and study work (learning a new language or training for a sport). He estimates that approximately half of people over age 55 are already pursuing portfolio careers even though they might not label them that way. Because this lifestyle can extend right into the period usually known as retirement, Handy contends that "retirement" is not an accurate term and will become obsolete.

Charles is a graduate of both Oriel College at Oxford and the Sloan School of Management at the Massachusetts Institute of Technology. Sandwiched between the years at Oxford and MIT was a decade that he spent as a personnel executive at Shell International and as an economist for the Anglo-American Corp. When he left MIT, he joined the London Business School, to start and direct the Sloan program in England and to teach courses in managerial psychology and development. He served as warden of St. George's House in Windsor Castle, a private conference and study center concerned with ethics and values in society.

Charles looks at the future of work and the obsolescence of retirement as we've known it. He puts his theories into practice.

"My teaching concentrated on the application of behavioral science to organizations of all types. In particular, I was dealing with the management of change, the cultures of organizations, and the theory and practice of individual and organizational development. My current thinking focuses on the future of work, and on the changes that demography and technology will bring to organizations and to all our lives."

Charles was ready to put his theories

to the test. "I was writing how the world would be. I was 49. It was time I bloody made some personal changes, and quick."

To make things happen requires a plan. "It is important to allocate the number of days and hours to be devoted to different segments of a portfolio career. I had to find ways to make money. In my case writing books has helped to build a reputation but hasn't exactly made me a lot of money. What makes money for me is running seminars and teaching managers.

"Elizabeth [his wife] and I are somewhat conservative, so we doubled the amount of money we thought we needed to support our lifestyle. How many days of teaching and running seminars would we have to work? The goal was not to maximize our income but to make enough so we could live somewhat more comfortably.

"Fortunately, Elizabeth is my manager. If I answer the telephone, I tend to say 'yes' to everyone. She keeps track of my hours. Every Christmas we review the hours we spent on different projects throughout the year to help us understand and manage the portfolio. It is a very disciplined approach."

Besides 150 days of fee work, Charles devotes 50 days to gift work—or as he calls it, "my causes," such as the Carnegie Inquiry into the Third Age. As the Carnegie Inquiry's unpaid consultant, he

> **"It is important to allocate the number of days and hours to be devoted to different segments of a portfolio career."**

has persuaded a number of foundations to provide $2 million to fund a two-year inquiry into a study of the Third Age. (The Third Age comes from the French idea that life divides into three sequential parts—learning, working and living.) His gift work also includes some church-related activities. "I'm very interested in religion. I make myself available at no fee to bishops to run seminars for the church."

He devotes another 75 days to reading and keeping current. This portion is expanding. "I'm now learning Italian because we own a house in Italy. Of all the things I do, learning Italian is by far the most difficult."

There's a lighter side in his portfolio—the 90 days devoted to home work and leisure. "We live part of the year in London, which is our public life; we also have a country place in Norfolk, where I do my writing. In Norfolk I'm housekeeper. Elizabeth and I reverse roles. I buy and cook the food, maintain the house and do everything. Elizabeth is free to devote her time to photography. This change is very good for me. It makes me aware of what it is like to go shopping every day. It keeps me as a human being and [saves me] from becoming arrogant.

"One can write great books, but the secret is learning to cook a tasty omelet. This is important. When friends come to stay with us in Norfolk, they're more impressed by my cooking than by my writings." As part of his portfolio lifestyle, Charles completed a one-week Cordon Bleu course in French regional cooking.

The portfolio career concept is starting to attract the children of the 50-plus set. The Handy children are no exception. Kate and Scott, who are in their mid twenties, heed to such a lifestyle. "It is silly to have a single job," says Kate. "One needs to have three or four different paying jobs because employment conditions are so poor."

COMBATING COMPUTER ILLITERACY

Louis Powell
PRODUCTION MANAGER TURNED EDUCATOR

Louis Powell's business card carries an unusual line: teaching computer skills to adults born before Pearl Harbor. Hardly a wise-guy comment. Louis supervises a computer boot camp for retirees.

A native of Minnesota and a University of Minnesota graduate, Louis worked for IBM for 34 years. When he retired in 1991, he was a production manager at the company's Research Triangle Park facility in Durham, North Carolina. By then, a one-time hobby of collecting antique cameras had by design already evolved into an active sideline business.

Once retired, Powell's Camera Exchange became his full-time focus. His business called for frequent trips to East Coast camera fairs and dealers. But as online computer systems became more universally used, computers and data communications lessened the need for face-to-face meetings as he increasingly did business by e-mail and over his own Webpage. Powell buys and sells cameras on the Internet or through e-Bay.

Then an unplanned event occurred in 1996, just about the time that he was looking for some more things to do. "I was attending an IBM Quarter Century Club when someone told me that the company was looking for people who enjoyed teaching to become involved in starting up a computer facility that IBM and Southern Bell were sponsoring. The next thing I knew I was one of the organizers of the SeniorNet Center being set up in Raleigh." Louis simply wanted to be an instructor, but he also became the Center's volunteer manager, a job requiring about 20 hours of work a week.

> **"My job is to get people over the fear of computers, and make them feel comfortable with a mouse and keyboard."**

The center opened in mid 1996, and during its first two years the team of teachers, including a number of former IBM managers and computer professionals, trained 500 to 600 retirees. The hands-on course is geared to retirees who might otherwise find attending a computer class at a community college with younger students to be somewhat intimidating. The SeniorNet approach is nearly one-on-one. In a room with six computers, two or three instructors are on hand to help students.

For approximately $60, students

progress to the point where they feel comfortable with word processing. They also learn how to develop a database, create an address book, run a spreadsheet, communicate via e-mail and access Websites. The intention, Louis says, is not to train people to get jobs, though some might use their new-found skills to return to the workplace.

"They take courses for practical reasons. Some want to use e-mail to write family, friends and grandchildren. Others are interested in genealogy, want to write family histories, keep track of their investments or do some form of research. My job is to get people over the fear of computers and make them feel comfortable with a mouse and a keyboard. When they say they can't type, I show them how I do it with two fingers. By the end of the first day's session, they know how to open a computer file, use the mouse and handle some of the other basics."

Most of the SeniorNet students range in age from 55 to 70. Occasionally, an octogenarian shows up. Many of the students, Louis notes,

recently retired and they're looking for things to do. The computer represents a new experience and a new challenge. It's a skill they can share with their children and grandchildren. Some already own computers, and others are planning to buy one. Louis and the other instructors show them how to select a computer to meet their needs.

Louis says that all the students are treated as beginners even though a few have some previous computer experience. At work, they may have used a terminal on dedicated assignments such as inputting or retrieving data. But these repetitious jobs, he says, did not prepare them to use a PC.

As an instructor, he has learned the tricks of the trade. "A number of husbands and wives are students. Naturally, they come together and attend the same class. But I don't let them sit next to each other. I place them in opposite sides of the room to avoid conflict. Otherwise, one would be instructing the other. If I could, I'd put seat belts on them to keep them in their seats."

THERE'S LIFE AFTER IBM

Larry Bumgardner

CORPORATE- TO SMALL-COMPANY SOFTWARE DESIGNER

For several years prior to Larry Bumgardner's retirement, IBM was offering early-retirement buyouts, and he was undecided whether he should stay or go. The dilemmas he faced—deciding if and when he should accept a buyout package, and what to do next—are being faced by countless other managers in the 50-plus set. Larry now admits that he should have accepted an earlier buyout package. But he remained at IBM because he hadn't yet determined the next step in his personal game plan. The factors that were involved in his decision-making are as complex and as typical as those of anyone weighing a buyout offer.

Change for change's sake wasn't in the cards for Larry. Contrary to one of IBM's many nicknames, "I've Been Moved," Larry's career and lifestyle had been rather consistent. "Same company, same location, same house and the same wife. As you can see, I didn't follow the 'grass is always greener' concept."

As a youngster, Larry thought about being a teacher or minister but found

Larry sums up the early buyout dilemma: "Taking the IBM package was one thing, but finding something I wanted to do was something else."

that he was better suited for and more interested in science. He received undergraduate and graduate engineering degrees from North Carolina State University and Duke University, joined IBM, and a few months later was activated as an Army Signal Corps officer. Other than two years of military service, Larry's entire life had been spent in North Carolina with IBM. Larry was officially classified as an IBM group leader in charge of designing software for retail-related computer systems. Ironically, as IBM downsized, his division achieved record sales.

Larry found it difficult to realistically consider any form of early retirement. He felt he was much too young, and retirement contradicted his philosophy that work is critical to survival—not in the sense of financial survival, but in usefulness. "I didn't believe in being idle. Taking the IBM package was one thing, but finding something I really wanted to do was something else." Initially, Larry felt that he couldn't leave until he decided on a new pursuit.

Prior to retirement, he was optimistic

about life after IBM: "I felt that when I left IBM, there would be a number of options." Larry had plenty of contacts through his work with retail computer systems and believed he "could join another software company or become an independent contractor and earn the difference between my IBM pension payout and my living expenses."

Larry also considered becoming an entrepreneur. He tried to purchase an auto machine shop from owners who wanted to retire. Hardly a newcomer to this field, he first learned how to repair cars from his father, who was a machinist. But the machining business had some serious environmental problems that would be too costly to remedy.

As a trained scientist, Larry considered teaching. "I only wanted to work in urban public schools where I could teach science to city and disadvantaged kids. Teaching in a private or church school didn't interest me. It wasn't where I was needed."

Practicing good works was nothing new to Larry. Besides his wife and their three children, his family includes several children he adopted from troubled families. He also donates 20% of his gross income to charity.

In his mid 50s, Larry retired officially from IBM in 1997 and since then has worked at three different jobs. Consistent with his preretirement plan, he became a teacher. Rather than seeking a safer haven in an independent school, he worked for several months at a Durham middle school teaching science and math, but his idealism was shaken by school conditions. Soon after he left teaching, IBM asked him to return as a contract worker, a relationship that lasted slightly less than a year. In early 1998, he joined QVS Software, a small company that produces point-of-purchase software systems, an area that he knows well from his IBM days. He describes it as the "best job I've ever had." As an IBM retiree, Larry is also a "double dipper," collecting both his IBM pension and a QVS salary.

Larry's children are self-supporting. His wife, Nancy, does not work. Like her husband, she is also a community activist involved in leadership positions with several nonprofit groups. "Even if I made less money, we knew that we could live on less," says Larry.

FROM MAINFRAMES TO WEB SURFING

Art Lebo

CORPORATE FINANCIAL MANAGER TURNED VOLUNTEER CONSULTANT

Art Lebo is comfortable with computers. There is good reason for his confidence. Over the past 35 years, he has worked with mainframe computers, timesharing systems and desktop computers. Now retired, Art uses computers wherever possible, as a volunteer in the U.S. and overseas, and in his daily retirement lifestyle.

Like Louis Powell (see page 49), Art was born in Minnesota and graduated from the University of Minnesota. He spent 25 years in the metropolitan New York area as a financial manager and controller with one company, General Foods, then with the merged General Foods and Kraft Foods operation, which as a result of acquisition subsequently became part of Philip Morris, and then spun off as a separate company.

When computers came of age in the 1960s, corporate financial departments became early converts. In the early days before the availability of software

Art and his wife, Nancy, planned an early retirement and a relocation, and he has embarked upon a series of paid and unpaid assignments that redirect his financial skills and acumen.

applications packages, Art, although a financial manager, designed Cobol and Fortran programs. In the '70s when General Foods switched to timesharing systems, Art became a timesharer. During this period, he received an MBA degree, and timesharing was the theme of his thesis. In the '80s, the desktop computer came of age, and once again he migrated to another computer medium and such financial and spreadsheet software packages as *Lotus 1-2-3*.

"Nancy and I always knew we wanted to retire at an early age when we were in good health and not wait until we were in our sixties. And we also knew that we wanted to move from New York to another section of the country. But we didn't want to return to Minnesota. It's much too cold in winter."

When they were in their early fifties and still years before they anticipated retiring, the Lebos started to look at possible destination spots in Virginia, Florida and North Carolina. They rated communities for what they offered in terms of culture, sports, weather and continuing education. Health care was not a priority item since they assumed any area they would select would have decent medical facilities. After repeated trips, they selected Fearrington Village near Chapel Hill, North Carolina. In 1990, Art left Kraft Foods and Nancy, also in her mid-fifties, retired as an elementary school teacher. Both would receive pensions, lifetime health-care packages, and in a few years would be eligible to receive social security payments.

To see Art in action is to see a model of the active retiree. Put aside the occasional paid consulting assignment; an active sports schedule that includes tennis, biking and swimming; and his numerous hobbies. Instead, let's see how Art applies his financial management and computer acumen.

In the mid 1990s, Art joined the Internal Revenue Service–sponsored Volunteers for Tax Assistance. Starting in early January and ending in mid-April, he works two days a week preparing computerized tax returns for elderly and poor people. As a result of a five-year relationship, Art was recruited to help launch the SeniorNet Center in Chapel Hill in 1998.

Nancy and Art are active internationalists. Through Friendship

> **Art's experience in Gdansk, Poland, in many ways, "was like running a 'finance for nonfinancial managers' course."**

Force, a crosscultural international organization, they have visited or had visits from Australia, Latvia, Finland, the Czech Republic, Greece and England. "It's a chance to meet different people and see life as it really is," he said.

Art's financial and computer skills resulted in several volunteer overseas assignments, whose American sponsors were Citizens Democracy Corporation and the volunteers for Overseas Cooperate Assistance, organizations funded by the Agency for International Development. While on assignment, transportation, lodging and living expenses were paid for both Art and Nancy.

In the late 1990s, Art spent one month in Moldova as a mentor and consultant to several small companies. "It's important to these companies to learn how to establish and maintain budgets, and to prepare financial plans if they expect to grow. Most of them use homemade bookkeeping systems that few outside the company could understand."

In 1998, Art took a positing in Gdansk, Poland. "In Gdansk, I worked with two companies and helped them design financial reporting systems. One company was in construction and the other in the production of point-of-purchase displays. I showed them ways to present financial information in a better format and how to prepare a financial analysis to go with the numbers. In many ways, it was like running a 'finance for nonfinancial managers' course." Nancy, who joined Art for two of his four weeks in Poland, was given a classroom assignment. She conducted an intensive conversational English course for business and professional people.

"A laptop was given to me for the Gdansk assignment. It permitted me to compile and analyze financial information. This way I could review information at the end of the workday and prepare spreadsheets," Art said. He also used the laptop to send e-mail letters home. He even kept up with U.S. news by reading *The New York Times, Washington Post,* and *Raleigh News & Observer* on the Internet.

Art's computer saga extends to his personal life. "I spend more time on my computer than watching TV. When my granddaughter learned that she had an injured knee from soccer and lacrosse, I used the Web to find what doctors had to say about the injury."

NO STRANGER TO SETTING HIS OWN COURSE

Hank Baer
LAW PARTNER TURNED PROFESSOR AND INDEPENDENT ATTORNEY

In this era of job and career uncertainty, it is critical to know when and how to take early retirement. At age 55, Henry "Hank" Baer felt it was time to make a change. He negotiated his way out of his law firm from a position of strength, while he had something tangible to offer his partners and they still needed him as much as he needed them. How Hank handled his planned departure could serve as an example to others.

Graduating from Brown University, Hank was commissioned in the Navy. Though he was not a lawyer, he was assigned on a number of occasions as a defense counsel. "From that point on, I wanted to be a lawyer. When I got out of the Navy, I applied to law school at Harvard but was turned down." He went to work first as a sales representative and then as sales manager for ten years with his family's business, Imperial Knife Associated Companies.

"I still wanted to be a lawyer, but I was now married and had two small children. I applied once again to law school. The only person who knew about it was my wife, Ellen. When I was deliberating over my decision, she said, 'Either go to law school or shut up.'" This time Hank was accepted at Harvard.

The Baers moved to Cambridge and Hank financed his education with the GI Bill, student loans, some savings and Ellen's salary as a hospital nurse. Hank completed law school when he was 36 and went to work for Skadden, Arps, Slate, Meagher & Flom, one of the few corporate law firms that hired middle-age lawyers directly out of law school. It was then a small law firm with only 41 lawyers, all based in New York. Hank was named a partner in 1978, and four years later, as a labor relations specialist, he became chairperson of the firm's labor and employment law practice committee.

Over the years, the firm changed. In 1971 it was "small and collegial, and run like a family business. As it grew, it became increasingly more businesslike and for me less fun." By 1990, its peak year, the firm employed more than 1,000 lawyers, including 225 partners, and a

> **At 55, Hank chose to give up his partnership and become "of counsel" to his law firm. Held to fewer billable hours, he can indulge his other loves.**

support staff of approximately 2,500 people in its U.S. and overseas offices.

Hank began to consider alternatives, all using his skills as a lawyer and arbitrator. One of his close professional colleagues and his immediate supervisor at the firm was John Feerick, a year younger than Hank, who had left the firm as a partner in his late forties in 1983 to become the dean of Fordham Law School. Hank, John and a third lawyer, Jonathan Arfa, had jointly written a legal textbook and collaborated on a number of legal articles. Perhaps subliminally, John had set the stage for Hank's departure seven years later.

Two dissimilar events, which occurred almost at the same time, triggered Hank's decision to change his work habits. Ellen's brother died at 47, and Hank and Ellen won an American Express around-the-world sweepstakes. They traveled for 60 days in Australia, New Zealand and Europe. "Until then, I had never been absent from the office for so long a time. I also decided to do things differently than my father, who was literally kicked out of Imperial Knife when he was 85. My brother-in-law's death forced me to face the fact that we're not going to last forever."

It was time to stop putting off things he wanted to do in law and in his

> ## It was time for Hank to stop putting off things he wanted to do. "My brother-in-law's death forced me to face the fact that we're not going to last forever."

personal life—things that could not be readily accomplished in a very demanding law firm practice. "I went to see John Feerick at Fordham and advised him of my plans to step down at the firm," Hank recalls. John told him that when a teaching position opened he would consider him.

In 1990, nearly 19 years after joining Skadden, Arps, Hank resigned as a partner, withdrew his capital investment and became "of counsel." In this new relationship, Hank maintains a professional relationship with the firm but no longer has a partner's vote or shares in the firm's profits. He does most of his work from an office that he maintains at his own expense in Florida. Some of-counsel lawyers receive a certain percentage of their legal fees, but Hank is a W-2 employee and is paid a salary. "I serve in a management position, as opposed to a legal position, dealing with human [resource] issues for the firm's 4,000 employees worldwide.

"I have an understanding with the firm that continues to be renewed. My income is less than when I was a partner, but I accepted the change so I could mold my life to my liking—a combination of law, teaching and other interests. I no longer want to bill the required thousands of hours a year and be accountable for the duties of a partner."

Hank was able to save and invest steadily as a partner in what was probably the nation's most profitable law firm during the 1980s, and his downshifting has not altered his lifestyle. With the money Hank got back from his capital investment in the firm, he and Ellen bought an apartment in Florida and invested the remainder. They remain on Skadden's health care and life insurance plans. Ellen, who retired as a professor of nursing at the University of Pennsylvania, now teaches nursing part-time at the University of Miami.

When Hank was asked to teach a labor law course at Fordham, he was once again a fledgling. "I had never taught before. It's different from giving an occasional lecture." Fortunately, Ellen and their son, who also had teaching experience, tutored him on classroom techniques. "Teaching is intellectually stimulating. Students keep me sharp. At first I would spend up to 18 hours preparing for a three-hour lecture. As a result, I have become a better lawyer." After moving to Florida, he taught for several years at Nova Southeastern University in Ft. Lauderdale.

Hank's new lifestyle means living in Florida six months a year and the balance of the year in New York and at his summer home on Long Island. He works as a lawyer in Florida and New York. His objective remains constant— to create a balance in his professional life as a lawyer, teacher and arbitrator.

PLANNING THE NEXT MOVE

Don DeBolt
TRADE ASSOCIATION HEAD WEIGHS OPTIONS

Don DeBolt has been a Washington, D.C., trade association executive for more than 40 years. He's also displayed an entrepreneurial streak since his early 20s, when he was a part-owner of a men's clothing store in his home state, South Dakota.

When Don retires within the next few years from his position as president of the International Franchise Association, he expects his penchant for and experience with smaller businesses should stimulate a number of post-retirement options.

The first of his family to go to college, Don left in his senior year without a degree. "I still have the lingering thought that that's something still unfinished, and it may get back on the radar screen again."

Besides his clothing store experience, Don was also a J.C. Penney management trainee and a commissioned salesman for a distributor representing a South Dakota machinery manufacturer. "I worked for the distributor for a couple of months in its Washington [D.C.]

> "**Retirement is an inaction word to me. My father said that retirement was the saddest mistake that he had ever made.**"

office before moving my wife and three-month old son out from Vermillion, South Dakota. I left my job, and I got 'keep body and soul together' type jobs—working in a restaurant at night and as a correspondence clerk by day, and showing model homes on the weekend. I was broke. That was the time in my life when the decisions were between buying razor blades to shave with or a pound of hamburger to eat."

As a result of his downward financial spiral and the need for a job with steady income, Don took what would be the first of four trade association positions, starting in 1962 with the Menswear Retailers of America (MRA). "When I left 18 years later, I was its executive director. By then, I was burned out. I asked the board to release me from my contract, which had another year to go. I planned to devote my efforts to real estate."

Instead, one of Don's uncles inspired him to start what became Credit Card Acceptor Corp., a company with a niche specialty—enabling trade associations to offer credit cards at discount rates to their member companies. "At our peak, we had 40 clients. I was a one-man band operating from our apartment. Little maintenance was required once the marketing was done and the deal made." The CCAC concept frizzled out a few years later.

It was time to look for another job. "After MRA, I never intended to run another association; I didn't think the skills were transferable." But Don's association experience became a lifeline. Over the next few years in the late 1980s, Don worked as director of the National Spa and Pool Institute, and the International Swimming Hall of Fame.

Once again, Don was bitten by the entrepreneurial bug. In 1990, he started what evolved into *CEO Update,* a biweekly, 28-page newsletter for executives in the nonprofit management field. It was a one-man start-up operation. Don did everything from writing the newsletter copy to pasting labels on the envelopes.

When he joined the International Franchise Association (IFA) as its president in 1995, Don stepped down as publisher of *CEO Update,* but became publisher emeritus and remained president of the company. These days, Don's involvement is limited to Sunday mornings, when he does bookkeeping and what he calls "financial things." "I see this work as my Sunday morning

golf game," says Don.

Now in his mid sixties, Don is considering a range of retirement options, although he has already eliminated the idea of a full-time retirement lifestyle. "Retirement is an inaction word to me. My father said that retirement was the saddest mistake that he had ever made."

"My present plans are to retire from the IFA in February 2005 when I'm 67. I doubt if I have another association gig in me. I plan to return to the newsletter for at least a few months before deciding whether that's going to occupy me long term. I have some really terrific younger people running the newsletter and I hope they continue on. If I return on a full-time basis, I might be in the way."

The IFA represents hundreds of franchisors, from the major players like McDonald's, Dunkin' Donuts and H&R Block to small newcomers such as Wireless Toyz and Drama Kids. Don believes that his knowledge of the franchise industry's players will give him an edge in shaping his retirement plans.

"I have a 17-year old grandson who plans to go to college. When he graduates, I might invest in a franchise. He'll do the work and I'll be his banker and partner. The idea is that he'll buy me out. After this job, if I can't figure out which franchise is the right one for me, I'll have been asleep at the switch."

PHASING INTO RETIREMENT

Pamela George
MOVES FROM CLASSROOM TO STUDIO

Pamela Georges learned a lesson on retirement from her mother, Ruby, who until her retirement at age 62 was assistant to the president of Centenary College of Louisiana. Ruby left the college when a new president was appointed. "She could have downshifted and taken another job at Centenary. To this day, she has rued her retirement, and says that she's been bored to tears ever since, says Pam."

Unlike her mother who retired abruptly and without a plan other than to take care of an ill husband, Pam, now in her mid fifties, has already started to unfold her new career as an artist. By 2005, Pam, a tenured professor of education at North Carolina Central University in Durham, North Carolina, will have completed the terms of her phased retirement.

"I've been painting since I was five. But being from a working class family, painting was not considered a profession but a hobby. One had to earn a living. In many ways, painting was my first calling. Even as a hobby, it was central to my life." Although Pam embarked on a different career path, she never lost her passion for painting.

> Pam can no longer think like a hobbyist. "In the past, I didn't have to paint to make a living."

Graduating from Louisiana State University in 1969, Pam got a master's degree in special education the following year at the University of North Carolina at Chapel Hill. Afterward, she spent two years in Samoa with the Peace Corps, where she met David Austin, who would become her husband. She traveled with him overseas for another two years before returning to the U.S. and a four-year stint as a middle school teacher. By 1979, she had earned a doctorate from UNC.

Since 1978, Pam has spent her entire academic career at Central as an educational psychology teacher, researcher and supervisor. For four years in the late 1990s, she chaired and taught four courses a semester in the Department of Leadership, Policy and Professional Studies, a job with a 60-hour workweek. "It kind of burned me out and got me interested in taking early retirement."

With a daughter about to start college, Pam has entered into a new phase of her professional life. "I'm now in the midst of a three-year phased retirement program. I paint three full days a week, spend another day doing research for my painting, and another day with my mentor who is actually my art teacher, and work 20 hours a week at Central. By 2005 when phased retirement ends, I would like to be appointed as an emeritus faculty member, but I won't know about this for another year or so." Under this arrangement Pam would teach one or perhaps two courses a year at NCCU.

Phased retirement was first offered through the University of North Carolina's statewide system about five years ago to encourage faculty retirement. The arrangement enables Pam to receive the equivalent of a full salary. The package consists of her pension, which is roughly 50% of her faculty pay, along with one-half of her faculty salary. Sales of her paintings produce another $6,000 a year. Pam's primary goal over the next few years is to replace the loss of academic income with increased revenues from her paintings.

With her painting taking on increased importance to her financially, Pam can no longer think like a hobbyist. "In the past, I didn't have to paint to make a living. I gave away paintings as gifts to local groups that could use them to raise funds, or I used them to illustrate the books I've written."

In beefing up her studio operation, P'Gale Studio, to function more efficiently and to be financially sound, Pam wrote a business plan with the help of Dub Gulley, who is director of Durham Technical Community College's Small Business Center. "Dub made me think of painting as a business, not as a

hobby. I now know what it costs to paint and have a gallery show. To sell a $1,000 painting entails spending several hundred dollars on oils, canvas and framing. I know that I can make up to $100 an hour teaching or doing consulting, while painting comes to only $25 an hour. One of my immediate goals is to complete several paintings a month—enough that I can have a one-woman show."

As part of her preretirement due diligence, Pam is accumulating data on different ways to operate a profitable studio. "When I'm attending educational conferences in other cities, I speak to artists about how they run their studios. I've come away with the impression that few artists make a living from their work." As part of this exercise, Pam is searching for ways to lessen her dependence on art shows, since galleries traditionally receive a 40% to 60% sales commission.

While creating her new lifestyle, Pam, along with a recently retired Central colleague, prepared this formula for retirement, which she calls her "Retirement E's":

- **Education,** including the need for a mentor, a painting teacher, and advisors like Dub Gulley;
- **Enterprise,** that is, operating her studio as a profitable business;
- **Earnings** from retirement, painting, and hopefully, a retirement position at NCCU and academic research;
- **Exercise** to stay physically well, and
- **Enlightenment** from involvement in her community and expression of spirituality.

PLANNING IS KEY IN HER TRANSITION

Marilyn Mellis Longman
RETIRED FROM CORPORATE AMERICA

Marilyn Mellis Longman no longer needs an alarm clock to get her going in the morning. Unlike most people her age, Marilyn is retired. She retired along with her husband, Doug, when she was 49, and he was in his mid fifties." In many ways," she says, "I'm the classic boomer."

After growing up in New York City, Marilyn went to the State University of New York at Stony Brook. The year after graduation she received a master's degree in education, which was followed by a brief career in the classroom. Five years later and after placing first in her Boston University class, she had an MBA degree and was ready to take the first step in her migration from classroom to corporate America.

In 1976, when Marilyn joined General Foods (which merged into Kraft, then with Philip Morris and more recently spun off as Kraft), Marilyn was part of the early wave of women who wanted line jobs (sales, engineering, or production) rather than staff corporate assignments (public relations, human resources, corporate law, and so on). At

> **"I was really looking for a lifestyle change so that I could have more control over my life, and achieve better balance."**

the time, the company had few women with MBAs. Over the next 23 years, Marilyn held marketing jobs with such brand-name food lines as Pet Foods, Maxwell House Coffee, and Kraft Cheese. In the years before she left the company, Marilyn was its director of corporate business development.

By the late 1990s, Marilyn and Doug were ready to jump ship. Doug, who has a doctorate in business administration, taught at the University of Texas in Austin and had worked for Citibank and General Foods, where he met Marilyn. The Longmans were living in Chicago.

"I had a heavy-duty job," says Marilyn. "For the past nine years I had worked a 12-hour day, from 7 to 7. Up to then I had never thought about retirement. My father retired at 65 and my mother died at 61. When my dad retired, he didn't do too much. He moved to Florida and now he's in his nineties. Not much of a role model there.

"Our goal was financial independence, so that we could do whatever we wanted, whether continuing to work at our current jobs, getting different jobs or not working at all.

"I was really looking for a lifestyle change so that I could have more control over my life and achieve better balance. I did not want to continue working so hard in my fifties, just in case I died at an early age like my mother. Rather than a rational perspective, it was purely emotional. At the time, Doug had left Citibank and was working as a consultant for Omnitech, and he felt that he could continue doing that from North Carolina. He also thought that he might want to return to teaching."

In planning her future lifestyle, Marilyn was guided by Gail Sheehy's book *New Passages* and its discussion of "the Second Adulthood": "Today there is not only life after youth, but life after empty nest. There is life after layoff and early retirement." Sound planning enabled the Longmans to walk away from well-paying corporate jobs. "We didn't think of ourselves as retiring in the traditional sense. We were just leaving the corporate world to do other things. Doug's children from his first marriage were grown and living on their own, the stock market was good, and we both had six-figure salaries. We could live very well, and we could maximize savings."

Long before the stock market

> ## "We didn't think of ourselves as retiring in the traditional sense. We were just leaving the corporate world to do other things."

meltdown, the Longmans had a balanced investment strategy. "It included both equities and fixed investments. We never had more than 5% of our portfolio in any one stock, which reduced our vulnerability. The bonds in our portfolio buffered the magnitude of the losses in equities, so we were not as vulnerable as others may have been. So despite suffering significant losses in the market, we still have a large enough investment base to support us comfortably. Now that we no longer have steady salaries to rely upon, it has been psychologically harder to stomach the big downturns in the stock market. But our philosophy has been to stay on the current course because we know that it will pay off in the long term."

Not asking for a lifetime health care package was the one mistake that Marilyn admits she made when she left General Foods. As a result and because the Longmans are too young to qualify for medicare, they must pay a large premium for independent health care insurance. What's more, Marilyn won't be eligible to tap her pension until she's 55.

Looking to relocate, the Longmans' criteria included an academic community in the eastern part of the U.S., with a four-season climate warmer than that of the Northeast or Midwest and a nearby international airport.

Because they were comparative youngsters by usual retirement standards, the Longmans were not overly concerned about medical facilities.

Once relocated to Chapel Hill, Marilyn handled a few nonchallenging commercial consulting projects for package goods companies; Doug had similar consulting experiences. Both were ready to move in new directions. Like a trained corporate planner, Marilyn set some goals: intellectual stimulation by taking college courses (on topics such as women in politics and the history of American women) and more physical exercise. "Another goal was to achieve emotional satisfaction," says Marilyn. "In the past I didn't have time for community work. Now I'm a mentor with the Blue Ribbon Mentor Advocate Program. I've been matched with the same young girl, an eighth grade student, for 3½ years. I spend three to four hours with her each week helping her however I can."

No longer a corporate manager, Marilyn discovered that she didn't really miss the job, and for the first time she feels she's in charge of her life. The Longmans rarely set the alarm clock, and Marilyn avoids early morning meetings, something that was endemic in her former corporate lifestyle.

SPENDS HIS LIFE IN THREE- TO FIVE-YEAR UNITS

Fred Cavalier
PREFERS RELAXING IN RURAL AMERICA

Fred Cavalier is a maverick. He worked 26 years in sales, marketing and management jobs for a number of small to midsize technology companies, followed by five years as an instructor and administrator for a community college. He severed these ties, and then relocated from Raleigh to a log cabin in the mountains of northwestern North Carolina. At 56, Fred was ready to live his dream.

Armed with a bachelor's and master's degrees in biology as well as an MBA, Fred sold pharmaceuticals for a few years, then joined a corporate conglomerate as a sales manager. By the mid 1980s, Fred shifted gears as he headed sales for an electronics and two biotech companies, followed by four years as president and general manager of a West Coast office equipment firm.

Each job was consistent with Fred's financial plan. Over the years, he worked for start-up and turnaround companies. He took risks. Instead of relying totally on a salary, he accepted equity positions. During these years, as Fred switched jobs, he lived in New England, North Carolina and California. "When I was

> ## "I look at my current life as another chapter. I don't know when the chapter will end."

in my mid twenties and already working, I learned that we pay little attention to how to accumulate money. I feel money makes me independent. I've learned how to manage money as one does other parts of one's life. I had to watch my assets and develop a plan, which ultimately had to include divorce, child support and education of my two children. Even so, when I got divorced, I left Connecticut broke. I lived simply. I had few belongings—a TV set and a bridge table."

By the mid 1990s, Fred was ready for his next move. This time he returned to Raleigh, where he already owned a home. He had a coach and mentor who suggested that he teach. His goal was to teach high school business courses, but he found that he was ineligible to teach because he lacked the required "how-to" education courses. Instead, Fred became a part-time instructor at Wake Technical Community College, and a year later he was named director of its Small Business Center.

Fred energized the Center with a series of self-help programs for current and wannabe business owners, but found that he wanted to embark on another adventure. "When I lived in California, I had dreamed of owning a log cabin in the mountains. But that wasn't possible because homes there were too expensive. After returning to North Carolina, I started looking for such a place no more than a 3½ hour drive from Raleigh. I thought it would be a weekend place." By mid 2000, Fred found a suitable mountain site and built a 1,500-square-foot log cabin that abuts the Blue Ridge Parkway.

Returning to Raleigh on Sundays, Fred asked himself the same question: Why live this dual lifestyle? Each Sunday night the answer was the same: He had a job in Raleigh. Fred solved that dilemma in 2002 when he resigned. He cut his ties even further by selling his house.

Fred's action was consistent with his approach to life. "I have a short attention span, and I get bored quickly. I look at my current life as another chapter. I don't know when this chapter will end."

What Fred is doing now represents a 180-degree change from his past corporate lifestyle. "I'm learning how to live in slow motion. It now takes me longer to do things I used to do quickly. I can spend an afternoon going into town for food."

Living by himself in the cabin costs less than it did in Raleigh or California. Too young for social security or pension income, Fred lives on income from investments. "I let my money work for me. I move things around to offset any drop in the market." Other than buying a four-wheel-drive car to handle the rough mountain terrain, Fred says that he's lucky that he doesn't need expensive adult toys.

"I love to walk in the woods with my two dogs, who are in heaven here. My children and friends visit me. What I'm doing is not retirement. I feel that I'm still active, but not in the traditional sense. I might very well do something different in the next chapter of my life, but I don't know when it will begin. In many ways, what I'm doing beats how I use to live. I don't miss living in motels more than my home, waiting for airport limos and driving rental cars."

His immediate aim is to complete four seasons. Then he'll consider if the current chapter will continue or he'll shift to something different. "In a year or so I might find work teaching at one of the two- or four-year colleges in this area, or perhaps even move off the mountain. Right now I haven't gotten myself to think that far ahead. For the first time in years, I feel that I'm in control."

> ## "I don't miss living in motels more than my home, waiting for airport limos and driving rental cars."

Back to School

THE 50-PLUS SET ARE COLLEGE-BOUND, BUT FOR them education often means more than collecting a degree. No longer do they need to play academic "show and tell." Just visit your local four- or two-year colleges. They teem with older students, a few of whom are degree candidates but most of whom are auditing undergraduate courses or participating in a number of noncredit learning alternatives available to older students. Only a small minority of the 50-plus set are getting professional or advanced degrees.

Unlike younger undergraduates, who are scrambling to decide what major to take or career to pursue, or who are grinding away at their studies to earn a grade-point average that will someday look great on their résumé, the 50-plus set are in school for their own reasons. For instance, they might want to:

- **Get a degree** because they didn't have time, couldn't afford to, or weren't interested in obtaining one before.
- **Study something** they were interested in as youngsters but didn't pursue because it didn't seem practical at the time.
- **Study in depth** something that they became interested in over the years.
- **Challenge themselves** intellectually and broaden their scope of interests.
- **Become "renaissance" people.**

- **Further their understanding of a public issue.** They might even put their newfound knowledge to work on behalf of society or their community.
- **Enjoy the ambiance** associated with a college environment.
- **Search for new meaning** in their lives.
- **Break the shackles** associated with a past career.

Adult-education programs geared to older or retired students often provide more than an intellectual experience. For many students, school is a social experience, a chance to make new friends or an opportunity to learn solely for the sake of learning. Since curricula are so diversified, classes attract birds of a feather—you'll meet others like yourself in whatever course attracts you. Husbands and wives frequently take the same courses. For many, it is the first time in their married lives that they have shared a nonfamily experience. Other students form new friendships to replace workplace relationships lost in retirement.

Those Who Do Seek Degrees

Despite all the scrambling for more education, the 50-plus set still make up only 3% of the total number of students obtaining undergraduate, graduate and professional degrees. And when they get their degrees, says the College Board (www.collegeboard.com), a monitor of adult education trends, they "seek degrees that have immediate utility. They deposit their learning into a checking account—not into a savings account—so they can draw on it without delay. To most adults, learning is a liquid resource, not a long-term capital investment."

Return to the Classroom

More significantly, the U.S. Department of Education (www.ed.gov) points out that nearly 9 million men and women age 55 to 64 take adult education courses, but only 9% of them actually earn a degree or certificate. They are taking courses to enrich their personal lives, learn new skills to qualify them for a different job or fulfill a lifetime dream. And it shouldn't be surprising to learn that twice as many of these students over age 55 are women. Consider that many women married, put their husbands through school, and in the process, sacrificed their own undergraduate or graduate education. Now many of these women are deciding that the time has come to obtain a long-delayed degree. As empty nesters for the first time in 25 years, they typically have the time and resources to start or complete their education, embark on a new and more demanding career, or learn for the sake of learning.

WHY ADULT EDUCATION?

- **Rekindle** the flame of knowledge.

- **Meet** other like-minded people.

- **Learn** on your own terms.

- **Master** a new skill.

- **Study** with a particular teacher.

- **Gain** an advantage at work.

- **Update** skills.

Getting Started

If you're interested in returning to school, start your search with your local community college. More than 1,700 public and private two-year community colleges are located within commuting distance of nearly 95% of the nation's population. Couple this with 2,400 four-year colleges and it is easy to see that higher-education opportunities exist at your fingertips. And to ease the financial burden for students who wish to audit courses, 42 states presently waive tuition at public-sponsored colleges for students who, depending on the state, are at least age 60 or 65. It's easy to find out whether your state has a tuition-free program. The registrar's office at your community or state four-year college will have the answer.

Even so, many in the 50-plus set feel uneasy in a traditional college setting—not because of the academic requirements, but because they are apprehensive about attending classes with students one-half to one-third their age. For many, it is the first time in school in 30 or more years. Yet age is frequently an asset in the classroom, as many 50-plus students attest. "Don't worry if you have gray hairs. My general rule is the older the student the better," says Don Higginbotham, history professor at the University of North Carolina in Chapel Hill. "I find that older students who audit my early American and colonial history courses are more serious-minded and better read, and I don't get blank stares from them in class."

While some undergraduates wonder why older students, often the age of a grandparent, take college courses, May Chrisman, a recent UNC graduate, finds that they give a different perspective to class discussions. In a course on the family and society, she said "it was refreshing to hear older students discuss pop culture. They speak up for their generation as we do for ours."

A Different Kind of Master's Degree

Imagine taking a college course called "Magic, Religion and Science in the West," "African American Music in the 20th Century," or "The Foundation of Modern Terrorism." These are just some of the courses available to students attending the 128 colleges and universities that belong to the Association of Graduate Liberal Arts (www.udel.edu/edu/aglsp/about.html). These schools were started for somewhat older students—men and women over 30 who want to pursue a nontraditional course of study and receive a degree in an academic environment geared to their workday schedules. The great appeal of these programs is the curriculum, which differs from traditionally structured master of arts programs. The curriculum is interdisciplinary, permitting students to design a personalized course of study. Typical of these programs is the one at Duke University, where approximately one-third of the 155 students in the program are 50 plus. At DePaul University, 20% of the MALS students are over age 50. "Graduate liberal studies, such as MALS, remain the best place for adult learners to find intellectual growth and challenge in an academic setting," says David Gitomer who directs DePaul's program.

While the association has not conducted a survey of its members since the mid 1990s, it noted at the time that 8,000 to 10,000 students were enrolled in member-college programs, with more than 1,000 receiving master's degrees each year.

Rather than base admission totally on past academic record or performance on the Graduate Record Examinations, school officials also consider the applicant's work experiences. Donna Zapf, the director of Duke's program and a board member of the Association of Graduate Liberal Arts, points out that added maturity, recent accomplishments and a determination to succeed may help offset a weak or outdated college transcript.

Students enter the program for intellectual reasons. They are graded, they are challenged by academic discipline and, above all, they are making a commitment—at least three years to acquire a degree for part-time students and usually a year for full-time students. While no thesis is required, students submit an essay based on original research.

> **Added maturity, recent accomplishments and a determination to succeed may help offset a weak or outdated college transcript.**

The tuition varies in MALS programs, ranging from the lower fees at public institutions to more costly tuition at private universities. Some students are reimbursed by employers or qualify for financial aid.

Alternative Learning

Walk across the Duke campus and you'll find an academic alternative to the MALS program—the Duke Institute for Learning in Retirement (DILR), one of the more than 220 similar college-sponsored adult education programs (www.elderhostel.org/ein), with nearly 52,000 enrolled students. Similar dual opportunities—MALS and Institutes for Learning in Retirement—exist on a number of other campuses.

The curriculum of the Institute for Learning in Retirement conforms to the academic interests of older students, and it's particularly well-suited to retirees who want to break with the past. An Institute is an ideal place for a retired engineer, for example, to explore a wide range of nonscientific subjects.

Duke students, like those at Institutes on other campuses, prefer art, music, literature, history and related social science courses. Even with a curriculum of nearly 75 courses ranging from the mathematics of music to a study of the history of Western seapower, as well as courses for developing computer skills, Institute for Learning programs at the participating colleges offer few how-to or hobby-related courses. Those can be taken at community colleges or through high school adult education programs.

The concept of peer learning is a pivotal part of the Institute programs at most campuses. Students often serve as the faculty, create the curriculum and help operate the Institute. Typically, Institute students have little interest in taking courses for credit or being graded on their academic efforts. The tuition and registration fees on most campuses average about $100 to $400 a semester.

Though anyone 50-plus is eligible for Institute for Learning courses, chances are you will find somewhat older students attending them. The average age of Duke students is 69, and it is slightly higher, 71, at the New University for Social Research in New York City. Enrollment ranges from fewer than 28 students at one school's Institute to more than 2,400 at Brooklyn College's.

Sara Craven, DILR's director, is candid when talking about her program: "Most of the nearly 1,300 people who take at least one DILR class a year do not want to attend class with younger students." Older students have often covered the issues that are new to younger students. DILR students include both high school dropouts and Fulbright scholars.

Institute programs offer more than educational opportunities. They have evolved into a social hub. In Durham, where many of the retirees are newcomers to the area, DILR provides the setting to make new friends. It sponsors duplicate bridge sessions, Sunday afternoon walks, brown-bag lunches and a two-day retreat in the North Carolina mountains.

Molloy College in Rockville Center, New York, has added another dimension to its program by permitting its 80 or so students to mix MILL (Molloy Institute for Lifetime Learning) courses with those taught in the college. "They can audit one course each semester. Nursing, education and a few other courses are out-of-bounds," says MILL director Marion Lowenthal.

SUGGESTED READING

Adult Students Today, by Carol Aslanian (College Board, 2001; www.store.collegeboard.com). The author, an expert on adult education, discusses the trends in adult education.

Going Back to School, by Frank Bruno (Arco Publishing , 2001). The book's title is also its theme.

Elderhostel Mixes Travel With Education

Just reading Elderhostel's 206-page U.S. and Canadian catalog and its companion international catalogs is an educational adventure. Elderhostel (www.elderhostel.org) offers something for everyone with a desire to study and live on campus at one of the 1,900 participating colleges in every state and 100 nations overseas.

The thrust of the Elderhostel program is nontraditional and noncredit education. Don't expect to find conventional college art, political science or music appreciation courses. What you will discover, for example, is a course in Kansas on springtime on the prairie, one in California on composer Scott Joplin, and another in Massachusetts on the history and art of Cape Cod. Overseas courses include one in France on the art and artists of Paris and one in Ireland that offers a chance to learn about Irish life.

Given living arrangements that are sometimes Spartan, the Elderhostel program tends to attract hardier and healthier 60- and 70-year-olds.

Hundreds of thousands of people participate annually in Elderhostel's U.S./Canada and overseas courses. Elderhostel students, who are nearly all retired, must be at least 55. A companion can attend as long as he or she is at least 50. Although accommodations may range from country inns to urban hotels, the cost of some courses are kept to a minimum by living and eating on college campuses—arrangements that are sometimes Spartan. Thus, the Elderhostel program tends to attract hardier and healthier 60- and 70-year-olds. Elderhostel's literature emphasizes that "it is important for participants to be realistic about their physical condition and ability to maintain an intensive schedule. Classrooms, dormitories and dining halls are best suited to people who are mobile and able to climb steps and walk distances without difficulty."

The standard cost for a one-week program, excluding transportation in the continental U.S., averages about $100 a day, slightly more in Hawaii, Alaska and Canada. The fees for the international programs, though less costly than most overseas

---

POINTS TO REMEMBER

- **College extension programs** are the prime educational route for the 50-plus set.

- **Extension programs are not for everyone;** some in the 50-plus set like the discipline of being a matriculated student.

- **Master of Arts in Liberal Studies programs** appeal to some retirees.

- **With Elderhostel,** education means a vacation, too.

- **Many older students feel more comfortable** attending school with their peers than with younger students.

- **Older students enjoy** the college campus environment.

- **Adult education** brings families together.

---

travel tours, vary depending on air transportation, length of course and the type of accommodations. You can access Elderhostel's domestic and international offerings online at its Website, and most local libraries also receive its catalogs.

Who Are These Students?

Here are a few people from the 50-plus set who became students, ranging from candidates for professional degrees to those attending a course for retirees. Each returned to school for a different set of reasons. They all admitted that learning was not as easy as it was 30 to 40 years earlier. For each of these students, college created intellectual challenges as well as new personal and professional opportunities.

SETS A NEW GOAL—OVERCOMING IGNORANCE OF THE LAW

Erle Peacock

SURGEON & PROFESSOR OF MEDICINE TURNED LAWYER & LAW INSTRUCTOR

"When I was an intern, I promised myself that I would stop doing major surgery when I was 65," recalls Erle Peacock, Jr. Forty years later, Erle kept that vow. He quit performing major surgery, though he continued with medical consultations. He also entered the University of North Carolina School of Law, fulfilling an ambition born of his family heritage and an earlier personal and professional scrape with constitutional law. "By then, the light had started to go out, anyway. It was time to move on and act on the promise I made 40 years earlier. But, even though I wasn't performing surgery, I didn't want to retire completely. Complete retirement is the first step to the grave."

Still, Erle thought he might be too old for school. "When I entered law school, a few students told me that their fathers had been students of mine when I taught at the medical school. And I was older than any of my law-school professors." Age, however, in no way deterred him, and while he was the law school's oldest student, his class had a number of other midlife career-changers.

But there was one hitch if he was to enter law school. Erle had never received an undergraduate degree and was short six academic credits. That's because he had been drafted into the Navy during World War II. So besides taking the law school entry exam, Erle had to make up the six semester hours. He was awarded his bachelor's degree in the spring semester of his first year of law school.

Erle discovered that his goal in seeking education had changed. "When I was in medical school my goal was to be at the top of my class, which I was. In law school, I didn't feel the necessity of being the best student in the class. My objective was simply to graduate from law school and pass the bar exam. My challenge wasn't competing with younger students. It was overcoming ignorance of the law."

As if studying to be a lawyer at any age isn't enough of a challenge, Erle faced an additional and unusual one. He had to learn how to evaluate clients and cases as a lawyer, not as a doctor. Hardly a simple process, that meant breaking past professional habits. A doctor evaluates problems in scientific terms,

> **Erle's law degree wouldn't just be another trophy. He would put it to good use, drawing on his background in health care.**

while a lawyer is trained in the social sciences. "Each profession has different disciplines, and each looks at the same situation differently. Now that I'm a lawyer, I need to think and act like one."

From his upbringing in Chapel Hill, North Carolina, it would seem only natural that Erle would be either a lawyer or a college professor. His father taught accounting at the University of North Carolina, and eight of his uncles were lawyers. "Yet I never remember when I didn't want to be a doctor."

After graduating from Harvard Medical School and completing several surgical residencies, military service and 13 years in a dual career as a plastic surgeon and a professor at the University of North Carolina's medical school, Erle was recruited as the first chairman of the surgical department at the newly opened University of Arizona Medical School in Tucson. Little did he realize when he accepted this position that it would have a decided influence on his decision to become a lawyer 20 years later.

His job was to recruit a faculty and to establish the curriculum to educate surgeons. "It was my goal to start a renaissance in surgical education. The program was to be patterned after those in the great European universities before World War II." Such an

> "When I entered law school, a few students told me that their fathers had been students of mine when I taught at the medical school."

educational approach would go far beyond the classical vocational training received by most American surgeons.

Though his program attracted many supporters, it also had its detractors and was abruptly scuttled in 1974 with the arrival of a new group of university administrators. They challenged his theories, then fired him. An eastern medical school wanted him as its dean, but Erle's dander was up, and he decided to stay in Arizona to fight "against overbearing administrators" and for academic freedom and the right of free speech. His case became an education and medical cause célèbre. The federal district court decision supporting the University of Arizona administrators was overruled on four separate occasions on appeal and returned to the district court for a new trial. Erle was supported in his fight for academic freedom by the majority of the surgical faculty and students and by the National Education Association.

Although in the end he was awarded $800,000, the trials were both financially and professionally costly. "But in the process I got interested in constitutional law and my rights as a teacher."

The litigation behind him, Erle left Arizona and joined the Tulane University faculty as a professor of surgery. Five years later, he returned to Chapel Hill and a private surgical practice, until he made the move into law school and his new profession.

Graduating these days as a lawyer—at any age—does not necessarily ensure a job. And while some retirees might view another academic degree as a trophy, with little intention of applying their education in a new career, Erle set his sights on an active legal career in private practice as well as teaching health care law. A large number of Erle's classmates have not found suitable jobs or are working outside the legal profession. But Erle was more fortunate. He was hired by Patterson, Dilthey, Clay and Bryson, a 12-lawyer firm in Raleigh that specializes in representing health care providers in malpractice suits, and several years later Erle formed what evolved into Hollowell, Mitchell, Peacock & Von Hagen, a law firm with a focus on administrative, business and health law.

The irony of Erle's "retirement" hit home his first day on the job as a lawyer when he attended a retirement party for a 62-year old lawyer in the firm. "I asked him about his plans. Did he plan to do what I did but in reverse and now go to medical school? He didn't think so."

ONCE A CLASSICIST, ALWAYS A CLASSICIST

Armando Henriquez, Jr.

HIGH SCHOOL ENGLISH TEACHER TURNED UNIVERSITY INSTRUCTOR

I met Armando Henriquez, Jr. when he was giving a lecture on the classics at a Duke University alumni workshop. His attire, a white toga and sandals, was consistent with the spirit of his talk.

Armando, better known as Mickey, was a high school English teacher in northern Westchester County in New York for 32 years. Born in Tampa, Florida, in a Spanish district, his parents and grandparents were cigar workers, and Mickey learned to speak Spanish before English. Following college and graduate school in Tennessee, Mickey, by then married, moved north and took his first and only teaching job in Katonah, New York.

The toga that he wore at the Duke seminar typifies the classroom style that Mickey used throughout his teaching career. "My job in a course on the Miracles of Greece was to convince high school students how little we all know and that we must come to grips with our own ignorance. I kept students alert by animating and enlivening the class with a bit of histrionics."

Now, as a retiree, Mickey continues to teach and uses his former high-school

> **"With older students, I have to really hold their attention; otherwise they'll walk out on me and go visit their grandchildren."**

classroom style in lecturing to the 50-plus set. When he retired in 1986, family and friends were making book that Mickey wouldn't succeed as a retiree, living a retirement lifestyle. Mickey remembered, however, that Thoreau said we have other lives to live. With that in mind, Mickey and his wife, Martha, moved to Durham to be near two of their three children.

"I could have stayed in Katonah and become an elder statesman. I knew everyone in town after working and living there for 33 years. But what good would that do. You become overly critical. Nothing is like the good old days. It was time to leave Katonah and not get into an old-age rut." Mickey and Martha sold their house and much to their amazement found that the real estate commission on the sale was more than the cost of the house when they had purchased it 30 years earlier. Profits from the sale along with a teacher's pension, savings and social security provide the bulk of their retirement income.

"Martha and I decided not to move to a retirement community. We wanted to live as we did before in an integrated community surrounded by people of all ages and where medical conditions do not dominate the daily conversation. At the time, both my parents were living so we decided to set them up in an apartment near us."

Unlike other retirees to North Carolina who typically play golf and tennis, Mickeys plays neither. Other than family responsibilities, as always, his world focuses on literature and the classroom. Durham and Duke's Institute for Learning in Retirement have become his new stage.

Over the past 15 years, Mickey estimates that he has taught about 40 different DILR courses. What he teaches would hardly fall under the heading of light reading: Plato's *Republic,* Ibsen's plays, and most recently a discussion course on Thornton Wilder's "Our Town" and Samuel Becket's "Waiting for Godot" to name a few. "Since most of my audience were in their prime during the 1950s, I used David Halberstam's book, *The Fifties,* as the theme of a recent premillennium course." Mickey says the book provided the setting to review events that took place in the mid 20th Century.

Mickey finds that teaching retirees differs from teaching teenagers for reasons besides age. "In Katonah, I had a captive audience. My students needed a good grade to get into college. With older students, I really have to hold their

attention; otherwise they'll walk out on me and go visit their grandchildren. And, unlike high school, many of my retired students know more than that I do about the subjects I teach."

Mickey's reputation as an articulate retiree resulted in a paid assignment, writing a monthly 600-word column in the *Raleigh News & Observer.* Appearing under the headline of "Our Lives," representatives of various generations reflect on lifestyle issues that personally affect them and other people their age. In discussing his monthly column, Mickey puts it succinctly, "I talk for the geezers."

Mickey's responsibilities also extend to his grandchildren. When his grandson's Latin class needed an additional chaperon on a school trip to Italy, he says, "I was recruited. We visited Florence, Pisa and Rome, and for Thanksgiving dinner we had pizza in Pompeii."

Even with a son who is a Duke scientific researcher and a daughter who relocated to Durham and works for IBM, Mickey is a reluctant computer user. He remains a classicist at heart. He recently bought his first computer and is corresponding with some friends by e-mail, but he's still not totally sold on computers, at least in his lifestyle. "I'm not altogether sure whether computers build or weaken the relationships between people."

"THE ONLY AGE GULF IS THE ONE YOU DIG"

Alfred Eisenpreis
RETAIL AND ADVERTISING MANAGER GETS DOCTORAL DEGREE

Alfred Eisenpreis enjoys keeping a number of balls in the air at the same time. It was his hallmark throughout a 40-year career in retail and advertising management.

Consistent with his concept of an active retirement lifestyle, Al enrolled as a doctoral student at Cincinnati's Union Institute, which permits students to work off campus, and he received his degree in public policy in late 1999.

"Don't worry if you're an older student," he advises others his age. "The only age gulf is the one you dig. The others students accept you when they know you're also a dedicated student. Going to class is like going to the office. I like the discipline and responsibility."

Formerly a retail and advertising consultant to newspapers, stores and shopping centers, as well as the editorial director of *Retail Ad Week,* for which he wrote a regular column, Al now concentrates on education, nonprofit and economic development projects, putting his business experience, doctoral studies and a long-time interest in public service

> *After working for New York City mayor Abe Beame and the Nixon administration on economic issues, Al gets his doctoral degree in public policy.*

to work for such organizations as the Archaeological Institute of America, New York's Congregation Temple Emanuel-El, the Explorers Club, and the Cancer Research and Treatment Foundation. In late 2002, Al organized and moderated a seminar on the history and authenticity of the Vinland map, which is valued at $25 million and claimed to be the earliest map documentation of the American coastline.

The seeds for Al's retirement strategy were planted early and nurtured throughout his career. Al started out in Wilkes-Barre, Pennsylvania, where his family settled after they fled Austria when he was a teenager. After graduating from St. Thomas College, he worked for 14 years for Pomeroy's, the area's dominant department store and a division of Allied Stores. In 1957, Allied brought him to its New York City headquarters to direct its regional operations.

In 1974, Al was invited by New York City's Mayor Abe Beame to head the city's economic development activities. This was Al's first full-time government appointment, though he had previously served as a consultant on economic stabilization to President Nixon's administration.

With the election in 1977 of Edward Koch as mayor, Al, rather than returning to Allied, became a senior executive of the Newspaper Advertising Bureau, a national trade group that promotes newspaper advertising. His assignment for the next 14 years was to act as a liaison between newspapers and retailers.

Retiring in 1991, Al had little intention of becoming idle. "When you retire, you actually graduate, and you should look to new levels of interests and activities.

"The worst thing for retirees is to stay at home. I even have a small office in midtown Manhattan besides one at home.

"I have computers in both places. The one at home is used to catalog my collection of American political pamphlets and autographs. There's little reason for retirees to be computer-illiterate. If you can work a telephone, why not a computer? You don't need to know how it operates. You go on airplanes, but do you know how they fly?"

It's all part of Al's retirement philosophy, which stresses "the importance of not living in the past, particularly the immediate past. It is my way to maintain my perspective. One thing I discovered, you don't shut off the brain when you retire."

COMBINES COLLEGE COURSES AND ELDERHOSTEL

Frederick Levitt
MANUFACTURER TURNED STUDENT

Even in his seventies, Frederick Levitt considers himself a college student. He's not out to obtain another degree or become an academic expert in any field. Rather, Fred finds it challenging to be on a college campus and take courses with students usually one-third his age. When he's not auditing courses, running his part-time business or playing tennis, he's vacationing with his wife and other seekers on an Elderhostel trip.

Fred's current campus is the University of North Carolina in Chapel Hill. But before he moved to North Carolina, he had taken courses for a number of years at several different colleges near his former home on Long Island. He received his only degree, in political science and economics, from Brooklyn College.

As a current college student, Fred is fortunate. Being over 65, he has only to pay a registration fee and get permission of the instructor to audit courses, usually two each semester. "Unless the course is filled, I usually get in. The courses that interest me rarely have a waiting list."

Unlike some retirees who attend

Institute for Learning in Retirement courses at nearby Duke University, Fred prefers going to class with younger students. "I like the mix; it's half the fun. I avoid taking survey courses because the attendance is too large and there's little interaction with the instructor and the other students. I've yet to find a situation where the students haven't been friendly." Fred brings to class a perspective on issues that comes with age, which many of his instructors and fellow students welcome.

Fred concentrates mainly on courses in the humanities and other topics that interest him. He recently audited courses on the Buddhist tradition in Tibet and India, the comparative economics of the East and West, and the history of Rome from 154 B.C. to 14 A.D. Previously, he studied the history of the Reformation, Moses and the Exodus, and the New and Old Testaments.

Even though audit students of any age are not required to take tests or write essays, Fred at times elects, strictly for his own satisfaction, to write a paper or

> **Fred brings to class a perspective on issues that comes with age, which many of his instructors and fellow students welcome.**

take an exam. Even as an audit student, he's expected to keep up with a demanding reading list. He spends several hours each week reading the required books.

Fred's life since he moved to North Carolina—and what was supposedly retirement with his wife, Claire—has not been limited to academia. A manufacturer of corrugated paper boxes for many years, he sold his business in the 1980s. Now he works from a home office, the equivalent of two days a week, as a broker in the same field. "Most of my customers have been with me for years and are located in the Northeast. Within the past few years, some of these companies have moved South." He services his current customers but rarely seeks new ones. Every few months, he makes a trip to the New York area to visit key customers and suppliers. The rest of the time, a telephone and fax machine are his primary means of communication.

Claire and Fred live eight miles from Chapel Hill in a three-bedroom home in Fearrington Village, a community with a large percentage of retirees. A positive factor in the Levitts' decision to relocate was the proximity to the University of North Carolina and its academic, cultural and health care facilities.

The Levitts' lifestyle is supported by Fred's income as a box broker, his social security, investments and savings.

Fred's busy academic routine is not limited to the University of North Carolina. Claire and Fred for the past several years have participated in at least one Elderhostel trip a year. They spent three weeks traveling and studying in Turkey, and at Mars Hill College, in North Carolina, they studied the politics of Latin America and China. On a lighter note, at Peninsula State College, in Washington, they attended an introductory jazz course, and they traveled to Fort Lewis College, in Durango, Colorado, to learn what takes place behind the scenes at a music festival. They attended rehearsals, met with the conductor and members of the orchestra, and were briefed on every facet of festival life. Attending Elderhostel trips is a way of life for the Levitts. It gives them the opportunity to visit other parts of the country and, in a number of instances, to attend nonconventional courses.

Fred's advice to others on adult education: "Age is no barrier to learning." He purchased a computer so he can cruise the information highway. And, in Fred's thirst for knowledge, he looks forward each semester to scanning the UNC course listings to determine what courses he'll audit.

BROADENS HIS HORIZONS AND SETS THE EXAMPLE

Gil Turcotte
MACHINIST RETURNS TO COLLEGE AFTER A 40-YEAR BREAK

Most folks start and graduate from college within 10 years of finishing high school. Not so with Gil Turcotte, who took a nearly 40-year break.

Born in Canada, Gil has lived most of his life in western Massachusetts, within 15 miles of Springfield. High school diploma in hand, Gil briefly attended college part-time in the late 1950s while he worked as an auto mechanic at Sears Roebuck. Marriage to his wife Anne, the arrival of the first of their seven children (now ages 21 to 33), and a job with Pratt & Whitney in East Hartford, Connecticut, spelled the end of college for Gil.

Gil worked for Pratt & Whitney as a machinist for 33 years. He started at $98 a week, and by the time he retired, his salary had increased nearly tenfold. "I retired rather quickly. I wasn't expecting it at the time," said Gil. "Pratt & Whitney had an early-out program. I was told about it on Friday and had until Monday to make up my mind." Making less money as a retiree presented few problems as the Turcottes already knew how to live frugally.

After taking Pratt & Whitney up on its offer, Gil decided to return to college and get a degree. He wanted to satisfy his own intellectual curiosity and, by setting the example, wanted to encourage several of his children who hadn't attended college to do so.

Westfield State College, about 25 miles from home, was the nearest college where, as a 60-year-old, he would qualify for half-price tuition. He majored in liberal studies. "Westfield accepted most of my past credits except for one course in calculus and analytic geometry where I didn't do too well. I went to college as many as four nights a week. The last two years I went full-time. I even made the dean's list.

"I was fortunate to have a good adviser. She told me what courses and instructors to take or avoid. This was good because, as I discovered, not everyone is good at teaching older students. When I asked two instructors for help, they refused and said that they were there just to teach. Gil's advisor discussed the issue at a staff meeting, and the college went one step further. A plan was designed to direct older students to more accommodating instructors.

"I wasn't at school for the social life.

> "Next to getting married, finishing college was the best feeling in my life."

Other than being polite, I ignored the other students; they weren't interested in me. I was there because I wanted to be in class, not because mommy and daddy were pushing and paying for it.

Gil received his degree in May, 2002, about the same time his son, now a nurse, got his. "Next to getting married, finishing college was the best feeling in my life. College opened my mind. I found that there was more to life than the job. When I retired, I left the company behind while the others couldn't make the break; they live in the past. I go to Pratt & Whitney retiree lunches and the other guys just discuss 'shop.'

"College broadened me in other ways. After one course in which we studied Turkey, Anne and I visited Turkey."

A part-time job that Gil had taken many years before his retirement from Pratt & Whitney supplements Gil's pension income. He and wife Anne share the job of animal control officer, serving their hometown of Wilbraham and a neighboring town, Ludlow. "We're always on call to remove dead dogs, cats, raccoons and skunks. Other than this work, Anne didn't have any other job. Anne works about the same number of hours as I do. We share the job and we go together on as many calls as we can. We earn about $20,000 from both towns. The job requires a lot of social interaction; the classes I took in ethics and sociology have really helped here."

Because of the income he earns from the animal control job, Gil expects to wait until he's 65 to receive social security. His Pratt & Whitney retirement package included a health care package that cost him nearly $900 per quarter. Through his job as an animal control officer, however, he can get medical coverage for $33 a month. When he leaves that job, he'll be eligible for medicare.

"Of the 20 people who retired from Pratt & Whitney when I did, most of them didn't know what they would do. I'm proud to say that I'm the only one who chose to finish my education and get a degree. For some reason or another, I think seniors are afraid of not making the grade."

> **"For some reason or another, I think seniors are afraid of not making the grade."**

ILLNESS IN THE FAMILY PROVIDES FOCUS

Mike Collins
MASTER'S DEGREE PROVIDES MORE LEVERAGE, OPENS MORE DOORS

Mike Collins, 50, has been an independent contractor for more than 15 years, and thoughts of retirement have no place on his agenda. Even so, Mike has taken some steps over the past several years—earning a graduate degree and becoming self-employed—that could be adopted as strategies by many of his contemporaries who are evaluating whether to retire early or are preparing for retirement.

Mike is from Lumberton in southeastern North Carolina and early on learned an important lesson from his parents. "My mother worked for a local car dealer, and my father was the transportation manager for an agricultural company. Neither seemed to enjoy their work. They looked forward to retirement, and work was a case of putting in their time." In contrast, starting in high school, Mike read "success" books. The concept that one had the power to shape one's life became his guiding light.

Mike should have graduated as a radio, television and motion pictures major from the University of North Carolina in Chapel Hill in 1974, but

> **"I didn't want to be the guy in his late 50s who looks at himself and says that I should have done this or that."**

because he was a student who did well only in the courses he liked, he flunked out. He worked for several years, returned to UNC and graduated in 1979. By then, Mike had demonstrated a maverick spirit that would guide his professional life thereafter.

After working for Bell South, 3M and the Standard Register Company, a publisher of airline magazines, Mike decided to switch from corporate employment to self-employment.

"It began when I wrote a book, the *North Carolina Jobhunter's Handbook*. I needed other work to support myself so I started a lawn-mowing service. Next, I convinced the North Carolina Association of CPAs that I could sell advertising in their directories. My commission was 25%. After those experiences, I realized that I could be self-employed and make money."

Additional doors opened up to Mike after he wrote a series of articles that ran in several local business publications. An administrator at Wake Technical Community College's Small Business Center saw one of Mike's articles and asked him to conduct a workshop, which was named "Dynamite Marketing on a Firecracker Budget." This occasional workshop led to Mike's forming a new company, The Perfect Workday, for which he gives about 120 seminars a year, many at industry and association meetings. "Just as long as I stay current I can do these workshops forever. I do change them regularly based on current events, trends and audience interest."

Even after establishing a steady source of income and gaining the freedom of self-employment, Mike looked for additional challenges. "In the early 1990s, I was told to get an advanced degree. I needed something to open more doors for me—a credential to work myself into larger programs. I didn't want to be the guy in his late 50s who looks at himself and says that I should have done this or that. I was pointed toward the MALS (Master of Arts in Liberal Studies) program at Duke."

Mike delayed his decision to get the master's degree until 1999, partly because of procrastination, but also due to family events, including his father's illness in 1994. However, that experience opened Mike's eyes to a new opportunity that would, in a few years, provide the thrust of his master's degree studies. "When my father got ill, he needed a caregiver. In this case it was my mother. But I saw an important vacuum that needed to be filled— understanding the role of caregivers."

When he started at Duke, Mike still was not sure what courses to take. Serendipity stepped in. In 2000, Mike spent several weeks with other MALS students studying at Oxford University, where he heard how welfare programs in Europe respond to the experiences of human development, especially aging. This exposure helped to solidify Mike's academic goals. Combining what he had witnessed during his father's illness with what he had learned at Duke, Mike chose to concentrate on topics related to caregiving. One of his papers depicted how feature films portray caregivers, and his master's thesis explored the various ways that caregiving can be handled.

As a result of his Duke studies, which culminated with his graduation in 2003, Mike also produced a 28-minute video, "Care for the Caregiver," which his new company, Caregivers 101, Inc., is marketing to people like his mother, who years earlier needed to know how to take care of herself while attending to his father.

"If nothing more, my Duke studies kept me from getting stale in my small business lectures. Even better, I can tell my students that I, too, have started a business, Caregiver 101."

AN EVENING COURSE STARTS NINE-YEAR EXPLORATION

Jay Feldman
FROM CORPORATE LAWYER TO MUSIC STUDENT AND DOCENT

When Jay Feldman met with his financial adviser to determine whether he could afford to retire at age 57, he told his adviser that two budget items were nonnegotiable—season tickets to the New York Giants' home football games and a Saturday evening subscription to the Metropolitan Opera.

Following graduation from Harvard Law School, Jay worked for 20 years as a corporate lawyer before joining Nynex (now Verizon), one of the "Baby Bell" companies created by the breakup of the Bell system in the early 1980s. He spent the next 11 years heading up Nynex's corporate and securities law department. In 1994, Nynex was trimming its executive staff, and Jay realized his days there were limited.

"I was not ready for retirement at the time, but I knew I couldn't survive with the company until I was 65. In some ways, I *was* ready to retire. The job no longer offered the same challenges as it once had, and I was spending a lot of time just administering the legal department and supervising other lawyers. Nynex sent me to a financial consultant so I would be prepared to respond to an offer. Before the financial plan was finished, Nynex made its offer. It was June 1, 1994, and I had 30 days to make a decision."

The incentive to retire was a pension and benefit package based on a number of years of service that exceeded those that he had actually worked for Nynex. It made retirement affordable. At the time, Nancy (his wife) worked in an alternative high school program; she would retire three years later.

When he left Nynex, Jay didn't have a plan. He considered but turned down some temporary consulting assignments. "I wasn't ready to go back into the workplace; I never looked back after that. Until then, I had never stopped to think about life in retirement. I knew I wouldn't be golfing everyday, something my father did when he retired as a dentist at 60. Fortunately, Nancy and I had a vacation trip planned for July so it gave me time to think. I knew my plans had to have a volunteer

> **Jay develops his love of music with a once-a-week course at the Juilliard School, and has returned to a love of history while teaching about the Holocaust.**

element—payback for my good fortune to retire with reasonable economic security, and I also knew that I wanted to learn more about classical music and opera. But, I had no idea what opportunities were available."

Jay's answer came via a *New York Times* Sunday advertisement promoting the Juilliard School's evening program. "I loved music and had been attending concerts and opera regularly since the late 1950s. But other than a few courses as a student at Colgate, I had never had any formal musical education. Most of what I knew about music I derived from concert programs and CD notes. I decided to take a course at Juilliard. My approach was experimental. If I liked it, I would take another one."

And, indeed he did. For nearly nine years, Jay has been a once-a-week, not-for-credit student, commuting about 25 miles to class from Port Washington on Long Island to Juilliard at Lincoln Center in New York. His course selection has varied: Mozart operas, Beethoven symphonies, the Wagner Ring Cycle, Mahler Symphonies, and, most recently, one in 20th Century string quartets. "I have tried to alternate between music that I know yet wanted to know more about, and less familiar

The local Holocaust Museum, a few miles east of Jay's home, needed help from two types of people—those who gave money and those who volunteered their time. "I fit the latter type."

genres or composers. One course on Handel's operas led me to attend concert and opera performances that I might otherwise have missed."

Jay's fellow students at Juilliard range in age from those in their 40s to elderly senior citizens. About half of them are retired, and the others come to Juilliard at the end of their workday. The cost for 13 class sessions—the typical number per course—of 90 minutes each is nearly $400 with a 10% discount for students who are 65 and older and another 15% discount for subscribers to the New York Philharmonic.

In keeping with Jay's experimental attitude, he also took seven semesters of a Judaic studies program at the United Synagogue of Conservative Judaism in New York, which was taught by instructors from the Jewish Theological Seminary. In 1995, Jay learned that the Holocaust Museum in Glen Cove, New York, a few miles east of his home, needed help from two types of people— those who gave money and those who volunteered their time. "I fit the latter type," said Jay. "I had always liked history. It was my college major at Colgate. If I hadn't gone to law school, I would have gotten a doctorate and taught history. When I started with the museum, it had about 5,000 visitors a year. Now, we're up to 35,000. Besides school children—and not just Jewish ones—we get visitors from college alumni organizations, senior centers and tour groups. Our job is to help them understand what a holocaust can do to a society."

When he first got involved with the museum, one of Jay's friends said that the relationship would last only a few years. Not so. Jay has volunteered as a docent for four hours a week over nearly eight years—almost as long as his relationship with Juilliard. "I enjoy teaching—the face-to-face relationships with the students and answering their questions. I'm also involved in training new volunteers, and I conduct workshops for teachers on how they should teach their students about the holocaust." Jay was invited to join the museum's board of directors, but turned down the offer. "I wanted to avoid the politics and administrative work. I had had enough of that when I worked."

Volunteerism: More Than a Workplace Substitute

WHEN MARVIN LEFFLER EXITED HIS PLUMBING supply business, he was not concerned about how he would occupy his time. He substituted volunteerism for corporate management. What's more, he had already identified the vehicle that could use his talents.

Having spent more than 40 years in sales and an equal number of years as an active New York University alumnus, Marvin naturally became involved in the restoration and operation of NYU's Town Hall as one of the city's premier public auditoriums. When Town Hall was spun off from the university as a separate nonprofit organization, Marvin was named president. Though this is a nonpaying job, Marvin works a nearly full-time schedule attending to the things he likes and does best—sales, marketing and getting diverse groups to work together.

Most early retirees, like Marvin, return to their roots when they choose to volunteer. Simply put, a former manager or professional has skills and experience needed by nonprofit groups. A doctor assists in a health clinic, an accountant advises start-up businesses, and an educator teaches nonreaders. One thing is certain: Whatever the assignment, 50-plus managers and professionals usually describe their volunteer work as "payback" time, a form of thanks for a rewarding career.

However, after 30 to 40 years of corporate life, the last thing many managers want to do is serve on a nonprofit organization's board of directors. If they are inclined to be volunteers, they often look for assignments where they can use their skills by working directly with people rather than as members of committees or boards of directors. Not that board work is less important, but many 50-plus managers and professionals want to break from their former corporate lifestyle.

Some in the 50-plus set prefer working in a hands-on capacity teaching handicapped children, delivering meals to the elderly at home, or assisting in a health or legal-aid clinic.

WHY VOLUNTEERS PARTICIPATE

The major reasons volunteers give are:

- For personal enjoyment and fulfillment

- Out of a sense of obligation, duty or responsibility to society

- Because people need help

- To stay active

Source: AARP

But even with a desire for one-on-one work, can you imagine being as adaptable as Mark B., who went from a high-profile publishing job to building homes for the urban poor, or Mary Pat Toups, who provides legal assistance to the needy in California and is one of the leaders of the American Bar Association's Senior Lawyer Division. Both are among the volunteers profiled later in this chapter.

"Helping others can be surprisingly easy, since there is much that needs to be done." So say Rosalynn and Jimmy Carter in their book *Everything to Gain*. "The hard part comes in choosing what to do and getting started, making the first effort at something different. Once the initiative is taken we often find that we can do things we never thought we could."

President Carter, at 57, was out of work and, like other retirees, he was looking for new relationships. "For us, an involvement in promoting good for others has made a tremendous difference in our lives in recent years. There are serious needs everywhere for volunteers who want to help those who are hungry, homeless, blind, crippled, addicted to drugs or alcohol, illiterate, mentally ill, elderly, imprisoned, or just friendless and lonely. For most of us, learning about these people, who are often our immediate neighbors, can add a profound new dimension to what might otherwise be a time of too much worrying about our own selves."

The Facts Speak for Themselves

Take a look at the demographics of volunteerism: Approximately 44% of the adult population in the U.S or nearly 84 million Americans are active volunteers, according to the Independent Sector (www.independentsector.org), which represents about 700 philanthropic organizations.

Those who are 50-plus are hardly slackers; a third of this age group spend 3.6 hours a week volunteering, about the same amount of time as given by younger Americans. The U.S. Department of Labor's Bureau of Labor Statistics (www.bls.org) points out that about 45% of people over age 50 volunteer in church-related work, followed in order of preference by work with civic or political, health care, education, social or welfare, and sport or recreational organizations.

AARP finds that retirees with "higher education and those with upper incomes are more likely to volunteer out of a feeling of societal responsibility than older Americans in general."

You might think that an even greater percentage of the nation's 50-plus set would be volunteering. The reasons more people do not volunteer vary, according to an American Association of Retired Persons survey. The primary reasons other than sheer disinterest include lack of available time, physical and health limitations and family concerns. AARP finds that retirees with "higher education and those with upper incomes are more likely to volunteer out of a feeling of societal responsibility than older Americans in general."

Would redefining volunteerism attract more participants? Some people think so. For example, the Experience Corps (www.experiencecorps.org) sponsors a program to pay $100 to $200 a month to part-time school volunteers who are age 55 plus. Experience Corps maintains that nominal payment is one way to attract volunteers. Reporting on this budding trend, staff writer Abigail Trafford of the *Washington Post* suggests that we drop the volunteer label: "Instead, talk about work—paid work, unpaid work, incentive work (earning health coverage or education aid), flexible work (working 10-hour units instead of the 40-hour week). Volunteerism is too narrow, because it excludes people who need some kind of compensation. It also has a negative image suggesting that unpaid work is not as serious as a 'real' job. But community service is serious work. Think of volunteers as 'not-for-personal' profit workers. They're still workers—no matter what the compensation, no matter what the age."

Help Fill the Volunteer Gap

Nonprofit organizations have an insatiable need for volunteers, one that's more difficult to meet than ever before. That's because the leadership and hands-on work in many volunteer organizations historically was provided by women who are now engaged in the workforce. The management skills required to direct a nonprofit group or head a committee were comparable to those used by their husbands in corporate jobs. But the scenario has changed. Women have entered the workforce, and volunteerism, once a substitute for the job market, has become of secondary importance. In response, some nonprofits have adjusted their operations, offering more flexible options so they can continue to attract working women as volunteers. Others are actively recruiting early retirees and nontraditional volunteers. The point is, if you are interested, someone needs your help.

> **"Instead [of volunteer work], talk about work— paid work, unpaid work, incentive work...flexible work."**

Remember, whatever your level of volunteer involvement, don't expect it to be a direct replacement of the workplace. It's not and never will be, but it is often the next best thing. Above all, take on a volunteer assignment with a positive attitude. Most times it permits you to continue to hone existing managerial or professional skills, and in many other instances to learn and perfect new ones. And there is always the opportunity to continue peer relationships.

A Nonprofit Sampler

Every base appears to be covered. Some volunteer groups are national organizations with membership in the millions; others are regional with more specific missions. Nearly all need more volunteer help. If you're concerned with homelessness, then Habitat for Humanity (www.habitat.org) offers some practical solutions. Want to use your management skills? Try either Service Corps of Retired Executives Association (www.score.org) or the National Executive Service Corps (www.nesc.org). If you have a particular skill and don't know how to become a volunteer, you can either scan the Yellow Pages for the names of volunteer organizations in your community or contact local volunteer clearinghouses like the Retired Senior and Volunteer Corps (www.seniorcorps.org) program, which brokers volunteers to dozens of community organizations and agencies. Local newspapers and magazines sometimes publish lists of agencies currently in need of volunteers, and public television and radio stations occasionally conduct volunteer sign-up drives. Here are just some of the possibilities.

Elderhostel Offers Community Service

Many organizations have added community service to their basic programs. Elderhostel (www.elderhostel.org), also discussed in Chapter 3, offers members more than the diet of personal enrichment that they receive on "learning vacations." In 1992, it introduced a number of programs in conjunction with Global Volunteers, the Oceanic Society and Habitat for Humanity (discussed later in this chapter). In 2002, 5,000 retirees enrolled in 80 Elderhostel domestic and overseas service projects.

Interested in Rhode Island and lighthouses? Elderhostel sponsors a one-week project at the abandoned Rose Island Lighthouse near Newport. Volunteers are helping to restore

WAYS YOU CAN HELP

- **Help the poor,** homeless or needy
- **Improve your community** or neighborhood, or the environment
- **Provide services to older people** through senior centers or other means
- **Help people cope** with their problems
- **Tutor schoolchildren** or do other work involving children or youth groups
- **Help out at a hospital** or engage in other health-related work
- **Educate people** on specific topics
- **Foster art, music or other cultural activities**
- **Promote the political process**

Source: AARP

the lighthouse as a museum and the adjacent property as a bird sanctuary. Elderhostel volunteers are involved in reclaiming the Upper San Pedro ecosystem, about a one-hour drive southeast of Tucson. Using skills similar to gardening, they replace vegetation with native plants or they help clear fire breaks. On the lighter side, outdoor enthusiasts can enjoy early morning bird- and wildlife.

Global Volunteers work primarily in rural communities throughout the world, including China, Poland, Indonesia and parts of the U.S. They concentrate on teaching and maintenance work in poor, rural schools.

The Oceanic Society offers a range of environmentally related research assignments, such as studying river dolphins in the Amazon or monitoring sea turtles in Suriname.

The all-inclusive fees for the Elderhostel Service Programs range from approximately $500 to $700 for a U.S. project to approximately $2,700 in Suriname (including round-trip airfare from Miami). Volunteers live in the community, generally in quarters comparable in quality to a college dormitory. Before being accepted in some of the programs, prospective volunteers are asked to sign a form indicating their awareness of the physical nature of the program.

Helping Small Business

The Service Corps of Retired Executives Association (www.score.org), better known as SCORE, provides management and professional know-how to potential, start-up and existing small companies. Funded nearly entirely by the Small Business Administration, which is also a source of a large part of its client base, SCORE offers start-ups and small businesses a menu consisting of one-on-one and team counseling, and workshops in sales and marketing, manufacturing, distribution and record-keeping. In 2002, approximately 10,500 volunteers in 389 local SCORE chapters counseled about 440,000 small-business owners. SCORE seeks volunteers from all levels of corporate life, ranging from managers and professionals to people who ran their own retail, service and manufacturing businesses.

Responding to client needs, SCORE also provides online consulting services. In 2002, 1,100 online consultants replied to 82,000 e-mail inquires, a 45% increase over the previous year. "I've been an e-mail counselor since November, 2001," says John Wyman (profiled in Chapter 8). "This means I go into a 'members only' SCORE Website and indicate my availability for receiving e-mails as well as how many e-mails per day or week I want to tackle. My maximum is one e-mail assignment a day. I receive about 15 new clients a month, and I respond to about 35 new e-mails and follow-ups. SCORE requires us to respond to each inquiry within 48 hours, but I generally do so within 24 hours."

In contrast with traditional one-on-one consulting, John selects the time when he will respond to queries, usually in the evening. When he will be away, he removes himself from the SCORE availability list.

"One of the reasons I like e-mail counseling is that I can go into the SCORE database and give my qualifications and the geographic areas where I would like to work. I've picked people living in central Virginia, North and South Carolina." In some instances, where clients are "local," John personally meets them.

THE SIX SECRETS OF VOLUNTEERING

People sometimes talk themselves out of volunteering or give it up for reasons that they actually have control over. They're afraid they will end up doing something that's helpful, but absolutely boring. Or they're afraid the organization will demand more of their time and energy than they want to give up. After all, they just got off the workaday merry-go-round. But before you write off the possibilities, try following these suggestions provided in a pamphlet distributed to volunteers in Minnesota.

- **Determine your reasons for volunteering.** This chapter will help you define them.

- **Determine your time limitations.** How much time can you reasonably offer, given your other commitments and your desire for leisure?

- **Seek agencies whose work you support.** Volunteer clearinghouses, like the one described below, can help you in your quest.

- **Communicate your goals and limits clearly.** If you plan to be away on vacation for a length of time, the organization should be aware of your limited availability.

- **Fulfill your end of the bargain.** As in business, if you say you'll head a committee or prepare a report, then do it.

- **Ask for an evaluation of your work.** It's nice to get a report card to measure your effectiveness.

The majority of John's clients ask fairly basic questions that require routine replies. The remainder he calls the "fun contacts," that is, those who desire a mentor to help them through a crisis or need on-going help to launch a new business, as was the case with a dermatologist who was setting up a new office in northern Virginia. John worked online with him on ways to set up and staff his new office.

Management Assistance for Nonprofits

The National Executive Service Corps (www.nesc.org) provides management assistance via 32 affiliate offices to nonprofit organizations in the U.S. In 2002, approximately 2,800 consultants furnished an estimated 126,000 hours of consulting services. NESC seeks individuals with a broad array of management and professional skills.

I've been an Executive Service Corps volunteer consultant with the Greater Triangle ESC since 1993. Our group started in 1987. We have approximately 40 consultants, and we handled about 30 different assignments in 2002, ranging in size from several large nonprofits to a number of mom-and-pop social service agencies. Projects have varied from organizing a one-day board and management retreat to nine-month or longer marketing, management or financial assignments. Client fees are comparatively modest, from a low of $50 for a small, start-up nonprofit agency with limited financial resources to several thousand dollars for larger organizations. ESC can afford to keep a lid on fees because its consultants are all volunteers. Over the past ten years, I've consulted with an AIDS residence group, an historical site, a mental-illness facility, a theatrical group and the Durham County Library. One of the by-products is a chance to become associated with different organizations. As a result of my library consultancy, I became one of its trustees and subsequently chairman of the board.

> **One of the by-products is a chance to become associated with different organizations.**

ESC volunteers advise social service, education, health care, cultural and performing arts, religious and governmental nonprofit agencies on such management fundamentals as how to prepare budgets and financial reports, create long-term strategic plans, recruit board members, improve the relationship between the board and professional staff, formulate fund-raising strategies, and improve personnel policies.

Nearly every assignment starts by matching a volunteer's skills to a nonprofit's specific requirements. When the New York Philharmonic requested NESC's assistance, it asked for someone

THE GRANDDADDY OF 'EM ALL

The Telephone Pioneers of America (www.telephone-pioneers.org), as its name indicates, is a pioneer in volunteering. A nationwide group started in 1910, its membership consists of more than 750,000 retired and long-term employees of the U.S. and Canadian telecommunications industry. The Pioneers, mostly AT&T and regional Bell operating company employees, donate nearly 30 million hours a year to volunteer work. Special attention has been given to projects that help the lonely, disadvantaged and disabled, such as building a 900-foot boardwalk that gives disabled and elderly people easier access to the wooded areas in Flat Rock Brook Nature Center, in Englewood, New Jersey. More recently, the Pioneers have focused on such social problems as illiteracy, homelessness and substance abuse.

who understood both music and marketing. William Selden was given the job. Many of Bill's corporate and personal skills were ideal for the assignment. Bill had been employed for almost 40 years by several retail and apparel manufacturing firms. A late 1980s leveraged buyout of the company where he was a principal put him into an earlier-than-expected early retirement.

The Philharmonic was a perfect fit because Bill played the viola and collected antique stringed instruments. His task was to review the orchestra's whole marketing operation and to help it find ways to attract more subscribers. The Philharmonic has adopted many of Bill's recommendations, including providing subscribers with more flexible ways to buy concert tickets.

Sergio Sedita had a different set of motives when he became an NESC volunteer. Sergio was a retail banker with the same bank—originally Chemical Bank, now JP Morgan Chase—for 39 years. "At age 60, I received a two-year buyout package. I thought I was ready for retirement, but, to my surprise, I wasn't prepared. My initial reaction was a feeling of being lost. I had a very empty spot in my life without the structure I had had in banking." After four years in NESC's Arts Group, Sergio finds that two days each week of volunteering has given him back the structure that he missed.

Mobilizing Professional Talent

ReSet (the Retired Scientists, Engineers and Technicians; www.resetonline.org), formerly a part of the now defunct Emeritus Foundation, mobilizes the time and talents of retirees with scientific, engineering and technical skills to assist in classrooms in the Washington, D.C. area. It typifies what a nonprofit can do in a single locale. The headline of ReSet's brochure states its goal: "McDonald's or McDonnell Douglas? Shouldn't we give our children a fair shot at a promising future?" Volunteers commit to one hour of classroom time per week over a six-week period. In a typical fourth-grade classroom assignment, an electrical engineer demonstrates how electricity is generated using magnets and wires, and then follows-up by escorting students on a field trip to a power generating station to see electricity at work. The organization's volunteers have included a geologist who helped plan the first moon landing and another who was a laboratory chief at Walter Reed Medical Center.

A Need for Health Care Services

You may think of Hilton Head Island, South Carolina, as a paradise for the island's 35,000 permanent residents and the annual 1.5 million vacationers who visit there. But a real-life problem exists: An estimated 12,000 residents and people working on Hilton Head receive few if any primary health care services. What's more, a significant number of the island's schoolchildren have never been examined by a physician.

Dr. Jack McConnell, a physician and, until his retirement, Johnson & Johnson's corporate director of advanced technology, along with a number of other retired health care professionals living on Hilton Head, recognized the area's health care deficiencies and in 1992 started the Volunteers in Medicine Clinic. The clinic's volunteer staff of retired physicians, nurses, dentists and chiropractors provides free vaccinations, physical examinations, primary healthcare, as well as care in the areas of pediatrics, gynecology, cardiology, ophthalmology, and dentistry for upward of 22,000 patient visits a year. The clinic also gives retired health professionals a chance to be professionally productive.

The Hilton Head clinic has nearly 160 volunteer health care professionals, but, says Dr. McConnell, a volunteer clinic could operate with only one physician and a nurse.

Before it opened, the clinic managed to get a bill through the South Carolina General Assembly creating a "Special Volunteer License" for physicians who agreed to practice medicine free of charge in a nonprofit clinic and to dispense drugs. In practical terms, the physicians, dentists and other retired health care practitioners are licensed to practice only at the Volunteers in Medicine Clinic. The clinic also obtained unlimited malpractice coverage from the South Carolina Underwriters Association for its staff of health care and lay volunteers for $5,000.

The retired physicians need to apply individually to the State Board of Medical Examiners for the special license. The Board then thoroughly searches the applicant's credentials. The protocol adopted in South Carolina, of course, would vary from state to state for similar types of volunteer clinics.

Some of the retired professionals in Hilton Head have an opportunity to continue in their medical specialties, such as gynecology, ophthalmology, pediatrics and dermatology, while others are assigned as primary-care physicians. A continuing education program is conducted at the clinic on a weekly basis. To many of the participating physicians, the clinic provides a chance to work directly with patients, use skills and be an active player in a medical facility.

According to the Volunteers in Medicine formula, the proper utilization of retired health care professionals should help to control health care costs by relieving hospital emergency rooms of the need to furnish high-cost, primary-care medical services. The Hilton Head clinic has nearly 160 volunteer health care professionals, but, says Dr. McConnell, a volunteer clinic could operate with only one physician and a nurse.

Hilton Head is the only U.S. town in which everyone who

lives there now has access to health care, says Dr. McConnell. To date more than 1,250 communities have either visited or contacted the Volunteers in Medicine Clinic, requesting information or help in replicating a clinic in their community. The Volunteers in Medicine Institute (www.vimi.org) was established to respond to these requests. Twenty other clinics are up and running in 11 states, and most likely an equal number are in various stages of development. Dr. McConnell's dream? "There is sufficient retired medical personnel (about 550,000 physicians, dentists and nurses), who if prompted to come out of retirement on a part-time basis, could deliver most of the health care services needed by the 45 million Americans who have been left with little or no access to health care."

> **A growing number of retired lawyers are providing free legal services to low-income people with everyday legal problems.**

What About Free Legal Services?

A growing number of retired lawyers, many among the 11,300 members of the Senior Lawyers Division of the American Bar Association (www.abanet.org/srlawyers), are providing free legal services to low-income people with everyday legal problems. Arizona, California, Florida, New York and Texas have already adopted pro bono participation programs whereby state bar association dues are waived just as long as the attorney receives no compensation for volunteer legal services. Other states are debating similar types of legislation for retired lawyers. Unlike the open policy in the other states, California does not grant emeritus status to lawyers previously not admitted to practice in the state.

Typically, members of the Senior Lawyers Division, who are age 55-plus, are involved in representing indigent clients in such areas as landlord-tenant and consumer matters, family law, senior citizen issues, public benefits and immigration law. The amount of time devoted to pro bono work varies greatly. As in all professions, there are some lawyers who do no volunteer work while others devote a full week at a time to representing those who are less fortunate. The Division sponsors educational programs dealing with the legal and personal issues of Alzheimer's, social security and comprehensive health care.

The Division also develops, publishes and presents educational programs and material to guide lawyers in making the transition from full-time to part-time jobs, changing careers or retiring.

Harnessing Corporate Leaders

Finding a volunteer program may be as simple as finding out what programs your company already sponsors. It can be a great way to stay in touch with your fellow retirees and at the same time serve the community. If you haven't been involved before, this may be the time to start. Your company may be able to help you get involved, and if it can't, you may be able to help it get involved. Here's how.

Imagine a volunteer organization that has a client roster consisting of 3M, Amoco, Citibank, Heinz, Hewlett-Packard, and Honeywell. The National Retiree Volunteer Coalition, which merged with the Volunteers in America (www.voa.org) in 2000, has just that and offers a novel twist to volunteerism. Its mission is to help companies mobilize retirees into volunteer groups.

To be sure, some companies go it alone, but others want to avoid reinventing the wheel when it comes to establishing and running a volunteer program for retirees. NRVC offers a high level of know-how and experience. It shows corporate clients how to recruit and train volunteers, meet meaningful goals and objectives, conduct long-range planning and develop community partnerships. A nonprofit organization, NRVC offers these services to corporations on a fee basis with 68 corporations in the U.S. and Canada presently operating under the VOA/NRVC umbrella.

Why don't retirees volunteer on their own? And why should companies start a new corporate service when they are in the process of reducing overhead expenses? Companies find that many of their retirees want to maintain collegial ties but typically don't have a history of volunteering. Past reports show that 70% of the people recruited by NRVC's participating companies have never before served as volunteers. These companies view community service as a beneficial and practical corporate activity. In short, volunteerism proves to be a sound community relations investment.

Honeywell, NRVC's charter member, reports that its volunteers over the past 20 years have contributed several million hours of service, handling a range of projects calling for different management, technical, administrative, professional and blue-collar skills. "[If you] estimate [the value of] the volunteer time," says James Reiner, Honeywell's former CEO, "at a very conservative $12 an hour, that's $50 million worth of value added to the community."

Typical of Honeywell's contribution is a design team of retired Honeywell engineers and scientists who created and assembled a hands-on electricity and magnetism kit, and a machine kit for use with third and fourth graders in schools in the Minneapolis area. Students learn about series and parallel circuits, and see how motors work. The role of the retiree is not to lecture or do the work, but to support, mentor and provide good adult role models.

Honeywell's Assistive Technology Project uses a volunteer core of nearly 60 retired Honeywell engineers, physicists and technicians who work with nonprofit agencies in the Minneapolis area designing and building special equipment for physically and mentally challenged people.

> ## SUGGESTED READING
>
> *Dynamic Boards,* by James Hardy (Essex Press, 1990). As a board member, I've used this book.
>
> *Starting & Running a Nonprofit Organization,* by Joan Hummel (University of Minnesota Press, 1996)
>
> *Successful Fundraising,* by Joan Flanagan (Contemporary Books, Chicago, 1993)
>
> *Volunteering,* by Hope Egan (Barnes & Noble, 2002)

Building for the Future

Amateur and skilled carpenters, plumbers and electricians alike are welcome at Habitat for Humanity International (www.habitat.org). Using a volunteer labor force of youngsters through oldsters in more than 1,900 affiliates throughout the U.S. and overseas in 83 other countries, Habitat for Humanity has built or rehabilitated more than 125,000 homes for people

WAYS TO MAKE A CONNECTION

Besides working through the volunteer clearinghouses discussed beginning on the following page, here are some proven ways of locating volunteer groups that need your help.

- **Many newspapers** publish "volunteers wanted" listings; TV stations feature them in public-service announcements.

- **Your library's reference desk** may maintain a file of literature from volunteer groups, or the librarians may know of other ways to search the field.

- **Scan the *Yellow Pages*** under categories including "Associations," "Political Organizations," "Volunteer Services" or "Social Service Organizations."

- **Read bulletin boards** in public places.

- **To make a quick connection** with the organization of your choice, call and ask for the volunteer coordinator.

who otherwise couldn't afford decent housing. Not every Habitat volunteer has the stamina or skill to build a house. One alternative is to work at the thrift stores operated by a number of affiliates.

Visit downtown Paterson, New Jersey, and you'll see Habitat for Humanity volunteers in action. The area looks like any other construction site—workers in coveralls, hammers pounding and saws buzzing. But on Wednesdays, the scene is somewhat different. The workers, mainly 50-plus retirees, including former managers and craftsmen, have helped to build more than 100 duplex and triplex homes since the Paterson affiliate began in 1984. Some of the volunteers made their living as plumbers and carpenters, others are skilled hobbyists, and some are novices like one retired physician, who said, "When I first went to work I just bent nails; now I can 'finish' them and work on my own."

Help to Find Your Niche

AARP (www.aarp.org) sponsors a number of community-service programs for its 35 million members. For example, in 1979, AARP started 55 Alive/Mature Driving, the first nationwide refresher driving course designed exclusively for people over age 50. Taken annually by 640,000 drivers, it spins off a tangible benefit. Insurers give discounts on auto insurance rates in 34 states and the District of Columbia. The program consists of an eight-hour classroom course with AARP volunteer instructors doing the training.

Each year AARP Tax-Aide (www.aarp.org/taxaide) places 30,000 volunteers in local offices to help low- and moderate-income older persons prepare federal and state tax returns. It also operates a national computerized-matching project that refers volunteers to AARP projects and other nonprofit agencies that are in need of their services.

A Giant Volunteer Agency

Recognizing that corporate downsizing and early retirement have increased the pool of potential volunteers, the Retired and Senior Volunteer Program (www.seniorcorps.org) has lowered its membership age from 60 to 55. RSVP, a part of the Corporation for National and Community Service, the federal domestic volunteer agency, is a massive broker of people, linking volunteers with organizations and agencies in need of volunteers. An estimated 500,000 volunteers spend four hours a week with approximately 65,000 local organizations such as childcare centers, libraries, parks, museums, outreach programs and hospitals. RSVP offers nonprofit agencies a base of volunteers with a range of business, education, administrative and blue-collar skills. Its mission is to enhance the lives of the volunteers and the communities in which they live. While RSVP has little difficulty placing accountants and marketing people, skills often in demand at nonprofit agencies, the organization finds it a greater challenge to place volunteers whose workplace skills are not in demand in childcare centers, libraries, parks, museums, outreach programs and hospitals.

POINTS TO REMEMBER

- **Giving back to the community or society** in which one has enjoyed success is one of the primary reasons that the 50-plus set work as volunteers.

- **There is no shortage of opportunities** to serve as a volunteer.

- **There's a volunteer job to fulfill every interest.**

- **Professional and management skills** are always in demand.

- **Many managers and professionals prefer** hands-on volunteer work—not administrative work.

- **You can learn new skills** as a volunteer.

- **Corporate America is packaging volunteer programs** for early retirees.

Volunteers in Action

The retirees who are profiled on the following pages devote large blocks if not most of their free time as volunteers. They share a common bond—they have applied their workplace enthusiasm and skills as volunteers. Some were active volunteers throughout their business careers; others became volunteers when they retired. A few had to learn new sets of skills to be volunteers, while others simply used existing skills to do their work. What you'll see are the range of opportunities available to the 50-plus set, including a retired executive-search consultant who gets retirees in their eighties enthused about computers.

SHE SPEAKS FOR THOSE WHO NEED HER

Mary Pat Toups
TRIAL LAWYER TURNED ADVOCATE FOR THE POOR

Many women in the 50-plus set have much in common with Mary Pat Toups and her mid-life career as a lawyer, which she has parlayed into a nearly full-time volunteer commitment in retirement. She specializes in serving the elderly poor and actively recruits other senior lawyers to the effort.

Mary Pat was married by the time she graduated from the University of California in Los Angeles, then for 20 years she was a homemaker, a civic volunteer and an elected school board member. Seeing the influence of lawyers in the governmental process, Mary Pat decided when she was in her early forties to become a lawyer. She was one of ten women in a class of 100 at Pepperdine University School of Law.

"My work as an elected school board official prepared me for law school by making me conscious of issues facing children, parents, the poor and the elderly. When I passed the California bar examination, I became a sole practitioner, taking any case that walked in the door." She also liked the independence of being her own boss.

When her husband, a civil engineer

> **"I want to empower senior citizens so they better understand the laws that impact on their lives."**

(from whom she was divorced in the early 1980s), was transferred to Washington, D.C., in 1978, Mary Pat decided to concentrate on a few legal specialties that personally interested her. "I first specialized in representing abused and neglected children, and then in 1984, I started to specialize in elder law." By then, Mary Pat had recognized that poorer elderly people received inadequate legal assistance.

As a practicing Washington attorney, Mary Pat never had a formal business office. "For $50 a year, my office was the library in the courthouse. All my child-abuse cases were assigned by the District of Columbia Superior Court. It was mostly trial work, which is like the theater. Both require acting and dramatic skill."

When Mary Pat turned 63, she decided to return to Southern California to be nearer her sons and daughters and grandchildren, though she fully intended to continue practicing law.

Leaving Washington meant selling her Watergate apartment and severing her ties with the Washington community, especially the Kennedy Center for the

Performing Arts. As a drama and music fan, she had performed as supernumerary and had had nonsinging, walk-on roles in several operas—*Tosca, La Boheme, Manon,* and the Royal Ballet's performance of *The Prince of the Pagodas.* "I'd be in court all day, then rehearse until midnight. We were paid a $70 honorarium and had to agree that we would only 'mouth' words, never sing them."

In California, she bought a two-bedroom home in an adult community in Laguna Hills, near Los Angeles. For more than a year, she commuted from the East Coast, living and working in both areas as she severed her professional and personal ties in Washington. Mary Pat financed her move and her "retirement" with profits from the sale of her home and income from investments, social security, and payments from writing and teaching. "In short, I'll never go hungry."

She practices multifaceted advocacy. Her legal practice is now totally voluntary. "I wouldn't consider it a good week unless I spend two days at the Legal Aid Society office in Santa Ana. I no longer accept fees. I only take clients on a consultation basis, referring them to other lawyers if necessary for additional legal help. Mary Pat estimates that she has helped an average of about 200 pro bono clients (defined by the American Bar Association as those who receive legal services at no fee or for a greatly reduced fee equivalent to the minimum wage) a year for each of the past ten years.

"I want to empower senior citizens so they better understand the laws that impact on their lives." This she accomplishes through her writing, teaching and active participation in the ABA's Senior Lawyers Division. Mary Pat has taught a how-to law course for the elderly at a local community college; wrote a column, "Legal Issues for Seniors," for the *Laguna Woods News;* and wrote a book, *Senior Lawyers Organizing & Volunteering: a National Profile,* which the ABA published.

Mary Pat is an advocate in the broadest sense, recruiting older and retired lawyers to work as volunteers with the elderly poor. Her goal is to convince them that, as retired lawyers, they can use their skills to help the elderly understand their legal rights. It might be difficult for some lawyers who formerly had large, well-paying practices to work at this level, but volunteering with groups like the Legal Aid Society represents one way for them to continue being active, practicing lawyers. Mary Pat provides a model; for her efforts, she was selected by the ABA to receive its "Pro Bono Publico Award" at its 2003 annual meeting in San Francisco. She was honored because her entire legal practice has been pro bono. Mary Pat made the awards ceremony into a family affair, with her four children, their spouses and six grandchildren, ages 3 to 16, attending.

SPREADS THE WORD ABOUT COMPUTERS

Herbert Halbrecht
EXECUTIVE RECRUITER TURNED COMPUTER LITERACY INSTRUCTOR

Herbert Halbrecht spent 30 years in the information technology field. He was neither a techie nor an information specialist. Herb was the founder and principal of Halbrecht Associates in Stamford, Connecticut, an executive search firm that recruited top-level managers in the information technology and telecommunications fields. Herb describes his forte as a "layman who understood the dynamics of the field." His industry experience enabled him to be one of the founders and a president of the Society of Information Management.

A former entrepreneur, Herb continues to convey the enthusiasm of the workplace in his approach to volunteerism.

Now retired, Herb continues to apply his understanding of technology in a different setting—helping retirees, many in their eighties, to go online, or teaching school children their computer ABCs.

After Herb sold his business and his house in Connecticut, he relocated to Durham, North Carolina, and started a personal mission to make more folks computer literate. "Before retiring, I had never used a computer, even though I was involved in the high-tech worlds of information, telecommunications and assorted exotica. I took several brief courses on computer usage at Duke, but I don't consider myself the typical user. I do very little word processing. I'm not a real computernik. I'm mostly interested in e-mail and the Internet. What I do doesn't call for being a computer techie."

Because he wanted to help the elderly learn how to use computers, Herb talked with gerontologists at Duke University. They convinced him that older people often suffer from severe loneliness and the related health problems that loneliness produces, namely depression and physical illnesses. To test this theory, Herb became involved with the Methodist Retirement Home in Durham. His goal was to get elderly residents to use computers.

A former entrepreneur, Herb continues to convey the enthusiasm of the workplace in his approach to volunteerism. To launch the project, he donated three computers to the Methodist Home. The 310 residents were asked to enroll in the computer course; 18 people signed up, 16 of them actually took the training, and 14 of them completed the six hours of training. Currently 35 residents at the Methodist Home are computer users. "One resident who is 69 met a 71-year-old from Texas on the Internet. When I last saw them they were engaged. Some residents use the chat rooms to exchange ideas on hobbies, or they play bridge over the Internet. Another resident sends e-mail letters to a son in Denver who rarely writes or calls her."

Herb feels that computers scare older people. Even so, they can enjoy many of the advantages of networking with new devices such as Web TV. Toward that end a program was initiated in Durham with the Jewish Family Service. "We installed Web TV in the homes of five shut-ins to help them decrease their loneliness. One of the five users was middle-aged but wheelchair bound, while the others were in their late sixties and seventies."

At the other end of the age spectrum, Herb also works with elementary schoolchildren. "I'm obsessed with education. It was my way up. For the past eight years, even when I was living in Connecticut, I've been an elementary-school tutor." Herb's interest goes beyond teaching youngsters to read. He works with students to make them computer literate. "If I can learn how to operate a computer then they can, too. We can teach almost any fourth- or fifth-grade student the basics of the Internet in 30 minutes; third-grade students take a little longer.

"In Connecticut, I tutored second-grade kids. In Durham, I've been a reading tutor at a local magnet school. Originally, I was working and assisting a reading-recovery teacher for three years, and two years ago I started teaching third- to fifth-graders how to use the Internet, how to access certain Websites and how to use search engines. Then I helped to initiate a program that sets up training tutorials for the teachers to essentially 'demystify' the Internet."

As a low-tech computer user, Herb is guided by a single principle in working with retirees and school children. "When older people say to me that they never could use a computer because they don't know how it works, I ask: Do you know how your car's engine works? Who cares? You just drive."

THE LIFETIME VOLUNTEER

Iris-Rose Ruffing

GIRL SCOUT EXECUTIVE TURNED CONSULTANT TO NONPROFITS

When Iris-Rose Ruffing graduated from Meredith College, she went to work for the Girl Scouts, an organization where women could rise through the ranks without discrimination. By the time she retired in the late 1980s, Iris-Rose had spent 26 years with the Girl Scouts as a paid professional and a score of additional years as a volunteer, with time off for marriage and raising two daughters. After a lifetime of either being a volunteer or supervising them as a Girl Scouts executive, she signed up as a volunteer with the Executive Service Corps.

As a former employee, her partiality to the Girl Scouts is based on the way the organization operates. "The Scouts are unique. There never was a glass ceiling since the organization is run by women. This has enabled women to fill leadership positions that were not open to women in industry until relatively recently."

Widowed at an early age, Iris-Rose, a North Carolina native, was living at the time in Greensboro, North Carolina. When she went back to work, she was named director of the regional council serving Girl Scouting in that community.

"After my council was merged with another council, I was no longer in charge. I was given a new job in the merged council, but frankly my nose was out of joint. I liked running my own show. I promised myself that I would stay in Greensboro until my youngest daughter went to college. When that took place, I was transferred to the Chicago area to head a council comprising 18 Chicago communities. I intended to stay for six years, but I ended up staying 18 years until I retired."

With a paid staff of 14, along with a cadre of volunteers, Iris-Rose learned most of the tricks of the nonprofit world from the Scouts. "You soon discover the importance of volunteers. Without them, a nonprofit organization can't exist. I had a board of 25 people who represented the economic and racial diversity of the 18 communities that we served. I had to learn how to work effectively with all of them if I was to succeed in my job."

About a year before Iris-Rose planned

> "You soon discover the importance of volunteers. Without them, a nonprofit organization can't exist."

to retire, she started preparing for her departure. She reached out to the Chicago affiliate of the Executive Service Corps to help her in the transition and to ready her board. "When I left the Scouts, I was not altogether sure whether I'd stay in Chicago or return to North Carolina. I liked Chicago and its cultural life," she says.

Following her retirement and still debating whether to move or stay put, Iris-Rose joined the Chicago ESC as a consultant, applying her know-how about the workings of the nonprofit world. Eventually, she left Chicago and returned to North Carolina. This was "home," even though her two married daughters with two daughters of their own lived in Florida and Georgia.

As an expert on effective management of nonprofit organizations, Iris-Rose's talents were soon put to work by the ESC affiliate serving central North Carolina. "This is a natural thing for me to do. It means sharing my past skills and my experiences that I learned as a Girl Scouts executive.

"Volunteering should mean more to retired executives than payback time, a way they can say 'thanks' for a successful career. More important, it is a way that retirees can feel useful by applying what they know best to help others," she says.

FROM SUITS TO COVERALLS

Mark B.

PUBLISHING EXECUTIVE TURNED HOMEBUILDER FOR THE POOR

"At 57, I was literally reorganized out of my company." That's how Mark B. frankly refers to his leave-taking in 1989 from his job as president of several departments in a major publishing company. Mark received job offers, but he didn't want to return to work. His immediate response to being downsized was to play.

Why not? Because of his employer's excellent retirement and benefits program, he could afford to continue his present lifestyle. He had little need to work to pay the bills. He lived the life other would-be retirees can only fantasize about. He scuba dived, sailed and played tennis. He biked in France, skied during the winter, and in the summer vacationed at his Cape Cod home.

Two years later, Mark was still living the life of Riley. It was enjoyable, but by his own standards he was, for the most part, idle and increasingly dissatisfied. Right after he returned from a summer vacation, his wife suggested that he broaden his interests beyond being a director of the local YMCA, singing in a local choral group and sailing. She wanted to know how he expected to spend his time. Knowing that Mark was a skilled home craftsman and do-it-yourselfer, she suggested Habitat for Humanity. "I called, and in two days they had me at work," he says.

Becoming part of a local Habitat for Humanity has furnished Mark with a vehicle for his various skills and interests. As a member of a Habitat construction crew, he enjoys working with his hands building small one-family homes in northern New Jersey. At first, Mark was satisfied to be just another Habitat worker, spending several days a week as a builder. After a corporate career that emphasized administration, office work, and obligatory meetings and conferences, he was glad to be doing hands-on work. But Mark couldn't totally escape his management roots, and he was elected to the affiliate's board of directors and served as chairman of its building committee. In his new role, he helped to systematize a number of procedures, including

> **After his company downsized, Mark was, the for the most part, idle and increasingly dissatisfied. Then he picked up a hammer for Habitat for Humanity.**

scheduling of construction materials so that they are delivered to the appropriate site when needed.

Construction had been a recurring theme, one way or the other, throughout Mark's work life. He grew up in suburban New Jersey, and he worked part-time in college on some construction projects. Mark attended Wagner College with the intention of becoming a Lutheran minister, but his career goals changed. Following graduation, he joined the Army and was trained as a Russian-language specialist. After the Army, he sold real estate, got married and, after a two-year stint at New York Telephone, was hired by a construction company where he was directly involved in supervising building projects. Little did he realize that 30 years later this experience would provide the thrust of his retirement lifestyle. The business, however, did not succeed and was dissolved.

As a married man, Mark needed steadier work. He landed at a major publishing company, where his varied experience led to a job selling advertising space in magazines. Promotions came rapidly, and by the time he left the company 26 years later, Mark had headed nearly every operation, from information systems to books and publications, including several professional and news magazines.

His downsizing from the company resulted in a two-year odyssey. "I had lots of time to reflect on current corporate conditions. With what's going on in business today, this is a wonderful time to be out of corporate life, since so much of a manager's time involves downsizing both programs and people. It is not a very creative experience."

Mark is long gone from the corporate roller coaster, and he's found the fulfilling outlets he needed in retirement. From the several days a week he spends on Habitat construction and board assignments, he has discovered that "there's nothing like seeing a neighborhood change and giving people the chance to live in their own home."

Despite Mark's immediate attraction to Habitat work, he feels other retirees might take longer to reach the point where they feel that they're making a real contribution as a volunteer. He suggests that they join several groups before they decide on the direction they want to go. "Experiment. Look around and you'll find your niche."

A PASSION FOR HISTORY AND THE ENVIRONMENT

Kurt Loesch
TREATS NONPROFIT WORK AS A FULL-TIME JOB

When Kurt Loesch retired in his late fifties, he didn't have a plan. "I didn't know what I would do, but I knew that things would take care of themselves." And so they did, because Kurt discovered his passion as a volunteer historian, organizer and spokesperson for Point Lobos Preserve, a California state park that overlooks the Pacific Ocean, south of Monterrey.

A native New Yorker, Kurt migrated to California in 1948 after graduating from Colgate University. By the mid 1950s, after several jobs as a department store buyer, he left retailing and got a job as a manufacturers' representative. Liking the work, he became a self-employed representative, specializing in the sale of fabrics to retail stores. Years later, new fashion trends changed the fabrics industry. "Women were wearing pants at home and work, and they had little time for home sewing. So I retired in 1984. I didn't know what I would do, yet I knew that things would take care of themselves. At the time, I played golf but playing golf all the time soon gets old."

Until then, Kurt had had little time for

> **"I find that many volunteers are not motivated, and have little commitment or passion. They need that to succeed in their endeavors..."**

hobbies or volunteerism. Being self-employed and living on commissions meant that business was his primary focus. But this all changed when Kurt and his wife, Betty, moved from Menlo Park to Carmel, and again in 2001 to a retirement community in Pacific Groves.

Looking for something to keep him busy, Kurt encountered the green-jacketed volunteer docents who guide visitors through the Point Lobos State Preserve. Kurt was fascinated by their work, which was surprising because Kurt is neither a tree hugger nor an environmentalist, according to a story featuring him in *The Colgate Scene*.

Kurt learned the ropes at Point Lobos through a mandatory docent training program. At the outset of his training, Kurt experienced a learning curve. "I knew nothing about whales, abalone or other local animals." And, despite his indifference to environmental matters, Kurt found himself intrigued with the natural history of the area and with the people who lived there.

"But what closed the deal for me was

connecting the faces of the present-day descendants to the names and stories of their ancestors who once lived in the area. In the process of reconstructing their stories, I became part of their families." For more than ten years, much of Kurt's energies were absorbed by helping to create a museum to house the artifacts left by past residents—of Chinese, Japanese, Portuguese and American origin—who had lived and worked over the past several hundred years in the Point Lobos area.

"From the beginning, Betty was of enormous help. She saw that what I was doing was important, and she made me keep it up."

While restoring a mid nineteenth–century cabin as a museum, Kurt researched libraries and microfilms and interviewed descendants of the earlier settlers. His work uncovered a personal interest in history that he had previously denied. Karl said he hated history when he was a student.

The opening of the Whalers Cabin in the 1990s stimulated Kurt to do more volunteer work on behalf of Point Lobos. He prepared a list of nearly 50 feature films that included scenes of Point Lobos starting with a 1914 silent film, "Valley of the Moon," as well as "A Summer Place," and "The Graduate." Based on this list, a local television station produced a 30-minute documentary on films that take place at Point Lobos.

Kurt's contribution to Point Lobos continued with his participation in the production of a one-hour documentary film. "For several years when the film was being produced, I was the go-between for the film people, researchers, Point Lobos group and the state government. Even though we didn't receive state money, we still needed their approval for the project." Even with its limited distribution, 900 copies of the film were sold within the first year. Kurt's next project was a 400-page book on Point Lobos, the Whalers Cabin and exhibit, researched by Kurt and written by a local college professor. Kurt is counting on it being published by late 2003.

"My goal is to get others involved in Point Lobos and the Whalers Cabin. I can't do all the work myself. I find that many volunteers are not motivated, and have little commitment or passion. They need that to succeed in their endeavors and to make nonprofit groups work. I treat my work as a full-time job."

Kurt's involvement has not gone unnoticed. In 2000, he was recognized as the Docent of the Year among California's 20,000 park volunteers. Nor have his efforts gone unnoticed in Point Lobos; the Whalers Cabin attracts 40,000 visitors a year.

"Looking back, I guess I'm what you would call an expediter. I'm the guy who gets things done. I have never been afraid to make 'cold' sales calls. It's something I did as a manufacturers representative. I pickup the telephone and get people to volunteer."

STILL SETS GOALS AND MAKES LISTS

Perry Colwell

CORPORATE EXECUTIVE TO FULL-TIME VOLUNTEER

As Perry Colwell anticipated the end of his 45-year career, he had two goals: To finish his career in a positive and productive way and then to decompress from a demanding corporate job in which he had worked 60 to 70 hours a week. Over the next decade, Perry subsequently found a substitute for the workplace by spending more time with two old "friends," namely cars and motorcycles, and discovering two new ones, volunteerism and travel.

Perry had begun his worklife as a navy seaman and college dropout and worked his way up career rungs that included telephone lineman, lower and mid-level telephone company manager, corporate staff executive and, just prior to retirement, AT&T's acting chief financial officer. "Starting about a year before my retirement, I retained a consultant. She helped me to plan my last year at work so that I would focus on the things that were important to AT&T and the people there. The goal was to help me feel good about the way I had completed

> In the nonprofit world, skilled corporate executives are a valuable commodity, especially when they're willing to apply their business talents in a different environment.

my career," said Perry.

Rather than remain in central New Jersey following his retirement in early 1992, Perry wanted to leave the area. He and his wife (see Betty Neese's profile in Chapter 5) selected Chapel Hill, North Carolina, a university town with good health care, and recreational and social activities. Influencing their move was Juanita Kreps, an AT&T board member, who was also an economics professor at Duke and President Carter's Secretary of Commerce. She helped Perry and his wife become established in the community.

Perry's goal was to keep busy in the months following their move to Chapel Hill. "I always wanted to build my own car. I bought a Caterhan Seven kit, and it took Betty and me about ten months to build it." When he finally drove it, Perry found that the interior was somewhat small for his six-foot plus frame. He ultimately sold the car a few years later, but building it had given him time to adjust to his new lifestyle and to find challenging replacements for his former 12-hour corporate workday.

Juanita Kreps provided two key introductions to organizations that would become the focal point of Perry's future community involvement: The first was the University of North Carolina's Ackland Art Museum, where Perry's AT&T skills were applicable to the museum's financial planning process. As a result, Perry was named to Ackland's national advisory board. Kreps, a board member of the National Executive Service Corps, in New York, also introduced involved Perry to that organization's local affiliate, the Executive Service Corps of the Greater Triangle.

In the nonprofit world, skilled corporate executives are a valuable commodity, especially when they're willing to apply their business talents in a different environment. For Perry, volunteerism would be a new experience. His previous nonprofit participation had been limited to being a board member of a New Jersey group that built reasonably priced retirement homes.

Perry is no token board member or one who rests on his past laurels. He's a hands-on worker who, so far in retirement, has served as both a board member and chairman of not only the Executive Service Corps, but Planned Parenthood and the Center for Child and Family Health. Perry was asked to join the Planned Parenthood board when it received a $1 million bequest. As with the Ackland Art Museum, he was

recommended to Planned Parenthood, based on his know-how in financial management. "My AT&T financial experience has been useful. And, as a manager, I knew how to work with diverse types of people."

By design and somewhat similarly to his old AT&T schedule, Perry puts in a full workday with the nonprofits. "I've tried not to change my work habits now that I'm retired. I organize myself as if I'm still going to work. Before going to bed, I put together a checklist of things I need to do the next day. I still get up early. I'm at the spa at 6:15, and I work out for 45 minutes to one hour."

Perry has two grown children from a previous marriage—Louise, a critical care nurse, and Chip, a career changer presently in law school. Perry's long-time interest in cars and motorcycles, still a part of his retirement lifestyle, has proven to be infectious: "Chip and I both like motorcycles. He owns five or six bikes; I have four. For the past nine summers, we've gone on bike tours in Europe. Our relationship was not always this way, but we've become friends as a result of these trips and our common interest in bikes."

Cars and motorcycles have also influenced some vacation destinations. In May, 2003, Kurt took time off from his volunteer endeavors and joined Betty on a car devotee's dream vacation—a ten-day Smithsonian Study Tour of northern Italy visiting Fiat, Lancia, Ferrari, Lamborghini, and Alfa Romeo design studios, factories and auto museums.

Hobbies: The Pleasure Is All Yours

STERLING "BUD" DIMMITT IS A RELATIVE NEWCOMER to his hobby as a "birder." Prior to retiring in the late 1990s, Bud was an outplacement consultant (his comments on that topic appear in Chapter 7). At home in semirural Sherman, Connecticut, he looked for new interests. His wife, Angela, a birding enthusiast, asked Bud to build some birdhouses on their property. His handicraft attracted new residents to the neighborhood—bluebirds and woodpeckers, along with bats. "My birdhouse construction got an 'I want one' response from friends. I started selling some but ended up giving them away at charity auctions."

Bud's newfound hobby led to his being elected a board member of the state's Audubon Society, which raises funds, lobbies on environmental and conservation issues, and supports related educational activities. "This is what happens when you take up a hobby, begin to understand a small piece of it, and grow intensely beyond your initial interest. We even spent our 25th anniversary in Belize, where we went birding in the jungles and on the waterways. Our group counted over 200 species in one week."

As many 50-plusers have learned, there are no fixed limits to a hobby. A hobby is simply defined as "a pursuit outside one's occupation." It can be manual, intellectual or creative, or all of these.

The listing of possible hobbies is nearly unlimited, ranging from active sports, such as tennis or skiing, to something more leisurely, such as gardening or cooking. It includes cerebral pursuits such as learning Greek or mastering Chaucer; dexterous skills like sculpting, piano playing, weaving or rebuilding colonial furniture; or sedentary pastimes such as calligraphy, reading or collecting 19th century apothecary jars. The National Endowment for the Arts (www.nea.gov) reports that the favorite arts activities of people over age 55 are weaving and buying art work, followed by making pottery, drawing, group singing and photography. Folks in this age bracket enjoy arts and crafts fairs, historic parks, art museums and musical plays.

Some hobbies are costly, requiring special equipment and training. Though books, craft hobbies and travel rank high in expenditures by the 50-plus set, other hobbies cost nothing but the effort of imagination. Hobbies can be done individually, in a group or both. Many are very time-consuming; others take only a few minutes a day.

Some hobbies fit best into the lifestyle of 30-to-40-year-olds, while the ones of interest to the greatest number of retirees can be pursued over a lifetime. You're more likely to find retirees walking than running regularly, and gardening than bungee-jumping. Even so, it seems that nearly everyone knows someone who's defying the odds—a 77-year-old who plays tennis regularly five times a week or an 82-year-old downhill skier. Witness also

WOMEN AS HOBBYISTS

The Hobby Industry Association (www.hobby.org) has a vested interested in hobbies, estimated in 2001 to be a nearly $26 billion industry. HIA members produce and sell craft supplies such as art supplies, needlecrafts and floral crafts. In its most recent industry analysis, the Association noted that 97% of adult women (age 55 to 64) participated in a craft activity in their lifetime, and 88% of them continue to do crafts as they age. Cross-stitching, crocheting, décor painting, scrapbook/memory crafts and floral arranging are the most popular crafts among women. The only thing that stops them is poor health, especially bad eyesight.

the success of the Senior Olympics sponsored for those 55 and over. Whether they are competitive athletes or just doing it for fun, chances are many of these athletes learned and perfected their sports skills long before retirement.

Countless numbers of retirees call travel a hobby. Even so, many members of the 50-plus set find that travel is only one part of a much larger leisure-time pattern that goes beyond cruises, overseas travel odysseys and other once-in-a-lifetime travel events. In some instances, retirees combine walking and hiking, or explore different areas by car and camper. Opportunities also exist to travel and study on an Elderhostel trip in the U.S. or overseas, or to build homes for Habitat for Humanity in a third-world nation. Besides affinity groups sponsored by college and university alumni associations, you'll find more about travel with an educational or humanitarian purpose in mind in Chapters 3 and 4.

In sum, a hobby is whatever you decide you want to make of it.

> ## FAVORITE SPORTS
>
> In order of preference:
> - **Exercise walking**
> - **Fishing (fresh and salt)**
> - **Exercise with equipment**
> - **Swimming**
> - **Golf**
> - **Camping**
> - **Bike riding**
> - **Bowling**
> - **Aerobic exercising**
> - **Billiards/pool**
>
> Source: SGMA International

Getting Started

Getting involved in a hobby is as simple as visiting a local library or bookstore, or attending an adult-education workshop given by community colleges, high schools or hobby organizations. As a first step, obtain the course listings from your local community college and high school extension programs. Hobbyists have their own "birds of a feather" groups, and they, too, sponsor workshops to attract and train new enthusiasts.

Hobby- and craft-supply shops, as well as other retail outlets catering to the clothing, equipment and literature needs of all kinds of enthusiasts, usually post notices of related classes, meetings and outings. If you're lucky, you might enjoy a productive chat with a knowledgeable clerk—also likely to be an enthusiast—in such a store.

"How-to" books and magazines abound in nearly every field, appealing to both novices and advanced hobbyists. To test this theory, visit your neighborhood bookstores. You'll find that easily one-third to one-half of the nonfiction books in stock are in hobby-related fields, including gardening, cooking, collecting, woodworking, crafting and painting. Such publications contain plenty of leads to hobby organizations and other prospective contacts for more information.

Selecting a new hobby depends to some extent on your income, aptitude and personality. Some hobbies, due to more costly equipment and training, naturally attract fewer people. But don't let expenses deter you. If your goal is to make pottery, for example, you can get instruction and access to wheels and kilns on a shared basis through community and extension schools and hobby-related clubs. This same cooperative spirit aids flying enthusiasts who individually can't afford the cost of buying and maintaining a plane.

There's no reason to limit yourself to one hobby. Why not enjoy several, with each selected to fit different moods and interests?

Or how about finding new ways to expand the scope of your current hobby? For example, bird watchers do more than track birds. They lead hikes, attend workshops and join environmental groups. A hobby can also broaden you, as Iris S., a retired New York City high school English teacher, has discovered. Iris grows African violets in her apartment, and is an officer in a group that

CRAFTY BUSINESS GUIDES

Barbara Brabec, a former publisher of Barbara Brabec's *Self Employment Survival Letter,* gave up newsletter publishing to concentrate on writing business self-help books for craftpeople who want to be self-employed and also work at home. Her titles include: *Creative Cash—How to Profit from Your Special Artistry, Creativity, Hands Skills and Related Know-How; Handmade for Profit—Hundreds of Secrets to Success in Selling Arts & Crafts; The Crafts Business Answer Book;* and *Home Money: Bringing in the Bucks.* Want to know more about these books? Visit Barbara's Website at: www.barbarabrabec.com.

SOURCES OF IDEAS

- **Browse through the Yellow Pages** of the phone book.

- **Visit the library.** Read books and magazines about an activity. Ask the reference librarian at your public library to help you find the names of associations, clubs and organizations in your field of interest, or consult directories such as the *Encyclopedia of Associations*.

- **Contact local recreation departments** for information about their programs and schedules.

- **Talk to retailers** who sell hobby and recreational equipment.

- **Learn as much in advance as you can** about the required initial investment and ongoing costs.

Source: New York University Center for Career, Education and Life Planning

---

meets regularly to discuss and show their plants. For those wanting to take the next step, she points out, there is a worldwide society devoted to African violets, which publishes a quarterly magazine and conducts regional, national and international meetings.

If you've been pursuing an avocation for years and have developed some expertise, maybe it's time to begin teaching others.

One admonition, however: How far you're willing to go with a new interest may be limited by your tolerance for "risk," and not necessarily in the life-or-death sense. "A man at 65 doesn't suddenly pick up a camera and revive himself with a second career as a photographer," Gail Sheehy noted in her book, *Passages*. "Whether one has a natural talent or not, any learning period requires the willingness to suffer uncertainty and embarrassment. Even in the fifties, one is apt to be too self-conscious to wait out such a period of trial."

Also, don't fall victim to the notion that you need to be an expert to enjoy a hobby. Listen to *Parade Magazine* columnist Dr. Joyce Brothers' assessment of someone lugging that burden: "You believe you have to do everything at an 'A' level. If you can't, you feel you aren't accomplishing anything at all. You may give up."

Right on Joyce. I'm a lifetime piano player. Wouldn't dare call myself a pianist. I no longer read music but I can play most tunes by picking out the melody. My approach is homemade. I play the melody with my right hand, and the same chords for all songs with the left hand. At times, the sound can be somewhat discordant. My wife is tolerant of my playing; my children have different views. The end result is I enjoy playing, and I try to play several times a week. A great way to let out tension, and relax.

Not a Substitute for Work

Some hobbyists personify perfection in their dual roles as professionals at work and hobbyists at home, with equal devotion to both throughout their lives. Others balance what they often consider lackluster or uninteresting careers with more spectacular extracurricular lives. Whereas a 9-to-5 job provides income, a hobby is the real focal point of their lives. Retirement offers an opportunity to put their priorities in order and act on them at will. But members of either group value their hobbies as a creative outlet that differs radically from day-to-day workplace challenges. Still others show more interest in hobbies in retirement than they showed in them during their workday lives. Even among the upper echelons of corporate managers, you'll find these differences.

Most assuredly, Alan "Ace" Greenberg, chairman of the executive committee at Bear Stearns & Co., and Norio Ohga, former president and currently chairman of Sony, will have little trouble keeping busy as retirees. Both fit the description of a dedicated executive and hobbyist to a T.

Besides being a principal in one of Wall Street's largest and most successful investment-banking firms, Ace Greenberg, a magician since he was 9, performs at fundraisers and charitable events, and is a member of the Society of American Magicians. For a change of pace, Ace plays bridge with similar vigor, having won a national bridge championship in the late 1970s.

Norio Ohga, who *The New Yorker* profiled as responsible for making Sony "emblematic of Japan's technical and economic domination," is a classically trained singer. He piloted his Falcon jet from Tokyo to New York, where he conducted an orchestra

SUGGESTED READING

How CEOs and up-and-coming entrepreneurs spend their free time is a topic that Marilyn Wellemeyer covered for ten years as a *Fortune* editor and then chronicled in *The Fortune Guide to Executive Leisure* (Little Brown, 1987). Her book, nowadays found in libraries or used book stores, spotlights a potpourri of hobbies and leisure-time activities from ballooning to barbershop quartet singing. Some of the executives she profiled pursued relatively inexpensive hobbies; others used their larger-than-average incomes to invest in costly photographic equipment, elaborate greenhouses or valuable antique pieces. The book is a great source of ideas and inspiration if you need them, and it is still the only book that chronicles how managers relax and enjoy themselves.

performing Beethoven's *Seventh Symphony* and Schubert's *Unfinished Symphony* in a fundraiser for Lincoln Center.

Top executives typically do not have hobbies, observed Jeffrey Sonnenfeld of Emory University in his book, *The Hero's Farewell,* a study on the retirement habits of CEOs of major corporations. "Their greatest gratification was generally in the job they left and not in deferred recreation or outside organizations." The executives interviewed by Sonnenfeld frequently asked, not at all rhetorically, "How much tennis can you play before you look for something bigger to do?"

A hobby has its limitations even for the most enthusiastic fans. As much as Russ Larson, publisher of *Garden Railways,* a monthly magazine (www.kalmbach.com), enjoys writing about model railroad hobbyists, he does not advocate "spending 40 hours a week on a hobby after retiring. I suspect that for most people a mix of more serious pursuits along with hobbies and games would be the most satisfying."

When you're working full-time, a career and a hobby are often in conflict as Pam George discusses in Chapter 2. Pam, who presently sandwiches college teaching *and* painting into her daily schedule, is about to change her priorities so that she can spend more time painting than teaching. The late Jules Willing, a human resources executive with Revlon, candidly wrote about the problems of trying to substitute a hobby for a lost job in his book, *The Reality of Retirement:*

"When work no longer provides activity, interests and hobbies are substituted. Early in retirement, there is a carry-over of attitudes—you tend to approach your hobbies as you did your work: intensively. The hobby gets the highest priority, the most time, the greatest energy, the extensive investment....In retirement, hobbies are not pursued at all in a leisurely way, but more as a matter of job replacement than of pleasure, the anxious need to fill an unendurable void."

> **"Hobbies may entertain or amuse and occupy, but they rarely make the adrenaline flow the way winning a budget battle did."**

Willing was quick to point out that successful managers normally find hobbies "unsatisfying as major preoccupations. Hobbies do not generate the kind of psychic satisfaction your work did. They may entertain or amuse and occupy, but they rarely make the adrenaline flow the way winning a budget battle did. With a hobby you generally have nothing to risk."

As a hobbyist myself, I understand the relationship between a hobby and work. I average about 12 to 15 hours a week on my hobbies—cooking, gardening, reading, playing the piano and walking. Yet I don't feel that I could ever find total satisfaction from these leisure-time activities. Work and work-related activities are still my main focus. I still have the mind-set that a hobby is something to be sandwiched into evenings, weekends and vacations; it is part of my lifestyle but hardly an end unto itself.

Many of you may view hobbies as a form of leisure-time smorgasbord, something layered between more important functions—somewhere between sleeping and working. That's a trait from a time when occupational tunnel vision was the order of the day. Your first priority was to the workplace, a habit that you may find difficult to break.

Only you can decide to what extent one or more hobbies can replace the demands and satisfaction of the workplace, and how much of your time in retirement you want it to fill. At the least, a hobby can be one part of your total portfolio of activities.

POINTS TO REMEMBER

- **Hobbies can be demanding,** absorbing large blocks of time.

- **Some people need several hobbies.**

- **Some retirees convert their hobby** into a new career.

- **Don't be disappointed** if you never build the same enthusiasm for a hobby as you did for your job.

- **If you don't already have one,** it might take a couple of false starts before you find a suitable hobby.

- **There's no shortage of opportunities** to explore a new hobby.

- **Schools conduct courses** to help hobbyists learn and perfect their skills.

The Hobbyists in Action

Bottom line, there is no such thing as a bad hobby. The worst scenario is that it does nothing more than fill a time gap in one's daily schedule or serve as a casual pastime. At best, hobbies can be vibrant activities, forming the basis of a new lifestyle or even providing the incentive to launch another career. Be aware that if your hobby should become your new career you run the risk of a wonderful hobby becoming a terrible new career—as much of a taskmaster as your employment of old.

Hobbies for some avid practitioners started as casual recreation and then flowered from there. Some hobbies call for intellectual and physical energy once reserved for a demanding career. The people you are about to meet have hobbies that serve as the cornerstone in their 50-plus-set lifestyle.

Chances are you will not become a consummate hobbyist like these folks, but you'll see how their hobbies have helped shape their lives and retirement.

LEARNED A NEW SPORT

Bruce Berckmans

CORPORATE EXECUTIVE TURNED COMPETITIVE ROWER

When Bruce Berckmans attended Princeton University, his mother discouraged him from trying out for crew. Though he had no health problems, she feared that rowing might do bad things to his heart. Ironically, Bruce suffered a massive heart attack about 40 years later, and rowing became an integral part of his cardiac recovery program.

Bruce points out that rowing has a comparatively small following among the 50-plus set, perhaps only 30% among the U.S. Rowing Association's 16,000 members who row at least three times a week. Unlike Bruce, most are veteran rowers, dating back, in most instances, to college.

Bruce played tennis and boxed in college, but later on became the ":the typical weekend athlete," he says. After graduating from Princeton, Bruce joined the Marine Corps and ten years later received a medical disability due to injury. Several years later he returned to government service, this time doing classified work overseas. In 1975, Bruce was back in the U.S. as vice-president for international operations for Wackenhut

Corporation, a guard and security company based in Coral Gables, Florida, and about ten years later he joined Cordis Corp., makers of high-tech medical equipment, as security director. He was working there in July 1987 when he had a heart attack.

"I came close to dying. Fortunately I got emergency balloon angioplasty, which relieved the blockage." While he was recuperating, a friend gave him a copy of David Halberstam's book *The Amateurs,* an account of four young men who competed to represent the U.S. in the 1984 Olympics. The book became a turning point in his recovery. "Maybe [the message] was subliminal," he says.

Another friend suggested that he try rowing as part of his rehabilitation and offered the use of his rowing shell. Bruce followed his friend's advice, but first he checked with his cardiologist, Ted Feldman, who he discovered had rowed on Harvard's freshman crew. "Ted knew what rowing was all about. He thought it would be a good aerobic conditioner. It would provide exercise

> **Unlike most 50-plus rowers, who were collegiate competitors, Bruce took up the sport for rehabilitation. It became a way of life.**

for the entire body yet involve no physical impact." Within a few months of his attack, Bruce started to row. Even with positive heart tests, he still feared that rowing might lead to another heart attack, and he also realized that he had too much to learn about rowing to tackle it alone. To acquire the basics, he enrolled in a four-day program at the Florida Rowing Center in West Palm Beach.

During his early recovery period, Bruce returned briefly to Cordis. But because he wanted more time and independence, he left the company and started Corporate Support Services, a consultant group that helps clients protect trade secrets and proprietary information.

During his recuperation, Bruce and Ted Feldman started the Cardiac Rehabilitation Rowing Project with a small grant from the U.S. Rowing Association to study the beneficial effects of rowing on recovering cardiac patients. They developed some health protocols and an odometer for cardiac stress testing.

At first Bruce rowed for aerobic exercise, but in mid 1988 he started to compete in the 50-plus age bracket in Florida and in such races as the Head of the Broad, in Charleston, South Carolina, and the Head of the Charles, in Boston, the nation's largest rowing regatta. Of the several thousand participants of all ages competing in the three-mile Head of the Charles, about 40 of the entrants were 50-plus and nearly all long-time

rowers. Within a few years, Bruce was entering six sprint races (less than a mile) in the spring and an equal number of three-mile races in the fall.

"There is more to rowing than racing," says Bruce. "It's relaxing. Most waterways are physically attractive, and it's a chance to be outdoors. I averaged about ten hours a week rowing or working out on a machine or lifting weights." Bruce found that rowing gave him new self-respect and a sense of accomplishment. "It's hard work, but exercise is a critical requirement for people recovering from most serious illnesses. You don't have to compete in races to enjoy it. I did because it matched my personality."

Rowing soon became a family event. Bruce's wife, Lee, enjoyed watching her husband compete, and the couple donated trophies for college competitions. The Head of the Charles regatta became an annual family reunion for Lee and their five grown children. Then, in 1993, Lee was diagnosed with terminal cancer, and rowing took a back seat in Bruce's life. "I gave up rowing and much of my consulting work when she became ill, so we could spend as much time as possible together." Lee died several months later.

Bruce returned to competitive rowing in late 1994. In subsequent years, however, congestive heart failure forced Bruce to eliminate rowing from his regimen. As a replacement hobby, he breeds and trains Vizslas, a Hungarian hunting dog.

THE REBIRTH OF DOMESTICITY

Betty Neese

WOMEN'S APPAREL SALESPERSON TURNED CLOTHING DESIGNER AND NEEDLECRAFTER

On some of the overseas vacation trips Betty Neese shares with her husband, Perry Colwell (profiled in Chapter 4), she carries one suitcase for clothes—and several empty ones to hold the unusual fabric and wool that she collects. Retirement has given Betty the ability to do the things she literally had neither the money nor the time for as a young divorced mother and for many years thereafter.

"I always liked to sew but it was usually out of economic necessity. With three boys I made all my own clothes and theirs as well." Sewing has since changed from a household chore to an active hobby. Besides spending several hours a day designing clothing, based primarily on modifying patterns or copying items she sees in catalogs and magazines, Betty sews clothes for her grandchildren. She also works two days a week in a local fabric store, not because she needs the money but to learn more about fabrics. Betty is also a quilter, and in her loft studio, she uses a computerized sewing machine and expansive work space to design, sew and assemble quilts.

"While Perry continues to be involved as a director of several nonprofit groups, I enjoy being by myself, doing the many things that I never had time to do when I was younger. Being a divorced mother, I sewed and cooked out of need. This is no longer the case. Now I can enjoy something as simple as making my own raspberry and strawberry jam. After all my years of working and saving, I enjoy a hobby based on domesticity. Making jam and clothes for my grandchildren is one way to be a super-granny."

Her life in retirement is a far cry from her earlier days in Indiana. Betty grew up there and went to work for Indiana Bell as a customer service representative at age 17. She was so young she needed working papers, issued by the local health department to minors to permit them to work. In her early forties, after an unfortunate management incident, Betty found herself demoted from a managerial to a staff position.

"Looking back, my downgrading at Indiana Bell proved to be one of the best things that ever happened." It made her examine her life and consider what she really wanted to do. For the next few years, she stayed at the company and planned the next step. By now, her sons

> "I enjoy being by myself, doing the many things I never had time to do when I was younger."

were self-supporting, and Betty knew she was self-sufficient and willing to take a risk. Like many women her age who have worked and raised children alone, Betty had an instinct for survival.

Pursuing her long-time dream of living in New York City, Betty asked for a transfer from Indianapolis and Indiana Bell to New York and the company's then corporate parent, AT&T. By working for AT&T, she would at least continue to be part of the AT&T employee-benefits plan, including its pension program. It was not a high-level job, but she was soon promoted to district manager of a department that prepared employee manuals and related personnel materials. "It was a hollow victory after what happened at Indiana Bell," she says. But the move to New York more than compensated for that.

A long way from Indiana, Betty became the consummate New Yorker. On her larger salary, she bought an apartment in a brownstone building. "I found life in New York exciting—with Lincoln Center, the art museums, the stores and parks."

Then came the company's divestiture in the early 1980s, in which AT&T split up into seven regional operating companies. The company offered early retirement and at 53, after 32 years' service, Betty left with a package that included one year's salary, pension, lifetime health care benefits and a goodly amount of AT&T stock bought as part of the employee purchasing plan.

"The first six months I did nothing but travel and enjoy myself in New York." Then, to keep busy and supplement her income, Betty found a job as a salesperson at Saks Fifth Avenue. She was soon promoted to the store's couture department selling high-fashion women's apparel.

In the late 1980s, Betty married Perry, a senior executive at AT&T. Even after Perry was transferred to AT&T's new corporate offices in central New Jersey and the couple moved, Betty continued to commute two days a week to New York and her Saks job. "I could have worked in one of Saks' suburban stores, but it was not the same thing as working on Fifth Avenue. I also found another part-time job doing word processing. It's easy to find part-time work if you're not too particular."

When Perry retired in the early 1990s, they decided to relocate. Their combined retirement incomes eliminated any need for future paid employment. "We wanted to live in a college town for its cultural activities yet be convenient to my three sons and four grandchildren in Indiana, and Perry's family in Philadelphia and Baltimore. Perry preferred a climate warmer than northern New Jersey, and I wanted a home within walking distance of the stores, craft outlets and post office." They chose central North Carolina.

In her approach to many of life's problems, Betty has demonstrated a willingness to learn and do new things. She sees no difference when it comes to acquiring a new hobby. She advises others to simply "learn it and do it.."

HIS FAMILY SPARKED HIS INTEREST IN PAINTING

Kemp Anderson
PUBLISHING EXECUTIVE TURNED ARTIST

You can take the boy out of West Texas but you can't ever take West Texas out of the boy—and you're likely to find that spirit in many of his paintings, too. That's the case with Kemp Anderson, who prior to taking early retirement as a vice-president of McGraw-Hill was a career journalist, fulfilling his teenage dreams and his professional ambitions. Now he aspires to achieve a style resembling the great western painter Frederic Remington, with his western landscapes, horses and cowboys.

Kemp characterizes himself as a rapid painter, working nearly exclusively in oils on both large and small canvases. He exhibits his paintings only at fundraisers for his church and local civic groups. "I usually give my paintings away to friends, but when they wanted to buy them at the show I asked that the money be donated to the church to pay for a new organ." To Kemp, painting is a creative challenge, not a source of income. Just as important, painting complements his lifestyle: "I'm not the type of person who can sit around on my hands all day."

Corporate restructuring sapped Kemp's energy. Painting— engaging in the "process of creation"—has given it back and more.

Painting gives him a chance to get out and do something. Now that he's retired, longer visits with family members in Texas and with his five grown children in other sections of the country give Kemp additional opportunities to paint. On nearly every vacation trip, he tries to paint as much as possible. He prefers to paint on site, a change from his working days and briefer vacation trips when he painted at home from photographs taken on location. He has done landscapes in northern New Jersey as well as in other parts of the U.S. and Hawaii while on vacation.

Born in Texas, the son of a Methodist minister, Kemp was captivated by journalism as a youngster. After graduating from Oklahoma State University, he followed a traditional journalism career route, starting with a small daily and working up to *The Dallas Times-Herald*. Recruited by a friend to McGraw-Hill's Dallas bureau, Kemp worked his way up and eventually became the first non-engineer to be named as *Electronics* magazine's chief editor. "I was a little familiar with the technology, but I did know how to cover the news." By the late '70s, Kemp was promoted, this time to vice-president of McGraw-Hill's magazine division supervising the development and installation of the publisher's first computerized editorial system.

Then and now, Kemp's hobby was amateur photography, a pursuit dating back to his newspaper days, when reporters on smaller papers wrote the story and took the photos. As a photographer, he knows how to frame the subject of a picture and how to use light to the best advantage—both factors he would learn were important to painting.

Kemp was introduced to art by one of his children, who was attending an art course. Kemp was soon taking Saturday classes at the Ridgewood (New Jersey) Art Institute. He found that painting gave him a way to express himself and engaged him in the process of creation. It was a change of pace from the editorial and corporate world. Frequent business trips gave him an opportunity to photograph scenes that he would copy at home on canvas. "At the time, I enjoyed art but didn't worry too much about its quality. But in the back of my mind, I knew that art would play a strong part in my retirement plans."

> **"Find something you like to do and plan ahead. Start doing it before you retire, so you have something to look forward to doing."**

Thirty-two years with McGraw-Hill came to an end. Kemp was a senior-vice president in McGraw-Hill's corporate offices responsible for the development of future computerized systems. While under no pressure to leave, he started to tire of the restructuring taking place throughout the company, and he looked forward to spending more time painting. Kemp worked out a favorable buyout package that permitted him to retire at 64 rather than 65. His retirement portfolio, which—no surprise—he manages on a computer, includes a pension, investments, savings and social security. His retirement package included health insurance benefits.

Retirement has changed Kemp's attitude toward his painting as he works to perfect his style. Until recently, he took lessons at the Art Institute and went on painting field trips. Though he continues to paint, he admits that his intensity has decreased. Now, he uses photographs from past trips to inspire the themes of his paintings.

When people ask him about retirement, Kemp's answer is direct: "Find something you like to do and plan ahead. Start doing it before you retire, so you have something to look forward to doing."

NO MORE NON DE PLUME

James Duffy
CORPORATE ATTORNEY TURNED MYSTERY WRITER

For several years before his early retirement, James Duffy lived two lives. By day, Jim was a corporate attorney and a partner in Cravath, Swaine and Moore, one of New York City's premier law firms. By night and at other times, Jim was Haughton Murphy (Haughton is a family friend and Murphy is the maiden name of his late wife Martha), author of the popular Reuben Frost mystery series.

> **Jim follows the advice so often given to authors: Write about what you know.**

Like many novelists, Jim draws heavily on personal experiences in developing the series. He definitely writes about what he knows. "I admit that most of the characters are composites of people I've met."

His principal character, Reuben Frost, is a 77-year-old retired Wall Street lawyer and one-time senior partner in a large firm. Senior citizen Frost is a good vehicle because he gets around, circulates in a legal environment and is intimate with New York City's professional, social and cultural worlds, an environment that Jim has known for more than 30 years. Frost's wife in the series, Cynthia, is a former ballet dancer who works for a nonprofit foundation that supports the arts.

Jim has a long-time interest in the ballet and modern dance, having been a member of the Mayor's Advisory Commission for Cultural Affairs and chairman of a committee advising New York's mayor on his annual awards to individuals in the arts.

When Jim moved the setting to Venice, Italy, for his seventh Reuben Frost mystery, *A Very Venetian Murder,* he once again drew on personal experiences. Jim and his wife, Martha, a senior editor at *Time* magazine, vacationed in Venice for many years until her death in 1997.

Reuben also gives Jim an opportunity to express some opinions about retirement. In *Murder Keeps a Secret,* Reuben is asked whether he still practices law:

"Not really, I go down to my little cubbyhole now and then, but for all intents and purposes I'm retired."

"Do you miss it?"

"Of course. You don't just erase 50 busy years from your memory."

"I'm interested. Barton died with his boots on, of course, and vowed he'd never retire."

"Most lawyers are like that."

Though, of course, neither Jim nor Reuben is like that.

While most creative people tend to do

their creative work in an at-home office or studio, Jim likes to separate his home life from his writing. He maintains a one-room office a few blocks from his midtown New York apartment to do his writing and much of his research.

While bar association and corporate meetings were once essential in his professional life, Jim, under his Haughton Murphy persona, spoke at conferences of the Crime Writers Association of the United Kingdom and the Mystery Writers of America.

Until Jim started to write mysteries, his career focused mostly on corporate law. In textbook fashion, he graduated from Princeton University and three years later from Harvard Law School. Following military service, he joined Cravath in the early 1960s and was named a partner in 1968. A specialist in corporate and financial law, he represented a range of domestic and international clients, including, in one transaction or another, nearly all the nation's major banks.

Jim's interest in writing dates back to Princeton, where he wrote for the literary and humor magazines. At the time, he considered a career in journalism but instead became a lawyer. His first writing jaunt outside the realm of corporate law came in 1978, when he wrote a book analyzing some of the current issues in American politics. His publisher, Simon & Schuster, would in future years publish the hardback editions of his mysteries.

Eight years later he wrote his first mystery. "I started to write strictly as a hobby, not in anticipation of retirement." He selected mysteries rather than straight fiction because they are more structured and they permit the author to feature one or more central characters in multiple books. While he reads a lot of mysteries as background, Jim does not consider himself a "mystery-book junkie." He thought at first that he would collaborate with his wife. They soon discovered, as many long-time married couples do, that collaboration of this sort would not work.

"From the start, I found that I could easily mix law and writing. I never let my books invade my professional life. I wrote on weekends and vacations, and I worked under different names to provide further separation of my two lives."

When Jim was 54, he retired from Cravath, about six to eight years earlier than most partners normally elect to leave. His goal was to write full-time. "When I left, I didn't know what life would be like. Other than writing, I had no specific goals in mind. If nothing more, writing would keep me busy." While Jim hoped to make money from his writing, he hardly needed the money for survival. He was assured his income as a retired Cravath partner along with income from his investments.

Retirement gave Jim not only more time to read, research and write but also the opportunity to drop his pseudonym. He finally gave it up when a *Wall Street Journal* review revealed his identity. "Even so, about half the people I know call me Haughton."

LIVES HIS DREAM

Jerome Zukosky
MAGAZINE EXECUTIVE TURNED SAILOR

Jerome Zukosky is living his dream. He has become a full-time sailor with plans to spend several years cruising New England waters, the Caribbean and perhaps even beyond. Living this lifestyle is the fulfillment of years of preparing for the day that he would make his 38-foot sailboat, the Herman Melville, a retirement home.

Jerome was in his mid fifties and *Business Week's* deputy chief in charge of the magazine's network of U.S. news bureaus when he started to formulate a new lifestyle as a dedicated sailor. Until then, Jerome, a graduate of the University of Rochester and Columbia University Graduate School of Journalism, had been a newspaper and magazine reporter and editor throughout his professional career.

In 1987, while many of his contemporaries were investing in second homes as their retirement retreats, Jerome bought his sailboat. He began to learn how to join that small world of full-time cruising couples who are serious year-round sailors.

Jerome first took an interest in sailing as a youngster at summer camp, where he learned the basics in a canoe outfitted with a sail. When he and his former wife were raising their two children in New York City during the 1960s and 1970s, the Zukoskys owned a small sailboat. "It was our summer home. Each weekend and on vacations we would take the subway to our boat, which was docked on the Long Island Sound in the Bronx.

"I never took a sailing lesson. I learned by doing it. I'm constantly reading how-to books and magazines on sailing. Before you're ready to make a boat your home, there are many skills to be learned, from astronomy to do-it-yourself equipment repair."

In 1991, he knew that his 15-year *Business Week* career was nearing an end, perhaps a few years earlier than he had hoped for. McGraw-Hill, the magazine's owner, was downsizing. Jerome accepted an early-retirement package that included an enhanced pension, a lump-sum severance payment and health benefits.

Next, he began to put into place an intricate plan involving his sailboat and another job as a journalist. There were

> For Jerome, early retirement was a chance for a complete change of lifestyle — location, job, home. Now it's full-time cruising.

some restrictions. He would only work where he could live year-round on his sailboat, thus eliminating jobs inland and in most northern cities.

While he worked for *Business Week* in New York, Jerome had dry-docked the Herman Melville for the winter in Annapolis, Maryland. Now Jerome familiarized himself with a number of the larger ports on or near the Chesapeake Bay, especially those with daily newspapers. His search ended with a job in Newport News, Virginia, at the *Daily Press*.

"I got a job working three days a week on the metropolitan news desk, editing copy, tutoring young reporters and consulting with the metro editors on their big news 'takeouts' and other projects." He also taught writing at Christopher Newport University as a part-time instructor and acted as faculty adviser to the student newspaper. For almost three years he lived aboard the Herman Melville—moored at a marina on the James River about 200 yards from the newspaper. Here he experienced what it would be like to make the boat his year-round home.

> **"I'm better off than others who spend their old age wishing they had been able to live their dream."**

As much as he enjoyed newspaper editing, Jerome had little intention of being permanently tied to the job. It paid the bills as he learned more about shipboard living. Then in 1994, Jerome left Newport, sailed to New York and planned the next step—three to four years of long-distance cruising.

For the first time in his adult life, Jerome is out of the workforce. Retired, he's living on his pension, social security payments and savings. Living on a boat is much like living in any community, and some marinas are more expensive than others. But other than boat fixtures and maintenance and travel expenses, he does not incur many of the day-to-day operating costs faced by traditional homeowners.

"I have only one regret—that I wasn't able to become a full-time sailor years ago. I always envied retirees from the military who had the time and the income to indulge themselves when they were in their early fifties. But I'm better off than others who spend their old age wishing they had been able to live their dream."

ATTENDING COLLEGE IS HIS HOBBY

Tom Sawyer
OPTHALMOLOGIST FINDS NEW PASSION FOR LEARNING

Tom Sawyer retired as an ophthalmologist in 2000 at age 72. But retirement didn't mean that Tom planned to reduce his workload. It simply meant shifting gears from practicing medicine to fully engaging in his long-time hobby—perennial college study.

A University of Michigan undergraduate and medical school student, Tom practiced for nearly 30 years in Milwaukee until 1985 when he moved to Pinehurst, North Carolina. "I was 58, and my office lease was not going to be renewed. I could easily have found a new office but didn't want to start investing in leasehold improvements. I made an offer to my associate to buy me out, which he accepted."

Even so, Tom wasn't ready to retire. He still enjoyed practicing medicine, and had experienced no loss of manual dexterity, which is critical in his specialty. Serendipity stepped in. Tom saw a classified advertisement in *Jama,* the *Journal of the American Medical Association.* A multioffice ophthalmology practice in south central North Carolina was looking for a board-certified specialist to join its staff. It was the first time in his professional career that Tom responded to an employment ad. He applied, was hired and joined the staff of the Carolina Eye Associates, which operates offices in more than 15 communities.

Tom and his wife, Marilyn, relocated to Pinehurst and bought a house and he went to work. By the early 1990s, Tom was ready for another change. He would continue to work, but at a slower rate—two days rather than four days a week. His views met the approval of Carolina Eye Associates, which reassigned him to a smaller office that is open twice a week. By that time, Tom had already decided to restrict himself to eye examinations and other routine medical work, an approach taken by many surgeons starting in their late fifties.

While Tom was starting to wind down his medical career—not because of any pressure from his employer and in spite of his mixed emotions about it—he latched onto a hobby that reflected his studious personality.

He found the seed in his recollections of the Sunrise Semester courses, an early morning program on public television in the 1960s, and he

> **Retirement finally allowed Tom to learn outside his formerly narrow field of professional interest.**

experienced a renewed and blossoming interest in learning outside the subjects in which he had had to stay professionally current. "I worked my career in a narrow professional field where the only thing I did other than spend time with my family was to stay abreast of what was happening in ophthalmology."

After moving from Pinehurst to the Chapel Hill area in 1994, Tom returned to college as a University of North Carolina student. He started to take advantage of the rule that permits residents over 65 to enroll in courses at state universities at no charge.

Tom usually audits two to three courses each fall and spring semester, and a single summer school course that meets five days a week during a shortened yet more intensive six-week semester. Tom takes tests, does laboratory work when required and writes papers—an unusual approach for an audit student. "Why not? I want to do the full course and 'duke' it out with the kids."

On campus, his dress is similar to most undergraduates—jeans, sneakers and the omnipresent backpack. "When I was taking biology courses, most of the students in my class at UNC had no idea that I was a doctor. I don't volunteer this information. To most, I'm just another old guy in class with them." Tom likes

attending class with younger students and listening to them talk about careers in science and medicine. When this occurs, he breaks silence and serves as an unofficial mentor to students interested in a medical career.

Tom notes that he has more passion for the things he's learning now than when he was a college student previously. Over the past eight years, he has roamed the UNC liberal arts curriculum, auditing a diverse selection of courses ranging from molecular biology, ecology and population genetics to astronomy, music, art, sociology and geography. Interestingly, a number of the current biology courses weren't given in his college days, and the lab equipment now taken for granted, such as the electron microscope, was a campus newcomer 50 years ago.

Tom says that doctors of his generation weren't trained to use computers. "When I moved to North Carolina, I wanted to learn about computers, so I took some courses at a local community college. But my computer needs are simple. I use the computer as a word processor to prepare spreadsheets for my reports. I sometimes log onto Medline, but I'd rather go to the UNC medical library and read the papers. I guess it's the way I was trained."

> **In spite of being an audit student, Tom does all the work. "Why not? I want to...'duke' it out with the kids."**

TREATS HIS HOBBY LIKE A JOB

Zen Palkoski

BIOMEDICAL DESIGNER BECOMES A WOOD CARVER

When Zen Palkoski was ten years old, he vacationed with his parents in Quebec, where on one occasion he was fascinated by a man carving a small figure out of wood. That fascination remained idle for 50 years. Other than carving a few pieces, such as a British grenadier soldier and a key rack for the kitchen wall, Zen didn't take up carving again until he retired.

As a Seton Hall University student, Zen's goal was medicine. But his dream was quashed when he did not get into medical school. Drafted into the Army for two years, he spent 18 months in Germany, and following his discharge, he was hired by Hoffmann-La Roche (now Roche Holdings), to work in a preclinical cardiovascular lab designing biomedical equipment. Over the next 37 years in the same lab, he both observed and participated in the evolution of medical equipment from somewhat crude equipment by today's standards to complex computerized and electronic gear.

Zen's watershed year was 1994. "I had no personal retirement plan. I was expecting to retire in another five years, when I would be 65. But I got a good buyout package, because the company wanted to cut costs."

After a short stint helping a friend start a picture frame business, Zen was at liberty to find new outlets. "I got involved in a carving club, which met one evening a week in a high school shop. It was called the 'Whittle Club,' and we drank coffee and ate Dunkin' Donuts, exchanged ideas, gained confidence watching others do their carvings, and picked up some new skills. I started to carve, mostly Santas and shore birds." Zen found that many of the hand skills that he had previously used to tie dry fishing flies and to design intricate medical equipment were similar to those required in carving.

Jane (his wife) and Zen decided to move from Ramsey, New Jersey. Their decision was forced by a jump in real estate taxes to more than $8,000 a year, and the need to live on a fixed income that was based on a pension equal to one-half of his final Hoffmann-La Roche salary. Only 60, Zen was not yet eligible to receive social security. Another factor

Zen puts to use skills and interests previously developed at work and in other outdoor hobbies to create his wood carvings.

was Zen's interest in the outdoors. A longtime canoeist and fisherman, he wanted to move somewhere more amenable to his interests while he was still young enough to carry a canoe and wade into streams.

The transition from New Jersey to North Carolina was not easy. "I felt detached. No job, no friends, and I even missed the harassment at work. When I worked, I complained like most people, but when I retired I missed the work and the way my day had been scheduled. I realized that those things had been part of my life for 37 years.

"Then a friend taught me a lesson. I was advised to treat my wood carving as a job. I built a workbench in one-half of our two-car garage. I go to work at 8 A.M.; about 9:30 I take a brief coffee break, and then return to work. I do this until lunch when I usually quit for the day. I've made it something like a job with my morning schedule. And, I work this way about 20 hours a week."

Carving requires more than skilled use of an array of tools. Research is important. If Zen is carving an owl to sit on top of a wooden fence post, he reads about owls to ensure that its proportions and features are accurate.

Zen is fortunate that he incurs few raw material costs. Cedar, his termite-resistant choice for outdoor pieces, and bass wood for indoor carvings are readily available. When storms rip through North Carolina, his backyard and neighborhood are filled with downed trees, an ample source for future birds, gnomes and other carvings.

The Palkoskis have decorated their home and yard with dozens of carved figures. Even though he sells an occasional piece, Zen prefers to give his carvings as gifts to family members, friends and garden groups. He's not in it for the money. As he puts it, "I can make more money as a part-time clerk in a store." Even so, the income from sales offsets the costs of entering the annual Chatham County House tour and buying new tools.

Several summers ago, Jane saw a notice in a homeowner's newsletter. The advertiser was looking for someone to housesit their suburban Paris home during the summer. Zen stayed in North Carolina the first summer but accompanied Jane the following year to the same Paris house. While in Paris, Zen became interested in Rodin's sculptures and was inspired to begin sculpting in clay. Returning home, he took several sculpting courses at UNC in Chapel Hill to improve his skill.

Wood carvings, however, remain Zen's primary interest. He's carving more abstract pieces that are larger and more creative than his earlier works. As an outdoorsman, he has applied his observations in his carvings. "I noticed how beavers cut down trees. I became bolder, and like the beaver, I work with larger chunks of wood when I do my carving.

"One thing is certain, what began as my retirement hobby in 1994, is now my passion."

RETURNS TO A CHILDHOOD INTEREST IN ART

Rita Spina
PSYCHOLOGIST TURNS SCULPTOR

Rita Spina says she has had three careers: mother of four children, psychologist and since the early 1990s, professional artist. The last one is a culmination of an early interest and an expression of her life's experience.

Rita grew up in New York City, where as a youngster she took Saturday art courses at the Parson School of Design. Art was originally her goal at Russell Sage College, but because she didn't like the college's art program, she majored instead in speech and English. She tucked away art for a future day.

In keeping with the times, Rita married soon after graduating from college and lived a peripatetic lifestyle with her first husband, an aeronautical engineer who moved the family with each job change. They had four children and divorced in the mid 1960s. At the same time, Rita took the first step in shaping a career. She returned to college part-time and earned a master's degree in school and community psychology from Hofstra University. She began her worklife with the Dreyfus Biomedical Foundation, but lost her job when the company folded.

> **The multitasking of earlier years is reflected in Rita's multimedia approach to her art.**

Now remarried and living on Long Island, Rita opted to take a job as a school psychologist. She worked for the Kings Park school system for 16 years, and by the time she left she was supervising an eight-person department. Rita was also a Hofstra adjunct professor. To enhance her career, she earned a doctorate and was licensed so that she could qualify as a clinical practitioner.

"I realized at that time that I could do several things well at the same time. Multitasking is reflected in everything that I do." That was true then, and still today.

Rita and her husband, Larry, often made what appeared to be capricious decisions. With the last of the four children soon to leave home, Larry, who didn't know very much about boats, bought a 52-foot power boat on a whim, and the couple lived on it for four years in Huntington Harbor on the Long Island Sound. Several years later, they sold the boat just as precipitously after deciding that boat life was incompatible with their careers. Besides a full-time job, Rita was spending up to 20 hours a week in her private practice. She worked for two years as director of Hofstra's Psychological Evaluation and Research Center Before retiring, relocating and leaving Long Island for central North Carolina in 1989.

When she moved to North Carolina Rita didn't know exactly what she was going to do, but she knew she wanted to start painting and working as a multimedia artist. For several years, however, Rita instead taught behavioral psychology at two community colleges. Three years after their move to North Carolina, Rita and Larry decided on another fling—a year-long driving trip around the U.S. ala Charles Kuralt and John Steinbeck. Their journey was cut short when Larry died in California.

Finally, Rita's childhood interest in art moved center stage and soon became more than a passive hobby. First thing on her agenda was to move to a different house in the same community, one that would better accommodate the work she planned to do as a multimedia artist. She built additional storage space inside and outside the house for metal and wood, the materials she uses to create, build and paint abstract wall hangings and sculptures. The materials are scraps that she finds locally in the woods and along the roadsides.

"A piece of me needs a creative outlet. My work is my way to show my feeling about the conflict between nature—represented by wood in my work—and machines and equipment—represented by metal. I try in my art to resolve the conflict between nature and current technology. I work on four or five things at the same time—multitasking in sculpturing and relating it to life."

Art seems compatible with Rita's approach to life, and her training and career as a psychologist. "All my life I've been a problem solver by bringing people and ideas together. Now I put together things and ideas. My work represents everything I've done all my life; art is my way of life.

"I don't look at my work as a hobby. My income from my work is not large, but it does qualify my work as a semibusiness. My art work gives me supplemental income along with a great deal of personal freedom. I spend four to five days a week in my studio. I have no set work schedule. I'm like the daily jogger; I need to do it regularly." When Rita travels, she gets ideas for new pieces, but she admits that she's always eager to return home and to get to work in her studio.

> **"All my life I've been a problem solver by bringing people and ideas together. Now I put together things and ideas."**

Staying Put, But Not the Same

IN ADVISING OWNERS AND MANAGERS OF SMALLER companies how they can stay put, management consultant William Buxton Jr. likes to cite an example in his immediate family. "My father, William Buxton (now deceased)—or 'Mr. B,' as he was called—was president and major stockholder in the Peoples Trust & Savings Bank, founded by my grandfather in Indianola, Iowa. Mr. B planned to step down as president and let my brother run the bank. But unfortunately my brother died, and Mr. B, then 75, was once again president. Soon afterward he sold the bank to Iowa National Bank in Waterloo."

Instead of stripping Mr. B of his lifelong career, the new owners gave him a small office in the bank. While no longer an officer or on the payroll, he went to the bank two to three hours a day. As the bank's volunteer goodwill ambassador, one of his unofficial duties was compiling a newsletter called *Words of Wit and Wisdom,* which the bank mailed to customers throughout the region. "The bank was more than my father's career, it was also his hobby," notes Bill Buxton Jr., a Carrboro, North Carolina business consultant.

By and large, Mr. B is the kind of person you'll find profiled in this chapter: Self-described "old workhorses" who can't imagine being turned out to pasture and for whom work is their abiding passion. These are the people who can't fathom retiring in any traditional sense. For them, hobbies and other recreation, volunteer work, going back to school and spending more time with family—are pale alternatives to the invigoration of the workplace. The motivation is the same for the chairman of a multibillion-dollar company, the owner of a hardware store, the partner in a law firm or the corporate manager—to stay involved, responsible and challenged.

These are the people who can't fathom retiring in any traditional sense.

In his book, *The Hero's Farewell,* author Jeffrey Sonnenfeld describes one group of CEOs who exemplify this attitude: "Monarchs do not retire, but wear their crown until the end....These monarchs led their enterprises for lengthy reigns that ranged from 20 to 60 years. They were often in office until the last day they breathed." Sonnenfeld portrays Justin Dart, who built United-Rexall Drugs into a national drug chain and proclaimed at 72 that "I want my death and my retirement to be simultaneous." Three years later, Dart got his wish. He died after merging United-Rexall with Kraft.

Or consider Dr. Armand Hammer, who literally "died with his boots on" at age 92 while still chairman of Occidental Petroleum. He had taken control of the then-unprofitable company some 30 years before and was still in charge until the day he died in 1990.

And what about Maurice Greenberg. Now 78, he has presided over American International Group, a large international insurance company, for over 35 years. In early 2003, Greenberg and the board designated but hadn't yet publicly announced the name of his successor. Greenberg, *The New York Times* noted, has "no immediate plans to leave, and he provided no further insights into his timing."

Then again, not everyone hangs on by choice. Some do it out of financial necessity. They can't or don't want to maintain their current standard of living from pensions, savings and investments alone. Perhaps a large part of their retirement nest egg is tied up in a business that they haven't yet been able to sell.

For others, continuing to work has additional benefits, including being able to take advantage of tax deductions on entertainment and travel, or enjoying the fellowship that comes with being an active member of the business or professional community.

For many old workhorses, staying on in the workplace is simply a matter of "not whether you win or lose but how long you play the game."

To Chris Crenshaw, who operates a financial services firm of the same name in Durham, North Carolina, the word "retirement" has a feeling of finality, and it's definitely not part of his vocabulary. "Before you put your feet on the floor when you get up in the morning, you need something to look forward to doing that day." Chris finds his answer in work, and along with his wife, Elena, who's in her mid forties, in raising their two children. Though he was previously married, Chris became a father for the first time in his mid fifties. Now age 66, Chris lives the lifestyle of men 20 years younger. He attends school events, travels to soccer tournaments, and occupies the driver's seat of his business.

> **"Before you put your feet on the floor when you get up in the morning, you need something to look forward to doing that day."**

Chris plans to stay active in his business for many years even though he's considering merging or affiliating with another firm. In any scenario, he will keep a strong equity position in the new enterprise. As part of his game plan, he expects to add a few younger people to do research and to work with clients. "This will leave me more time to bring in business, and be the firm's rainmaker."

The Risks They Run

One of the privileges enjoyed by an Armand Hammer—or just about anybody who is self-employed—is the greater likelihood of staying put, adapting their role at work to their needs, and continuing to work if they want to. Why retire? Chances are they have more control over their fate than most corporate employees do. But even they may encounter inhibiting forces.

Even if they continue on by choice, some old workhorses may encounter resistance to their decision by a board of directors that

RULES FOR SCALING DOWN YOUR BUSINESS

- **Start off** with a business plan.

- **Maintain** a core of dedicated customers.

- **Make sure** you're running your business on at least a break-even basis. It doesn't make sense to sap your financial resources with a dying enterprise.

- **If you can, move** your business to your home, or at least to less expensive office space.

- **Invest** in good office equipment. Chances are you won't have a staff to do routine office work.

- **Don't downscale** your business at the risk of being bored.

maintains the company needs new blood and new direction. Other times, there is an heir apparent who's champing at the bit. Perhaps those reasons explain why "the average age of CEOs has held steady at 56 for the past four years (1998–2002)," according to *Chief Executive Magazine* (www.chiefexecutive.net). Older CEOs are actually becoming extinct. In 1980 more than half of the CEOs of Fortune 100 companies were in their sixties; today barely a quarter are.

Although their lives, souls and egos may be wrapped up in the business, many workhorses remain in family-owned businesses and professional services at a cost to the firm. More often than not, the operation is reduced in scope, size and quality of service as the owner gets older and less aggressive.

Retirement-age professionals who want to stay on in midsize to larger firms have little choice but to produce. They're allowed to remain with the firm just as long as they are "rainmakers," bringing in new business. The logic goes that the day-to-day professional work can be done by younger partners for less money. But in the small wholesale enterprise or the one- or two-person professional firm, there may be no one looking out for the best interest of the business—say, if it fails to update and install the latest in computer or manufacturing equipment, or if it continues to operate with outdated methods.

Many professions recognize the danger of getting into a rut and have instituted educational programs to improve quality performance among all members, not just the 50-plus set. The accounting profession, for example, requires that certified public accountants enroll in continuing education each year to maintain their professional credentials. But, in effect, the requirement particularly affects some older professionals who might have a tendency to let ongoing education take a back seat.

Ideally, the sole proprietorship or professional firm can take steps to assure continuity and to provide an opportunity for the owner to work past "normal" retirement age: Bring in a younger associate. Share responsibilities. Agree to take home less money in return for working fewer hours each week. Sounds good, but more often than not it doesn't work. Egos get in the way. After years of running the business, the owner still wants to be boss even though he's working less. Too many times, the associate ends up leaving because the owner was not totally committed to changing his work habits or to sharing the profits or ownership.

Some "die with your boots on" advocates face this possibility and take a more realistic approach. By design rather than attrition, they reduce the size of their operation and run a truncated law or accounting practice, or choose to operate a small and usually not too dynamic retail or service business.

One Man's Story

Harold T. maintains nearly total control of a closely held, $25-million, industrial-testing company that he started about three decades ago. Harold prefers to remain anonymous since it would hardly be in his best interest to tip off competitors on his corporate strategy. "Not a month goes by when I don't get a call from someone who might like to buy the company. We've even had some serious talks with two companies. Sure, I would get some money and stock, but they would want me to remain with the company after the takeover. I'd end up working harder than ever for the new owners so I could collect more money if my company increases sales and doubles profits. It would mean changing the friendly yet effective way we run the company. As you see, I'm not too interested in retiring and selling out." Harold feels that time is on his side. His father, a Nebraska farmer, retired when he was 75.

But Harold is also a realist, and he's concerned about the company and its future. His two sons are approaching college age and he estimates that even if they were to become interested, it would take five to ten years before they would be ready to enter the company. By then Harold will be in his late sixties. He's hedging his bets. He's setting up an employee stock-ownership plan that permits his 50 full-time employees to buy some of his holdings. "At least this way, the ownership will be shared by our people."

It's Harder for the Corporate Workhorse

Corporate or government managers, and partners in professional-services businesses normally don't have the options that are available to the self-employed or owners of smaller businesses. Employment contracts may force them to leave. Or they are forced out by downsizing or lured out by early-retirement packages. They can be pushed out by diminished rewards, unwelcome transfers, or work rules that make any sort of flexible or creative approach to retirement impossible. It might be nothing you could call age discrimination per se, but the message is still clear.

SUGGESTED READING

50 Plus!: Critical Career Decisions for the Rest of Your Life, by Robert Dilenschneider (Citadel Press, 2002). A public relations expert challenges readers to consider career and related decisions.

Reengineeering the Corporation, by Michael Hammer and James Champy (Harper Business, 2001). This bestseller will help you look at the same old problems differently.

POINTS TO REMEMBER

- **Many in the 50-plus set** want to continue working.

- **Additional income** is only one of many reasons for working.

- **You can work** without being a workhorse.

- **There are ways** to continue to work on your terms.

- **Flexible work patterns** are one answer.

- **You may want to pass along your business**—or you may not, or

- **You may want to stay involved,** but take on a different role.

That's unfortunate when you consider that, given the option, those in the 50-plus set prefer to work, an observation confirmed by the Commonwealth Fund (www.cmwf.org), a nonprofit group that studies social issues. More than half of workers between age 50 and 64 would extend their careers if their employers provided training for a different job, continued pension contributions past age 65, or offered a position with less pay but fewer hours and responsibilities as a transition to full retirement.

According to author Betty Friedan, most 65-plus men who continue to work are either at the "top or the bottom of the occupational ladder." It's mandatory for some men to hang on just to pay the bills, though she noted in her book, *The Fountains of Age,* "The increased availability of pensions has decreased the proportion of older men who work simply because they need additional income." More people at the top of the ladder would work after age 65 if they could find a position commensurate with their ability.

The possibility of staying in the corporate workforce would be enhanced if both employer and employee accepted such practices as flexible work schedules, telecommuting and job sharing. But the pros and cons of flexible staffing and scheduling notwithstanding, these corporate programs usually don't extend to most mid- to higher-level managers and professionals. At best, we hear the occasional anecdote about, say, a 62-year-old executive who wants to continue working but would like to avoid commuting three hours a day to and from work. To keep him in the work-force, new arrangements are made so that the executive can work three days a week at home and commute the rest of the week.

Those Who Are Keeping On

Professionals and self-employed people have many options if they want to continue working. They can go at full throttle or at a reduced pace. Above all, they find work to be a stimulant, more uplifting and challenging than retirement. The people you are about to meet have fashioned a lifestyle in which their work continues to be pivotal.

SHE'S NOW A MUSICAL INSTITUTION

Olga Bloom
MUSICIAN AND IMPRESARIO

Chamber music performed on a barge? On the East River in New York City, just opposite Wall Street? Despite the unlikely setting, Olga Bloom had a dream that she made come true.

But as rewarding as a Bargemusic concert is, part of the joy in attending the year-round, twice-weekly performances is watching Olga in action. Olga, who started the concerts in 1977, is Bargemusic's lifeblood. As its president, she is actively involved in management, taking on fundraising and public relations duties. But she also attends to the details. She sells and collects tickets, positions folding chairs in the auditorium, serves refreshments and personally greets the 130 or so people who attend a typical performance. Olga plans to stay put and has no intention of retiring anytime soon. But she is making sure that others will be able to take over for her once she's out of the picture.

"It takes as much energy doing things in retirement as it does to work. Going dancing or playing golf takes energy. If

Music—playing and sharing it—has dominated Olga's life, exemplified through her creation and eventual legacy, the Bargemusic concert series.

you like your work, why retire?" Her own schedule gives testimony to her words. She works six days a week, from 8 in the morning to 4 in the afternoon. She takes off Saturdays to do her personal chores.

"I still don't have a job description. When I clean floors, I'm the floor cleaner; when I'm raising funds, I'm a fundraiser. Other than music, I have few interests. My life is identified with the barge."

Even with her hectic schedule, Olga is still a performing musician. About once a month in a concert not open to the public, she invites three other musicians to join her on the barge in an evening of chamber music.

Olga never expected to get rich from her music or from Bargemusic. She admits to living rather simply on less than $40,000 a year, her income from Bargemusic. She lives by herself in a small house that she owns in Brooklyn—an improvement over the late 1970s, when she lived on the barge. If she ever does bother to retire, she will collect her social security, as well as her own and her deceased husband's pension payments.

Born in Boston, Olga attended Boston University to study music. "I left when my mother got sick. This was deep in the Depression years. I played in WPA [the Works Projects Administration, a federal agency supporting the arts during the 1930s] concerts, and in chamber music groups—first the viola and then the violin."

She moved to New York in 1943. "I decided it was time to stop being a student and to work as a musician. I met my first husband, who was then a violinist in an Army band. He had more noble purposes and did not want to spend the war years as a musician. He switched into the air corps and was killed in action in the South Pacific."

For the next 30 years, Olga played wherever she could, from symphony and ballet orchestras to chamber music. During this time, she recalls, "my philosophy about music was developing."

One of her observations was that music as a profession was being restricted to the wealthy, who could afford to buy costly instruments. She knew this firsthand. Her second husband, Toby, a violinist in Arturo Toscanini's National Broadcasting Company Symphony Orchestra, mortgaged most of his possessions to buy more-expensive violins.

Olga and Toby were living on Barnum Island, off the south shore of Long Island. They gave chamber-music recitals at their home for friends, and at these informal concerts Olga began to explore the relationship between music, water and the environment. Toby encouraged her to pursue the idea that would eventually become Bargemusic.

After Toby's death, Olga read in a newspaper ad that a barge was for sale. That seemed like an answer to everything—a concert hall on water. The first two barges that she bought had acoustical problems due to heavy planking that absorbed sound. On her third try, she found a 102-foot, 80-year-old steel barge, lined with cherry wood, that made the difference. A year later, in 1977, it was refurbished and towed to its current mooring in Brooklyn. The location, a few hundred feet south of the Brooklyn Bridge and directly across the East River from Wall Street, proved ideal. Getting a mooring in Brooklyn was no easy task. But Olga by then had a number of influential supporters and the ability to attract "friends in high office who could look after us."

Her intention in the late 1970s was to present concerts by students from New York's leading conservatories. That

> **"When musicians finish their studies, they need a place to perform. There are more good musicians than we can absorb. The barge is my answer."**

changed when violinist Ik-Hwan Bae was named as Bargemusic's artistic director. He convinced Olga that they should not rely exclusively on students for the level of performance that sophisticated New York audiences demand. Nowadays the pool of nearly 100 musicians are all professionals with an ambitious year-round schedule of four concerts each week, which is matched by few other classical music venues. The program is also consistent with Olga's original concept that Bargemusic concerts should, above all, further a young musician's career. "When musicians finish their studies, they need a place to perform. There are more good musicians than we can absorb. The barge is my answer."

In the late 1980s, Olga began to think about ways to operate Bargemusic more efficiently. She appointed a board of overseers consisting of professional musicians, a board of directors drawn from community leaders and a business manager to administer the organization, all calculated to leave Olga with more time for fundraising. The scheme partially fell apart when a number of board members resigned as their plans to institute managerial systems came into conflict with Olga's impresario style. After the rift, friends and patrons who consider Bargemusic synonymous with Olga Bloom, contributed $30,000 at a dinner and concert on the barge to help pay off debt and meet expenses.

Olga's dreams extend beyond her Brooklyn Bargemusic concerts. She would like to see other cities with waterside locations and a source of talented professional musicians develop similar chamber-music concerts on the water.

THE MIND IS IN HIS EYE

William Normand
PSYCHIATRIST

When William Normand talked about his 50th college reunion, the natural response was, "You're putting me on, Bill—you're much too young." But Bill did attend his Harvard College reunion. And unlike nearly all his classmates, who had fully retired, Bill still carries a full workload that includes both a private psychiatric practice and a part-time position in a New York City hospital.

Practicing psychiatrists Bill's age aren't rare. Within the medical profession, psychiatrists as a group continue to practice many years longer than other medical specialists. Psychiatry is less demanding physically than, say, surgery. And, as Bill puts it, "perhaps psychiatrists—like good wine—improve with age." Nonetheless, Bill's private practice has shrunk in recent years. "Perhaps I'm not getting as many referrals as before. Some of the doctors who used to send me patients have retired. Some patients come in for a preliminary consultation and never return. People who are considering long-term psychotherapy may be

> **Bill enjoys a mixed bag of private practice, teaching and outpatient-clinic management. But some things do change with the years.**

uncomfortable in starting with an older psychiatrist, who may desert them because of illness or death."

Bill likes the balance in his professional life. At Bronx Lebanon, a hospital affiliated with Albert Einstein College of Medicine, he teaches psychiatric residents and third-year medical students and manages the grand rounds program in which guest speakers present lectures on various psychiatric topics.

"Since I finished my training, I have had a half-time job teaching and managing outplacement clinics, and a private practice. I like the mix and I enjoy teaching."

The practice of psychiatry has changed since Bill completed his residency. At that time, nearly all psychiatrists were trained in psychoanalysis. Nowadays the approach is more chemically and biologically oriented, and most psychiatrists emphasize short-term psychotherapy, biological methods and shock treatment. Over the years, depending on the patient, Bill has changed his approach to psychiatry to include both biological and psychoanalytic treatment.

Bill grew up in Missouri and entered Harvard prior to World War II, intending to become a writer. He graduated in 1943, but the last semester was cut short when he joined the Army. Bill was assigned to the Army Specialized Training Program, spent nine months learning to speak Chinese and was trained in cryptoanalysis. At the end of the war, he entered Columbia University to continue studying Chinese.

"At the same time, I started to take an interest in my own neuroses, and I considered becoming either a psychiatrist or a psychologist." A trusted friend from Harvard, who had been exempt from military service, was already a physician and he advised Bill to become a doctor, too. Bill dropped the Chinese program and took the basic science courses needed to apply to medical school. At that time, medical schools were swamped with applicants because of the GI bill. Bill entered the University of Kansas, where he received an MA in physiology and an MD. He returned to New York City for his residency and the start of a lifelong association with the Albert Einstein College of Medicine and its affiliated hospitals.

Bill, who married when he was in his late thirties, has three grown children. His wife, Marjorie, a lawyer, is ten years younger, a factor that has favorably influenced his youthful professional and personal demeanor. She became a lawyer in her early forties and thus has practiced law for 20 some years. What's more, many of Bill's friends are near Marjorie's age, encouraging him to think and act younger. He plays tennis year-round and skis regularly during the winter.

"As for retirement, it never crossed my mind or Marjorie's. Our friends have not retired, so why should we? And, anyway, we like our work."

ONCE A JOURNALIST, ALWAYS A JOURNALIST

Pete Johnston
UNIVERSITY PROFESSOR

No sooner had Donald "Pete" Johnston retired from the faculty of the Columbia University Graduate School of Journalism than he walked across campus and joined the faculty of another Columbia graduate school. Teaching is Pete's forte, and his love, and he doesn't see giving it up just because he's in his seventies.

Pete's approach to college teaching has stayed constant over the years. Despite the way that computer technology has changed the processing of data, it hasn't much changed how a journalist reports and writes. "I spend a lot of time with the students, criticizing their work and helping them reach decisions relative to their careers. I have always let a job expand beyond its normal dimensions," says Pete.

As an adjunct faculty member, Pete officially works half-time, but keeping to official working hours has never been his strong suit. Pete enjoys helping students improve their basic communications skills, something he does in his "off" hours in one-on-one sessions. "Ever since I've been a teacher, I have felt I'm contributing something very useful in motivating my students."

For a change of pace, he serves as the volunteer editor of the Columbia Journalism School's alumni newspaper.

Born in Buffalo, Pete served in the Air Force during World War II. He graduated in 1949 from Cornell University and the following year from Columbia's journalism school. He worked as a reporter with the United Press International bureau in Buffalo for several years, then was transferred to the foreign desk in New York, where he covered the UN. *The New York Times* then hired him for its Sunday "Week in Review" section to report on national and international events and on trends in social issues.

"I always wanted to be a journalist. Little has changed. When I worked for UPI and the *Times,* I commuted from Westchester. The other commuters, who made more money than I did, sounded disgruntled with their work and their pay. They couldn't wait until

> **Pete knows that tools may change, but the essentials of his craft are enduring. He anticipates teaching them indefinitely—wherever.**

the weekends. I never felt that way toward work."

While at the *Times,* Pete taught journalism part-time at one of the colleges in the New York City university system. The experience encouraged him to apply to Columbia Journalism School as a full-time faculty member.

Pete found his true challenge as a teacher and mentor. "I like people, I like the Columbia environment, and I particularly like working with younger people— they make you feel younger." Students enjoyed his enthusiasm. He gave more time to the job than was required. His comments on their writings were both critical and helpful. None of that changed over the years.

During the mid 1980s, Pete, then an associate professor, was promoted to associate dean for academic affairs as well as director of admissions. When a new dean was named, Pete was replaced as an administrator, and he returned to teaching. His effectiveness as an instructor aside, Pete had an academic problem: He had neglected scholarly research, a critical factor in receiving tenure. Years earlier, he had been denied tenure but his faculty position wasn't jeopardized because he was also serving as associate dean, a position protected by university regulations. When he reached age 65 and lacked tenure, it

appeared his teaching career was at checkmate. This time he would have to leave the journalism school, with lifetime health care benefits and a pension based on 15 years' service.

At that point, Pete knew one thing. He did not want to stop working, unlike his older brother who worked as a sportswriter for 40 years, retired to Florida and has not written a word since. "He is content to play tennis, walk, read, ride his bike and watch TV. I'm not ready for that yet."

Fortunately, Pete's teaching credentials did not go unnoticed. As an associate dean, he knew other Columbia administrators, including those in the Graduate School of International and Public Affairs. They asked him to join the faculty as an adjunct professor, teaching basic journalism courses and working part-time as director of the school's International Media and Communications Program. In that capacity, Pete has run United Nations–sponsored training workshops for journalists from developing countries and has served as the editor-in-chief of a four-volume *Encyclopedia of International Media and Communications.* So long as Pete works no more than half-time, he can earn income and continue to collect his pension.

Pete's experience with an apparently seamless switch from one faculty to

> **Students enjoyed his enthusiasm. He gave more time to the job than was required....None of that changed over the years.**

another on the same campus has carryover value for many managers and executives exiting the corporate workplace. Rather than retire, perhaps they, too, can find another department within the same organization that can use their skills.

Pete's five children are all grown. His wife, Jane, a former high school English teacher, is a published writer of murder mysteries. Jane brings in a small pension, social security benefits and some book royalties.

Some time ago, Pete thought that at 70 (he's now 79) he and Jane would leave New York and move to their summer home on Cape Cod. Jane spent about six months a year there, and Pete lived there during the summer months. But any consideration of Cape Cod as a full-time home has been dropped. They found it too quiet and lonely in the off-season. Consistent with their desired lifestyle, the Johnstons have rented an apartment within walking distance of the Columbia campus. "We like the energy and action in Manhattan, and we plan to stay here indefinitely."

WORK IS A FAMILY TRADITION

Sally Rhine Feather and Bill Hendrickson

SHE'S A CLINICAL PSYCHOLOGIST; HE'S A BUSINESSMAN

Meet Sally Rhine Feather and Bill Hendrickson. They were college classmates, went their separate ways after graduation, married other people, raised children, pursued different careers, faced family traumas, and in the mid-1980s, they met again and were married the following year. Now, more than 15 years later, when most of their contemporaries are retiring, Sally and Bill are active workplace participants. They pursue separate careers and participate together on one rather demanding project, the Rhine Research Center.

Sally gave up private practice to follow in her parents' footsteps, while Bill turned over his business to his son and begins consulting.

SALLY

Looking back, it seems that Sally's future was somewhat predictable. As a youngster, she was interested in her father's research in parapsychology, which is commonly referred to as extrasensory perception. Photographs in magazine articles from Sally's youth show her playing games to test ESP.

Sally's father, J.B. Rhine, a Duke University psychology professor, along with his wife, Louisa, another psychologist, made ESP their academic and research focus. After 38 years on the Duke faculty, J.B. Rhine founded the Rhine Research Center in the mid-1960s when he neared retirement.

"After I graduated from the College of Wooster in 1951, I got a job as a technical writer in Washington with the Library of Congress doing abstracts on Department of Defense materials. Perhaps, in the back of my mind, I was interested in my father's work at Duke, but I was not too goal-directed at the time."

Like many women college graduates of that era, career took second place to marriage. Sally married, and she worked to put her husband through medical school. The couple returned to Duke for his residency.

In 1962, Sally enrolled at Duke in a research and experimental psychology doctoral program. "It took me five years, and I got my degree the same year I was divorced. My aim was to work full-time at the Rhine Research Center."

Sally found that a research job did not fit the needs of a single mother. "I needed a 9-to-5 job, a steady income and benefits. I was hired to run an adolescent clinic in Charlotte, but I stayed only two years because a job opened up in Durham." She worked until the early 1980s with several mental health clinics until she felt it made financial sense to become an independent clinical psychologist. Sally continued her practice until 1987, when she married Bill and moved to his home in Ridgewood, New Jersey. "The hardest part of the move was getting patients. I took assignments from the courts and had a part-time practice."

Six years later, Sally and Bill moved again— back to Durham. As soon as they settled in, she set up a private-practice office in Durham and one in her home in Hillsborough, north of Chapel Hill. She established new ground rules for work by limiting her load to 20 hours a week. "First, it is hard to regain a full-time workload when you've been away, and secondly, I was in my early sixties and I didn't want to work that hard. It's nice to choose and do what you want within the framework of your career path, but still be able to devote more time to volunteer work, gardening, family and other things."

But Sally's relationship to the Rhine Research Center moved front and center. Her father and mother died at ages 84 and 91 respectively, and both had worked nearly to the end of their lives. Their deaths had left a leadership hole at

the Center that was filled for nearly 20 years by a series of directors.

In January, 2002, Sally, who had been a Center board member since the mid-1960s, was named full-time director. As such, she now averages 30 hours a week of work, which is presently unpaid because of a budget crunch. Sally's goal is to get the Center on a sound financial basis within the next few years, expand its academic research and get it more involved in consumer-related ESP programs, and attract more grants and contributions. New responsibilities have meant a flip-flop in Sally's work schedule. As she has expanded her work with the Center, she has cut back her private practice from 20 to four hours a week.

Retirement is not part of Sally's (or Bill's) vocabulary. "Even though it might be wonderful to have more time to relax, retirement is for sissies." She plays tennis a few times a week, but finds that even a sport that one enjoys has its limitations in one's retirement plans. "How many times a week can you do it," she asks?

One part of the Feather-Hendrickson's lifestyle, however, might change. Living in a home on a multiacre rural site poses physical limitations. As a lifestyle alternative, the couple is considering moving into a retirement community in a few years. "That still does not mean that I have to play

> **"Even though it might be wonderful to have more time to relax, retirement is for sissies."**

bridge; I can still work. Like my parents, I expect to be involved professionally and in the community wherever I live," says Sally.

BILL

The son of a Presbyterian minister, Bill was born and lived in Ohio, and like Sally graduated from the College of Wooster. "I thought I would teach history or I would go into radio broadcasting." Like many other 1951 college graduates, however, he went into the army and worked in counterintelligence for two years in Europe. Three months after his discharge, Bill was married.

Over the next 34 years, Bill became a employee benefits specialist for several insurance companies, ending his career in New York with Marsh & McLennan as a sales and marketing vice president.

When he left Marsh in 1988, retirement was not part of Bill's plan. His pension income was limited due to having changed jobs in an era before portable pensions. As a career alternative to retirement, Bill formed Hendrickson & Company, which specialized in selling employee benefit insurance to small and midsize firms and to members of trade associations. He launched the company about the time that he married Sally.

Six years later, Bill faced another hurdle when he relocated to North Carolina. "At first, I commuted to New York about every two weeks, then every three or four weeks, and by 1999, every six weeks; now, it's more like two to three months."

Bill's lessening involvement reflects the increased involvement of his eldest son, Doug. In the mid-1990s, Doug, who was an executive with Chemical Bank in New York (now JP Morgan Chase), came to work with Bill with the idea that he would like to join, buy, and take over the business. "Doug's decision made sense to me because it would provide for an orderly succession consistent with my own plans." Following the takeover, Bill became a Hendrickson & Co. consultant.

Make no mistake, though. Fewer business trips to New York does not mean that Bill is retiring. Hardly. He does much of his work from North Carolina via telephone, fax and computer. He spends about 40% of his time on insurance matters. Until mid-2003, he owned an interest in a local land development company, Red Hill Farms, which he subsequently sold. He continues as the Rhine Research Center's unpaid treasurer. Tennis and travel round out the balance of his schedule. Bill's slate of involvements might change, at least temporarily, if the book that he's writing on corporate culture is published.

Unlike Sally, Bill has no role model when it comes to retirement. His father died in his mid sixties. "My idea on retirement is to continue to work and enjoy the psychic benefits of my income and fees. I'm also following the advice of one of Sally's uncles: 'Don't ever retire.'"

HE DROPS THE UNIVERSITY WORKLOAD

John Shelton Reed
OFFICIALLY RETIRED, BUT STILL AN ACADEMIC

John Shelton Reed spent his entire professional career as a member of the University of North Carolina faculty. In retirement, John's lifestyle is in many ways still colored with a strong academic hue, with his career skills adding a focal point to his retirement picture.

By 2000, John, in his late fifties, felt he was ready to retire. His plate was full as a tenured professor and director of the Howard Odum Institute for Research in Social Science, a position he had held for 12 years. Previously, John had been one of the founders and then director of UNC's Center for the Study of the American South. Besides the usual academic papers and books, John had written and edited a number of books for general readership, including *1000 Things Everyone Should Know About the South* (Main Street), which he cowrote with his wife; *My Tears Spoiled My Aim and Other Reflections on Southern Culture* (Harvest Books); and *Whistling Dixie: Dispatches from the South* (Harvest Books). And, John proudly claims that he's the only sociologist to be included in Southern author and humorist Roy Blount, Jr.'s, *Book of Southern Humor*.

This professor leaves academic administration behind and gets back to the basics.

"I left UNC after 31 years. I enjoyed teaching, but due to my administrative duties with the Center, I was spending about half my time in committee meetings and writing reports. In many ways, I had a great job. There was little supervision and one-half my time I could do what I wanted. Now I do it all the time."

John admits that he spent his first retirement year in leisurely fashion. "I had little trouble adjusting to my new lifestyle. Unlike some other people that my wife, Dale, and I know, my life and identity had not been tied up completely in my job. We spent the spring semester at Stanford University, which is only 30 miles from our 'number-one' daughter, and in our drive to and from California we visited our number two daughter in Houston." While at Stanford, John worked on a number of articles and a few book chapters. After returning home and continuing his research, John admits that he spent more time in the UNC library than he had spent in the previous ten years.

The tempo picked up the following year. "We only spent two months in Chapel Hill. I taught four weeks in January at Centre College in Kentucky, and then from February through June, I taught an American studies course at the University of London. That was a great deal. I didn't get paid, but I got free airfare for Dale and me, plus a free apartment near the university." During the fall semester, John taught a graduate course at East Tennessee State University, about 20 miles from where he was raised. It gave him a chance to visit regularly with his parents who are in their eighties.

Growing up in Kingsport, Tennessee, John, the son of a small town surgeon, was not planning on an academic career. He went to the Massachusetts Institute of Technology to study mathematics, drifted into statistics, and drifted once more into statistics and how it relates to sociology. This led to a doctorate in sociology from Columbia University and a thesis on the sociology of the South. It was only logical in 1969 to return south, and join UNC's sociology department.

The Reeds live modestly. Dale, a piano teacher, retired when John did. Their source of income is John's UNC pension, slightly more than half of his faculty salary. John also retired with lifetime family medical benefits. In several years both he and Dale will be eligible for social security. In the years before he retired, John also taught summer school, which increased the size of his pension.

In his early retirement, John discovered a new endeavor, unrelated to academia. A vacation in Mexico triggered what John calls his first serious hobby, collecting Mexican silver pieces. So that they can spend more time in Mexico, the Reeds are trying to learn Spanish. In early 2003 they spent a month in Guatemala taking a Spanish-immersion course.

John also expects to revisit England and Oxford University in 2004, where he had a year-long fellowship earlier in his career. "I'll be a visiting fellow at All Souls College for eight weeks working on a project—perhaps a book or maybe a couple of journal articles—that relates to my 1996 book, *The Cultural Politics of Victorian Anglo-Catholicism*."

The Reeds are also looking at different lifestyle arrangements. "In ten or so years, we might move to Carol Woods [a retirement community in Chapel Hill and the home of many retired UNC faculty members]. We're not ready or old enough yet, but someday we might want to give up housekeeping and live with some of our friends."

> "In many ways, I had a great job. There was little supervision and one-half my time I could do what I wanted. Now I do it all the time."

ADVISES OTHERS ON CAREERS AND RETIREMENT

William Stanley
OUTPLACEMENT AND COACHING CONSULTANT

William Stanley practices what he preaches. A career coaching consultant, Bill, now in his late sixties, advises men and women who are ten to 20 years younger than him on the strategy that they should follow if they've been pink-slipped or given the option of early retirement. Bill's decision was easy—continue to work.

Providing this type of assistance is not new to Bill. Since graduating from Princeton and completing his military obligations as a naval officer, he has focused on human resource issues. Bill spent 20 years at Connecticut General Life Insurance Company (which merged into Cigna) and 13 years with an outplacement firm. Since 1995 he has worked as a self-employed outplacement and coaching consultant.

"Retirement is not a very useful word; it means withdrawal. I expect to do what I'm doing as long as I can. I find that my clients [presently a large communications industry equipment supplier and a metro New York hospital] don't care how old I am. They like my experiences, and want to learn more

This former human resources manager, now self-employed, helps others come to grips with the last third of their lives.

about how to deal with the last one-third of their lives. I try to give them the feeling that what I'm telling them *is* me. It's the way I live. In this way, age has its advantages.

"My job is to get at each person's personality and show them how to fulfill their needs, but when I coach some people, I get a blank stare and rolling eyeballs.

"I try to stay in touch with some of the people I coach. Some have developed consulting businesses. Others have used their energies in hobbies or as volunteers. Others just give up and escape into the lifestyle of a gated community."

Because of Bill's expertise, he has twice been invited to speak to his Princeton classmates at their reunions. At their 35th reunion, he asked them to describe their plans for the last third of their lives. By then, the class was balanced between those who had already retired and those who were still working. Their primary questions, other than those related to health, were: Why retire when there's so much left to do? How do you find structure in retirement? How do you learn a new routine? How do you stay busy yet not feel stressed or rushed?

After more than 30 years of working a structured business day, Bill discovered that becoming an independent consultant in 1995 and working from an at-home office in Ridgewood, New Jersey, called for some fine-tuning. No longer was his 9-to-5 day scheduled with meetings to attend, reports to prepare and "make work" assignments to handle. His independent consultancy posed another challenge— keeping his network going. "That has become more difficult as people who I knew in the corporate world have retired. My Princeton classmates, who are now mostly retired, can no longer refer people to me."

Consistent with his business and personal plan, Bill works three days a week. Despite his reduced workweek, revenues from coaching are surprisingly strong—boosted somewhat by an unsettled job market where people in their fifties are asking themselves, "What's next?" Besides consulting fees, Bill's income consists of social security benefits, income from a few 401(k)s and

Bill finds that networking has become a challenge as his contacts in the corporate world have retired.

a Cigna pension from which he's been receiving payments since he was 55.

Interestingly, when Bill was a Cigna human resource manager he recommended that the company lower the pension age for retirees to 55, recognizing that by that age, employees may have already worked for 30 years, be able to retire, but not be able to collect on the money.

Bill's wife, Viola, is in her mid fifties and teaches fifth grade in a neighboring community. She has every intention of working another nine years until she's eligible to retire on a full pension. In consequence, when Bill is between coaching gigs, he has other responsibilities to keep him busy. He calls himself a " house husband," an assignment with many roles: cooking, a long-time hobby; maintaining their home; and taking care of his 94-year old mother-in-law, who lives in another house in Ridgewood, and his mother, 93, who lives in Wallingford, Connecticut. Besides all that, there's constant maintenance to do at their 150-acre rural retreat in upstate New York, which the couple enjoys on weekends and in the summer.

NOT READY TO EXIT HER FIRM

Pat Kosak
PROVIDES ACCOUNTING SERVICES TO SMALL BUSINESSES

The death of Pat Kosak's mother in the mid 1990s made her take a look at some career options and change her professional direction. "I felt that if I didn't go into business for myself at this time, I would never do it. I never liked working for other people anyway."

At the time, Pat was in her mid fifties and already had 23 years of accounting experience. Her husband, Roger, worked as a technical manager for IBM, and her daughters were both married, had jobs and were parents. With nothing to lose, Pat made the plunge, and launched Accounting & Business Solutions of N.C.

Raised in Rockville Center, New York, Pat graduated from the University of Wisconsin with a major in sociology. Working in a job related to sociology would have required obtaining an advanced degree. Instead, like many women of her generation, Pat got married, put her career on hold, and was a stay-at-home mother until her daughters were 10 and 7½.

"We were living in the Washington [D.C.] area, and I was hired by an insurance company. Five years later I went to work in the accounting department of a large law firm where I did my work on a memory typewriter. The firm was in the process of computerizing how it did business, and I was asked to help install and use an IBM System 32 computer." At the same time, Pat took a few accounting courses at George Mason University to enhance her employer's on the-job-training.

Life changed once again for the Kosak family. Roger was transferred in 1986 from Washington to Raleigh, North Carolina. Pat held several accounting related jobs until she joined the League of Municipalities as its chief financial officer. Eight years later her mother died, and Pat was ready to put her dream to work as an entrepreneur.

The dream was encouraged by her son-in-law in Washington who runs a midsize accounting firm that specializes in serving smaller businesses. Andrew became Pat's mentor while she made the transition from employment to self-employment as an accounting and small-business specialist.

> **Prompted by her mother's death, encouraged by her son-in-law, and working with her daughter, Pat's business is a family affair.**

"I started out at home, and I could have stayed there. But within two years, I added new clients, hired a few people and ran out of space. I rented a separate office, five minutes from home. I've grown every year since I've been in business, and we now have four people working here, who serve about 55 small-business clients. I don't know how much more I want I grow. I do know that I'm not making as much money as I made in my last job as CFO, but that doesn't bother me."

Pat's goal from the outset was to work with smaller businesses. Her forte is to get clients at their inception and help them set up their accounting, financial and business systems. During the winter and early spring months—an accountant's busiest time—Pat works up to ten hours a day plus weekends.

"Work keeps my mind active; I don't have time to think about retiring. I know one thing; I don't have the patience to stay at home all day. Roger recently retired from IBM, but he's busy doing some consulting and his own things."

Even so, Pat, has set the stage for her retirement. Daughter Anna, who spent four years as the bookkeeper at Quail Ridge Books, Raleigh's largest independent bookstore, now works with Pat, and Anna's husband, Edward, is the part-time telemarketer for Pat's firm. Anna is being groomed for the day when she'll take over the business. It's been a learning process for the entire family, and especially for Anna. "I never worked for my mother before. We have different styles. I tell it like it is. At work, I'm an organizational freak, but not the same way at home, while Mom is better organized at home. One of our strong points is that we know each other's personal shorthand. We try not to discuss business when we all get together as a family."

When she does retire, Pat will receive a small pension of several hundred dollars a month from the League of Municipalities. Roger has his IBM pension, its health care plan, plus social security, which Pat will also receive when she comes of age.

The Kosaks are ardent cooks, and for the past eight years they have been members of the American Institute of Wine and Food, a nationwide gourmet group. Food and wine tasting and attending gourmet events notwithstanding, Pat's workplace skills caught up with her: she serves as the local chapter's unpaid financial officer.

> **"Work keeps my mind active; I don't have time to think about retiring. I know one thing; I don't have the patience to stay at home all day."**

ADAPTS TO A PART-TIME WORK SCHEDULE

George Krassner
ACTIVE AS CONSULTANT AND TEACHER

"**M**y retirement lasted from April to June, and then I moved to North Carolina to be semiretired," says George Krassner. He then embarked on a routine that includes consulting, teaching business workshops, and representing a legal services company as a commissioned marketer. Now in his mid seventies, George admits that he's the type of guy who likes to be active, whether he's running a company, lecturing or calling square dances. But he also likes to be in charge, and that's reflected in his approach to his workday routines in semiretirement.

Continues his consulting business, but sets his own work rules.

George grew up in New York, went to Music & Arts High School (now High School for the Performing Arts) and as a youngster gave a concert in Carnegie Hall. In college, he trained as an engineer, and while in graduate school at the University of Michigan, he began teaching. His diverse interests came into play when he applied his violin training to fiddling at square dances. "When I learned that the caller made more money, I switched over."

Early in his career, George worked in satellite communications. As a corporate manager, he held a number of management positions, primarily with midsize companies. For seven years he was the president and general manager of three operating units of Simmonds Precision, which at the time was Vermont's third-largest private employer. While at Simmonds, he wrote *Introductions to Space Communications* (McGraw-Hill, 1964), believed to be the first book on the subject. "The publisher approached me when they learned that I had headed the first government satellite communications group. I also had lots of notes and materials from a course I had taught at Fort Monmouth, New Jersey [a long-time Army telecommunications center]."

After George left Simmonds, he bought a consulting firm, Corporate Profiles, where he specialized in the purchase and sale of companies, turnarounds, and the development of sales and marketing strategies. About the time that he sold Corporate Profiles, one of his consulting clients recruited him to manage one of their operations, Streeter Amet, which produced street and highway counters. When the parent company was acquired 11 years later, George left, moved to Connecticut and in 1984 set up his own consulting company, GK Limited.

The direction of GK Limited was similar to Corporate Profiles. In addition, George began to teach. "It's the extroverted side of me. When I was getting my master's at the University of Michigan, I was a teaching fellow. As a consultant, I would run workshops and handle all the details—book the room, do the advertising."

George and Judith, his wife, relocated from metropolitan Boston to North Carolina in the mid 1990s. They preferred a four-season climate, near to universities and a metro center where consulting assignments would be more readily available. The couple chose to live in a 34-home development called Solterra (which refers to sun and earth) that features passive-solar-heated homes. A side benefit of the community is that it attracts people like George who for various reasons adhere to a macrobiotic diet. Diet became critical to George in the late 1980s after his diagnosis with prostate cancer. Pursued as an alternative to surgery, a macrobiotic diet eliminates certain foods while emphasizing others. The diet is important in other ways. It emphasizes eating slowly, relaxing and exercising. Following this routine gives George time to smell the roses and allows him to balance work with his interpretation of a retirement lifestyle. He continues with his earlier

> **"I feel I can be a part-time worker for as long as I want."**

endeavors, but he sets the ground rules.

George has reduced the scope of GK Limited, once a full-time endeavor, to a few assignments. "I don't advertise for clients; I get them by referrals. Three or four clients is all I want to handle. I want to spend January in Florida and one month each summer in Maine.

"I gave up being a Small Business and Technical Development Center consultant because I didn't want to work a fixed schedule.

"Once I moved to North Carolina, I got involved with both Durham and Wake Technical Community Colleges teaching business courses. I do the same thing at Duke in its community education program." The themes of George's courses vary: "Build and Maintain a Successful Consulting Practice: Yes, You!" and "Jumpstart Your Business and Ramp Up Cash Flow." Another workshop theme relates to franchising (see Chapter 7 for George's views on franchising), where he draws upon his experience as a former owner of a Huntington Learning Center. "I could teach at other community colleges, but I try to avoid workshops, particularly evening ones, too far from home."

The next step in his agenda is to write a series of how-to books based on his seminar presentations and workplace know-how.

Within the past few years, George became a commissioned marketer for

Pre-Paid Legal Services, which provides legal assistance to individuals, families and smaller businesses. It's all part of his plan to live on the revenue that he's generated from teaching and consulting, social security, and a small pension from a former employer. "I feel I can be a part-time worker for as long as I want. As I get older, I might eliminate some evening workshops and cut back on consulting, and then if I need the money, tap into our investments."

Starting Over

YOU'RE 50- OR 60-SOMETHING AND YOU'VE JUST been pink-slipped. You definitely don't want to retire. Business is your lifeblood. What's the next step—do you look for another job (the subject of Chapter 8), buy an existing business, start your own, purchase a franchise, begin a new career, become a consultant?

Chances are the 50-plus set won't find a friendly welcome mat at most Fortune 500 companies. Many employers, while respecting your credentials, assume that you've been overpaid, that your work skills have plateaued or that you're no longer as aggressive as a 42-year-old.

Now's the time to downplay the traditional job market and consider some form of self-employment or career change, an idea that fictional Rabbi David Small contemplated in *The Day the Rabbi Resigned*. "Because I'm 53, it occurred to me that in a few years I'd be too old to be considered for a teaching job. Maybe I'm too old now, but I'd like to give it a shot."

The rabbi's not alone. According to the Small Business Administration (www.sba.gov), about 8% of workers of all ages are self-employed, but by the time workers reach age 65 and over, the rate nearly doubles. Perhaps one reason for this spurt is that owning a business has become a prime way to remain employed. That does not mean that all older entre-

---

TAKE THEIR ADVICE

Outplacement consultants and financial advisers offer these warnings and suggestions to retirees who are thinking about going into business.

- **Do become** a consultant in your field of expertise.

- **Do acquire** a business under a game plan to earn the difference between your former take-home pay and your current income.

- **Do keep** your business simple. Let it challenge but not overwhelm you.

- **Do develop** a practical business plan commensurate with your age. Sixty-two-year-olds should avoid overly ambitious corporate objectives.

- **Don't refinance** your home and invest the capital in a business.

- **Don't risk** pension income and investments in a business in which you have no expertise.

- **Don't bankroll** younger family members in a business in which neither of you has any expertise.

- **Don't involve** yourself in a new business that requires upward of 60 hours of work a week.

---

preneurs are putting in a 60-hour workweek. Some operate seasonal businesses; others are consultants who work two or three days a week.

Want to Own Your Own Business?

You've probably daydreamed about owning your own business. But before taking the plunge, be hard-nosed. Starting a business calls for enormous amounts of energy and endurance, a tough hurdle for anyone but more so for new business owners who are 50-plus, and especially so for those past 60. Above all, it means risking capital—rather little for an at-home consultancy but much more for buying or starting other types of businesses. Surely, your lawyer or accountant will point out the pitfalls of jeopardizing retirement-related resources on any new business venture.

As an entrepreneur, George Krassner (profiled in Chapter 6) personally knows the risks shared by most owners of start-up businesses. "They fall in love with an idea yet fail to do adequate research. They underestimate the cost of being in even the most modest type of business, and at the same time overestimate their market potential." Krassner finds that retirees go into business for many reasons: "They're bored with retirement, or they have an "A" type personality that needs to be stimulated."

Is it a risk worth taking for the 50-plus set or, in fact, for would-be entrepreneurs of any age? It probably depends on whether you're an optimist or a pessimist. The SBA estimates that about one-half of start-ups terminate within the first four years of inception. Yet, at the beginning, each of those start-up business owners was probably convinced that his or her venture was a sure-fire winner.

At age 54, 60 or 65, you hardly want to gamble a life's sav-

MUSTS FOR NEW BUSINESSES

- **Do your homework** before going into business.

- **A preliminary, one-year, realistically written business plan** is mandatory.

- **Avoid blue-sky proposals;** they accomplish nothing. Remember, the planning is not an exercise in fiction writing. You want to set realistic and achievable goals.

- **Prepare a tentative operating budget.**

- **Decide whether you need additional financing.**

- **Decide whether you have the income** to support the business and your personal needs during the start-up period.

- **Decide whether the business needs** any other full- or part-time employees.

HAVE YOU CONSIDERED?

- **How much money** you need to earn

- **How much money** you want to earn

- **Growth potential**

- **Risk**

- **Liquidity of the business.** How quickly could you sell the business if you needed to?

- **Location**

- **Competition**

- **Physical working conditions**

- **Status and image**

- **People intensity,** or the degree to which you'll be required to interact with other people. Are you a loner, or do you get your energy from other people? Make sure the business suits your personality.

Source: Lee Hecht Harrison

---

ings on a new business. Of course, there may be exceptions: a former executive with capital to spare as the result of a golden handshake, or the seller of one business who is in a favorable cash position to invest in another. Or how about retired high-income CEOs like Chrysler's Lee Iacocca, who started ventures including a food and wine company? Or Marvin Traub, past chairman of Bloomingdale's, who formed his own consulting firm, Marvin Traub and Associates? Occasionally you will find people such as former telecommunications manager Bill Gower (profiled later in this chapter) and his wife, Denise, who left corporate America and became novice bed-and-breakfast innkeepers. Simply put, a retiree should think twice before launching a start-up business. There are other ways to become an entrepreneur.

If you get the itch, be aware that you most likely would fetch a better return on your money in any number of safer investment vehicles. This may be beside the point if you are intent on owning a business, but it's a critical consideration as you approach retirement age. The three to five years it will likely take to establish the business may seem like an eternity to you. Also consider that you no longer have the luxury of 20 to 30 years to recoup any money that you may ultimately lose. Business turnaround expert William Buxton, a business consultant in Carrboro, North Carolina, does not court retirement-age people as prospects to purchase businesses up for sale. "Other than those people with extra money to spend or who know a specific business 'cold,' I advise people in their late fifties to sixties to avoid risking it all in buying or starting a business."

Aside from the financial risk, there are serious questions to consider:

- **If you've spent 25 to 30 years working in corporate America,** how prepared are you for the rigors of self-employment?
- **How well do you know the business** that you hope to start or buy?
- **If you are a newcomer to the field,** who is going to teach you the ABCs?
- **Are you mentally and physically prepared** to be your own boss?
- **Are you ready to work longer hours** than you most likely did in a previous corporate job?

In spite of the possible financial and personal risk, Sterling Dimmitt, until recently a senior vice-president and director of entrepreneurial services for Lee Hecht Harrison, found in the late '90s that about 18% of downsized executives of all ages surveyed by his firm opted to acquire or start their own business, compared with a 12% rate in 1990. These potential entrepreneurs tend to be in their mid forties or older and were earning more than $100,000 when they left their last job. "Survival in your own business generally requires significant capital and business know-how, which many of these older, experienced people have," said Dimmitt. But unless the individual has sufficient capital to risk, Dimmitt would seriously question the wisdom of starting a business from scratch in one's late fifties. Exceptions are service and consulting fields, where the capital requirements can be rather modest and the entrepreneur is already an expert in the field.

Buying a Business

A more practical alternative is to buy an existing profitable business, with enough sales (perhaps as little as $1 million to

$3 million) to provide you with an adequate income. "Although it takes a lot of up-front money, this is the self-employment path most likely to succeed," says Dimmitt. "In purchasing a business and its positive cash flow, people are, in effect, buying a job and a return on their investment." Buying an ongoing business makes sense just as long as the purchaser is in good health and has a desire to work harder and longer than the previous owner has worked in years. This rule has even greater application to retail businesses, where six-day workweeks are standard. If you are considering retail or restaurant ownership, get experience working in the industry beforehand or find a partner who is experienced. According to Dimmitt, running these businesses is an art, and experience is essential. "To succeed, the person should know the field very well, know how to run a business and have had experience operating a similar type of business." In short, we're still not talking about novices flying blind. He also cautions retirees against investing a large part of their retirement savings in a new business venture. The personal risks are obvious.

Is a Franchise a Better Choice?

What about franchising for "wannabe" entrepreneurs? Many new-business experts feel that franchising represents a strong start-up opportunity for the 50-plus set with risk capital resulting from severance or golden-parachute payouts to invest. The risks are sharply lower than in starting a business from scratch.

Franchise-industry growth figures are impressive: Depending on who does the counting, there are approximately 600,000 U.S. franchise-owned businesses with an estimated $1 trillion in industry sales. A new franchise unit opens somewhere in the U.S. every eight minutes. Name a retail or service chain of business and most likely it's a franchise. The roster, according to the International Franchise Association (www.franchise.org), includes food retailers, such as McDonald's and Dunkin' Donuts; tax service companies, such as H&R Block and Jackson Hewitt; and executive search firms, such as Management Recruiters International and Dunhill Staffing Systems.

Despite the numbers, however, franchising is not for everyone. Watch out for possible culture shock, especially if you're shifting from a corporate lifestyle to a "mom and pop" business environment. Gone are the 9-to-5 workdays. Hands-on work begins with the boss and is the order of the day in most franchises, as well as in any other start-up business. It can be especially shocking to a former white-collar administrator turned fast-food franchisee. Interestingly, the transition may be easier for older and more seasoned professionals who are less interested in frills and titles, have their feet firmly planted on the ground, and are more willing to do what's necessary to get the job done.

A franchise at best represents an entrepreneurial compromise.

A franchise at best represents an entrepreneurial compromise. The buyer obtains what hopefully is a proven business formula and a strong marketing image, along with training and an array of ongoing support services. In return, the franchisor sets the ground rules on fees, use of the company's logo, quality control, product marketing, advertising and purchasing.

Buying a franchise is not forever, says John Hayes, a consultant to would-be franchisees. "It is not like a family-run business passed along from generation to generation, but rather a business that might be sold after eight years, hopefully at a profit. This might become your retirement nest egg, or you could use the money to buy another franchise." Other franchise owners leverage their investments. They parlay a single franchise unit into a regional chain or create franchise mini-conglomerates. Nearly 20% of franchise operators own more than one unit— sometimes with the same franchisor, other times in different businesses to increase diversification and lower risk if one franchise concept goes sour.

Some franchise operators actively seek former corporate managers as franchisees. ProForma, a distributor of printed items (including promotional printing and advertising specialties), indicates that the owners of 240 of its 310 franchises had prior sales and management experience. What's more, 60 of them are age 50 plus.

It's little wonder that franchise operators run recruitment advertisements in the *Wall Street Journal*. In one ad,

AlphaGraphics, a digital publishing specialist, proclaimed that its 330 franchisees "come to us from a variety of industries, professional services and consulting firms."

Some franchise operators look for franchisees with related industry know-how. The Golden Corral chain prefers to recruit experienced restaurant-industry personnel. "When they aren't food people and they still want to invest in our franchise, we get them to partner with a food guy," says Golden Corral's Stephen Fortlouis. Since a single Golden Corral might gross up to $3 million a year and serve about 3,000 meals a day, the franchise company believes it is imperative that franchisees know the restaurant business, so it provides food-service training to the staffs of each franchised restaurant. UPS Stores (previously Mail Boxes Etc.) has trained approximately 3,300 U.S. franchise owners in two-week sessions at its in-house "university" in San Diego.

Learning how to run most franchise businesses is not that difficult. The good franchisors have developed easy-to-learn oper-

KNOW THE ANSWERS BEFORE BUYING A FRANCHISE

- **What type of experience** is required in the franchised business? with similar franchises from other franchisors?

- **Do you have a complete description** of the business?

- **How many hours and what level of personal commitment** are needed to run the business?

- **Who is the franchisor?** What is its track record? What is the business experience of the officers and directors of the company?

- **How are other franchisees** doing?

- **What are the start-up and licensing costs?** How do they compare

- **Are you required to buy supplies and business services** from the franchisor?

- **What is the turnover rate** among other franchisees?

- **Do you know the terms and conditions** under which you can terminate or renew the franchise relationship?

- **Is the franchisor** in good financial health?

Source: International Franchise Association

ating formulas, and they are experienced in training recruits. If you're interested in someday buying a franchise, why delay learning about it? The education and training in the practical day-to-day operations can start long before you retire or contact any franchisors. Work part-time in the evenings or on weekends for a franchisee in a field that interests you. You will soon learn whether that type of franchising is for you.

Start-up costs vary. It is safer but more expensive to be part of a proven, successful franchise company than to join a newly established franchise operation. Some franchises, due to their success, are naturally costlier. Expect to invest approximately $409,000 to $650,000 for a McDonald's franchise. To get going with a Subway sandwich shop plan to invest between $66,000 and $188,000, with 50% of the cost payable in cash. The ServiceMaster Company charges a $21,000 to $41,000 fee for its home-cleaning-service franchise, and 20% of the purchase price is due in cash. Storefront fast-food and retail operations are generally more expensive to acquire than most behind-the-scenes business-to-business and customer-service franchises.

> **About 15% to 20% of franchises are resold annually. Some potential owners prefer buying an accepted winner, and they don't mind paying a premium for it.**

More often than not, the franchise fee represents just a part of the start-up costs. If it is a retail operation, there may be the cost of building or renting the store. Bona fide franchisors provide checklists that show the average cost for training; store design; inventory and equipment; leasehold improvements; working capital; opening-day advertising; legal, accounting and licensing fees; and insurance. In talking with franchisees, ask them to compare their experience on opening-day charges with the franchisor's checklist.

You can also get into business by buying an existing franchise outlet. About 15% to 20% of franchises are resold annually. Some potential owners prefer buying an accepted winner, and they don't mind paying a premium for it. Distressed or marginal operations are less costly to buy, but turnaround situations are best left to the experts. One suggested buyout formula: The buyer should expect to pay three to four times net earnings plus depreciated value of assets, the current franchise fee and the liabilities as of the closing.

A Franchisee Speaks Out

At age 49, Tom (who otherwise prefers to remain anonymous) faced a dilemma, one familiar to many men and women his age. He lost his job as a marketing executive at a subsidiary of a Fortune 100 company when the company was sold. At the time, Tom was earning more than $125,000 a year, plus an excellent benefits package. As part of his severance package, Tom's former employer gave him severance pay equivalent to one year's salary and referred him to the local office of one of the nation's larger outplacement firms.

Tom was married, and his wife worked. One son had already graduated from college, another was completing college and a daughter was in high school. What direction would Tom go— take another job, or start or buy a business?

"When I went to outplacement, I was looking for a job, but I was also seriously considering the alternatives. My outplacement

---

TAPPING FRANCHISEES FOR INFORMATION

- **What was the quality of training** that you received?

- **What kind of ongoing support** and counsel have you received from the franchisor?

- **Have there been regular innovations** and upgrades to the program to make it more timely?

- **How effective is the advertising** to which you contribute?

- **How much money is realistically necessary** to have as working capital?

- **How many months did it take** to break into a positive cash flow?

- **How long was it before you could take a salary** from the business?

- **If you could do it all over again,** knowing what you know now, would you acquire this franchise?

---

counselor advised me to use a business broker. I spent some time with a broker who told me about the companies he had for sale. I also met with my accountant and asked questions about ways to finance a small business. Both the broker and accountant introduced me to a couple of bankers who were small business finance specialists.

"I looked at some franchises on my own. Why franchising versus another type of business? At 49 to 50 years of age, I was very concerned about the prospect of failure. I felt that franchises offered me the most insurance against failure. I didn't have any special business management skills, and I felt that a tried-and-true franchised formula would be better than 'hunting and pecking' on my own. I also looked at nonfranchised businesses—a sports clothing and equipment store, a couple of liquor stores and even a store that cashed checks. Each one had its own risks. I dismissed all food-related businesses because I had no food experience and the cost of entry was too high. I dismissed liquor and check cashing due to their long hours and personal risk—they get robbed.

"I became interested in a franchise in the 'pack and ship' field. It was a business that I thought I could understand and, I had become somewhat familiar with these stores and their business model in my last job. I went to the company's Website and read its literature. I read franchise magazines, read the 'business for sale' ads in my newspaper, and talked to everyone that I could. The price of buying a start-up store was a bit steep compared with buying an existing store, an option that the franchisor never told me about. So, I visited and talked with a couple of owners of existing stores.

> **"At 49 to 50 years of age, I was very concerned about the prospect of failure. I felt that franchises offered me the most insurance against failure."**

"I finally decided to buy an existing store from an owner who was retiring. It had a central location with a residential and commercial mix of business in a town about 15 minutes' drive from my home." Instead of financing his purchase through the seller over six years, Tom worked with his local bank, which offered a better rate of interest.

"I think I made a smart decision" said Tom. "When I went for training at the franchisor's corporate offices, I met guys who were building new stores who were frustrated with zoning issues and construction and had no customers. One guy was suppose to have his store up and running by August, but its completion was delayed for three or four months. That was something I didn't have to worry about."

Tom took over his franchised store in June, 2002. After six months, he reached the point where he could pay himself a nominal salary, although he has had to take other steps to meet his personal obligations. He has refinanced the first mortgage on his home at a favorable rate, borrowed on his credit card, and opened a line of credit from his bank. "In a nutshell, I'm leveraged beyond belief, but I'm betting this will all work out.

> **By buying an existing store, Tom already had a base of existing customers; the secret was to keep them as customers and obtain new ones.**

By buying an existing store, Tom already had a base of existing customers; the secret was to keep them as customers and obtain new ones. On his first anniversary, he reported that the franchise had done about 20% to 25% better in his first year of ownership than the previous owner had done in his last. Offsetting the sales rise was an investment in equipment, advertising and supplies, plus a lot of mistakes on Tom's part. Hopefully, he says, "I'm getting better at it, but there isn't much margin for error."

"I still worry about revenues, net income and cash flow, and bad weather that adversely affects the number of customers served each day. The enjoyable part is helping customers, and watching their packages leave the store on a truck."

Protecting Yourself

Due diligence should be the order of the day before making any commitment.

Now's the time to study the marketplace. Attend regional shows where franchisors exhibit. This is a chance to increase awareness of the range of different franchise businesses. Start to read how-to business books on franchising available in most bookstores and public libraries.

Prior to purchase, the franchisor is obligated by law to send all prospective buyers either the Uniform Franchise Offering Circular or an extensive disclosure document, which discuss such basic issues as the history of the franchising company, any bankruptcy records, fees and royalties. For fear of potential liability, most franchisors will avoid being specific about an anticipated return on investment from a franchise.

The UFOC guidelines were revised in 1995. This ensured that potential franchisees have a much easier time understanding the disclosure documents they receive because the information can't be hidden behind "legalese" but must be provided in plain English. The guidelines also require franchisors to reveal the names, addresses and telephone numbers of franchise owners, including all franchisees who have sold out or gone bankrupt. Franchisors must also reveal any litigation in which they have been involved. No longer can they list only the names of successful franchise operators.

Will you receive some form of market exclusivity or will the franchisor have the right to open additional outlets in your area?

Personally check out the franchisor. If the franchisor still operates a company-owned outlet, spend some time there assessing his or her day-to-day operation of the business. Or spend a day or two at the company's headquarters, getting a feel for how management interacts with its franchisees and perhaps even reviewing the UFOC with the principals.

Determine whether you will receive some form of market exclusivity or whether the franchisor has the right to open additional outlets in your area.

Most important, visit other franchises licensed by the same company you're interested in and talk to the owners.

In short, as in any new venture, do your homework and do it thoroughly.

Consultants Abound

Question: Who is a consultant? Answer: Any unemployed person 50 miles from home wearing a suit and carrying a briefcase.

There is no shortage of consultants. It doesn't take any particular skill to call yourself a consultant: Just print some business cards and letterhead. Except in a few specialty areas, consultants do not need a state license or professional accreditation.

The reasons for starting a consultancy vary. Sometimes the incentive is purely defensive. Downsized managers and early retirees become consultants as a shelter against further job loss. The start-up and carrying costs are minimal. You establish your own work schedule and business plan consistent with your lifestyle objectives. Above all, a consultancy permits you to sell your expertise to others.

> **The start-up and carrying costs are minimal. You establish your own work schedule and business plan consistent with your lifestyle objectives.**

Consultants are independent contractors who work for various employers, with whom the consultant shares certain advantages based on the consultant-client relationship. The client pays no fringe benefits or payroll taxes, and the consultant receives tax advantages and business exemptions. For example, consultants (and any business owner or self-employed person) may shelter up to 25% of their compensation or $40,000, whichever is less, in the most popular types of Keogh retirement plans. This money is fully deductible regardless of how high your income is or whether you or your spouse is covered by another retirement plan. Another fully tax-deductible alternative is the simplified employee pension (SEP or SEP-IRA), which is even easier to set up and maintain than a Keogh. This allows you to contribute as much as 15% of your net self-employment earnings (in practice, about 13% of earnings after subtracting your contribution and any social security taxes) up to a maximum of $40,000. Starting in 1998, a new form of IRA, the Roth IRA, became available. Although contributions to a Roth IRA are not deductible, this new plan has several advantages. While investors in a regular IRA or Keogh plan usually can't withdraw any contributions until they reach age 59½ without paying a penalty, Roth investors can take their own contributions out before that age tax- and penalty-free, thus offering a potential source of funds for business start-ups, a possible incentive for early retirees.

And all earnings from the Roth ultimately can be withdrawn tax-free, while those earned in regular IRAs and Keoghs are fully taxed. In addition, investors don't have to start withdrawing money from a Roth at age 70½, as regular IRA and Keogh investors do, and there are further tax-saving benefits that come with the death of the investor.

The Internal Revenue Service cautions employers to avoid using consultants on a nearly full-time basis while specifically excluding them from their tax roll and benefits program. Similarly, consultants should avoid any relationships with clients that appear to be a subterfuge designed to avoid tax consequences of full- or part-time employment. That could affect your status as an independent consultant and your ability to take business-related tax deductions.

Some ex-managers in the 50-plus set flower as consultants, with incomes eclipsing their highest corporate achievements. They're able to market their services and do the work. Other consultants are only marginally successful. In fairness to them, strong financial performance may never have been their primary business goal. To many retirees, a consultancy represents a way to stay active, maintain business or professional skills, and, most important, bridge the earnings gap between their former salaries and their retirement benefits and investment income.

To many retirees, a consultancy represents a way to stay active, maintain business or professional skills, and bridge the earnings gap between their former salaries and their retirement benefits and investment income.

Consulting, though a practical entrée into business for retirees, is not for everyone, says outplacement consultant John Challenger of Challenger, Gray & Christmas (www .challengergray.com). The upside is that, depending on how much the individuals want to work or earn, they control the decision whether to work part-time or full-time. But there is some risk. While the investment might be small for starting a consultancy, the business can easily dwindle unless there's an infusion of new business. "It's not know-how that gets the new business," Challenger says, "but the willingness to spend 70% of one's time selling."

SOME COMPANIES AVOID "DOUBLE DIPPERS"

Retirees interested in being consultants or part-timers often have to surmount an extra hurdle. They may discover that their former employer shuns hiring its own retirees as consultants, referring to them as "double dippers" because they have received a severance package to leave or are receiving a pension, as well as a consultant's fee. This is probably more true in the case of a severance or other buyout agreement. Your company may feel that if you had really been needed, it shouldn't have paid you to go in the first place. So if it did, there's no reason to hire you back as a consultant. If you're interested in consulting after retirement, check with your employer's human resources department beforehand to find out what your company's policy is.

The consultant's lifeblood is new business. The consultant's first rule of survival is to obtain business. Signing the first client is usually not the problem. Many times, it is a former employer. For example, if you're a recently downsized corporate public-relations director, your former employer has an immediate problem. Who is going to write its annual report—the one you wrote for the past five years? Your former boss contracts with you to write it. Client One surfaces. But a consultancy needs other clients and their business, perhaps writing annual reports for other companies or offering a range of public relations services. Where will they come from? You'll have to learn to market yourself.

Avoid doing battle with the "big guys." Consultants come in all shapes and sizes. The large national and international firms can afford to be generalists, offering clients what seem like an unlimited range of services. Smaller consultancies need to pursue a different strategy because they can rarely compete across the board with the larger firms. The successful one-person consultancy wisely becomes a niche specialist and, more often than not, a sub-niche specialist, obtaining new business by convincing clients of its unique expertise.

The consultant must be self-sufficient. Many consultants go into business directly from a sheltered corporate environment. Staff assistants previously handled simple tasks like ordering stationery, maintaining office equipment and billing customers. A consultancy and, in fact, nearly all start-up businesses operate differently. Unless you do your own word processing, printing, photocopying, faxing and telephoning, nothing gets done.

The consultant needs to know more than his business. Take nothing for granted. Know the basics of running a consultancy. You may be an authority in your area of business or technical expertise, but chances are you are not an authority on running a consulting business. Develop new checklists for yourself, and don't overlook things you most likely never did as a corporate employee, such as billing and collecting fees. Learn the consultancy fundamentals well in advance of opening day. Take a trip to the library or bookstore and get an array of books and magazines on running a small business or consultancy (see the list on page 196). Talk with other consultants. And consider taking courses at a local college or community college.

How are your writing and presentation skills? Consultants need to express their views on paper and on their feet. Do you like to lead and command? Do your people skills need polishing? Only in Hollywood movies do consultants pound the table to make a point. Effective consultants use tactful terms such as "suggest" and "recommend," and they take charge by "counseling" and "advising." If you're too heavy-handed, you might be a consultant without any clients.

It pays to be frugal. Control your expenses. Remember, it might take up to 90 pays to get paid by some clients, and cash flow can be a problem. Don't overspend on equipment and supplies. One alternative is to lease office equipment and furniture for a few months with an option to buy. By then, you'll know whether you really need the equipment. Though you might have been taught in corporate America to "think big," this caveat works in reverse for start-ups. If you mail five letters a day, why rent an automated postal meter? Postage stamps will do.

THE AT-HOME OFFICE TOOL BOX

There's no need to overspend when you equip an at-home office. Buy the basics; avoid the frills. A good basic start-up package costs under $5,000, including the following items. Add to this stationery and other consumable supplies, such as printer paper and note pads. Also, budget for office furniture, though this is one area where you can make do with what you've got or purchase it used. Once again, don't be excessive.

- **A desktop computer is a must,** but for some businesses a good laptop makes more sense. Buy the maximum amount of computer memory that you can afford.

- **Word processing and application software packages as needed.** Whatever comes loaded on the computer may be sufficient.

- **Printer.** Pay for what you need. If you print out just a few sheets at the time, the printer you already have in the family room may suffice. If you intend to print out documents equivalent to a whole book, you will probably want to purchase your own printer—one with good speed and abundant memory. With e-mail, fax software, and the ability to convert documents to .pdf files, you may find that you can get by with no printer at all.

- **A self-standing fax/copier /scanner.** An "all-in-one" machine provides all three functions. For big copying jobs, take a break and run to the local office-supply, quick-print or packaging store.

- **Appropriate Internet service.** If you're accustomed to a blink-of-the-eye connection at the office, you'll want to find out if you can get a cable or DSL connection at home—if you don't already have one. It's hard to go backward.

- **Telephone answering device or voicemail service** from the phone company. With the latter service, you can create separate voicemail boxes for your business and home phone calls.

Life in a Home Office

Whether you are an engineer or technician starting a high-tech company in the garage, or a marketer who launches a consultancy in the den, you've probably considered the immediate advantages of an at-home office. Folklore aside, not everyone wants or is suited temperamentally to work at home. Thomas Roeser, a retired Quaker Oats executive and now a Chicago-based columnist and public affairs consultant (profiled in Chapter 8), enjoys commuting from suburbia to a downtown office on Michigan Avenue.

But the at-home office has become an acceptable venue for many 50-plus-set consultants, as well as for start-up entrepreneurs of all ages. There are some obvious advantages, such as eliminating office rent, avoiding a commute and enjoying the ambiance that comes with a more informal business lifestyle.

There is also a slight home-office tax advantage, but it is hardly enough motivation for working at home. You can deduct only that portion of your home—determined by square footage or number of rooms—that is totally dedicated to an office. For example, if you live in a seven-room house and devote one room to your work, and your work only, then you may deduct 14% of the operating costs for the home, as well as 14% of your monthly mortgage payment minus the interest, which you deduct separately.

The availability of low-cost computers and communications equipment means that even the most remote home office is only microseconds away from customers and important business hubs.

Before you start to redesign an attic or spare bedroom into an at-home office, alert yourself to some of the realities and myths of this workplace.

- **Find out whether your community, condominium or landlord permits your business to operate in the home.** Zoning regulations, for example, may prohibit posting a business sign or causing increased traffic or parking in front of your home. Environmental rules usually ban chemical processes in residential areas.
- **Working at home is more than trading in wing tips for Docksiders.** Business is still the order of the day, despite the informality of attire.

SUGGESTED READING

CONSULTING

- *The Complete Guide to Consulting Success,* by Howard Shenson (Enterprise/Dearborn, 1993)

- *The Concise Guide to Becoming an Independent Consultant,* by Herman Holtz (Wiley, 1999)

- *Independent Consulting,* by David Kintler (Adams Media, 1998)

FRANCHISING

- *Achieving Wealth through Franchising,* by Robert and Vincent Justis and William Slater (Adams Media, 2001)

- *Franchising: The Complete Guide to Evaluating, Buying and Growing Your Franchise Business* (Dearborn, 1998)

- *The Franchise Survival Guide,* by Carol Green (Probus Publishing, 1993)

OWNING YOUR OWN BUSINESS

- *Starting on a Shoestring,* by Arnold Goldstein (Adams Media, 2002)

- *Starting Your Own Business,* by Rieva Lessonsky (Entrepreneur Press, 2001)

- *210 Great Ideas for Your Small Business,* by Jane Applegate (Bloomsbury Press, 2002)

- *The Unofficial Guide to Starting a Business Online,* by Jason Rich (Wiley, 2000)

WORKING AT HOME

- *The Best Home Businesses for the 21st Century,* by Paul and Sarah Edwards (Tarcher/Putnam, 1999)

- *The Work at Home Sourcebook,* by Lynie Arden (Live Oak Press, 2002)

- **Can you resist the temptation of the 24-hour workday?** With an office across the hall from your bedroom or in the basement, you may find it hard to separate your business from your personal life. Modern technology can help you on that front, too. After-hour telephone calls can be intercepted by an answering machine, and the fax machine can operate unattended.

- **There's no reason to be a recluse.** Unless you are a peripatetic consultant who only returns to the office to read mail, make telephone calls and prepare reports, you may find it lonely working at home. Make a point of meeting regularly with business friends and associates. Also, keep up with trade and business groups, and attend their meetings. This serves another purpose, too; networking usually leads to new business prospects.

- **Don't be defensive about your at-home office.** If you are a consultant, you are supposedly an expert in your field. The location of your office was rarely a factor when you were considered for the assignment before. It's no more important now that you work for yourself at home.
- **Avoid routine household chores during working hours.** This is another angle on separating business from home life. It is as fundamental as refusing to answer the family telephone during business hours. It went unanswered when you worked outside the home, so why change the pattern? The same guidelines apply to trees that need pruning and closets that plead for cleaning.

Changing Careers

The media thrive on publicizing dramatic career changes, but they are the exception in the 50-plus set (see Erle Peacock's profile in Chapter 4). Few people in their fifties or older are prepared to face the academic demands, the dual rigors of learning a new trade and obtaining professional accreditation, or the cost in time and money in order to change careers.

When someone does switch to an entirely different field, it usually involves shifting gears from a demanding job to a less pressured one. That's the route taken by Roald Young, a one-time bank officer in Arizona who described himself as burned-out and seeking a fresh start after a 32-year banking career. He took a nine-month program in restaurant management and has been employed as a cook and baker ever since. After so many stressful years in banking, he says, "I feel as if I've been let out of the cage."

Or, take Dale Graff. He just turned 50. "I was working 65 hours a week, and my wife, Paula, and I weren't getting a chance to play golf and enjoy life." A nuclear engineer with an MBA, Dale worked for Argonne National Laboratory on reactor safety, then for Bell Labs as a project manager, followed by ten years with Fujitsu and another two years with Lucent. Dale has a desire to more fully develop another aspect of himself—a certain psychic ability that he strongly experienced in a couple of instances.

FOR MORE INFORMATION

- **For additional information on how to obtain public-school teaching accreditation,** contact your state's department of education.

- **If you're interested in receiving information on teaching careers in independent schools,** contact the National Association of Independent Schools (www.nais-schools.org). The NAIS holds an annual conference that includes several days of workshops on such topics as leadership, teaching and learning, and career paths. The conference provides an opportunity to network with administrators and teachers from independent schools across the U.S., as well as the Employment Exchange, a job bank that can put you in touch with potential employers.

On September 9, 2001, Dale had a psychic sensation. He acted accordingly the following day when he sold his stock holdings. He had had a similar sensation 11 years earlier when Iraq was about to invade Kuwait, and he sold stock then, as well. "I always liked things that were strange and wacky; the difference is that I now live it."

Dale is building his psychic awareness in the hopes that it might lead to a new career. He attends workshops at the Rhine Research Center, a nonprofit parapsychology institute in Durham, North Carolina, as well as other psychic-related meetings. "I've done more than 100 free readings over the past few months on the telephone. I've done them for people of all ages. I hope I'll get to the point where I might charge a fee to help people understand their psychic experiences. But I'm not ready for that yet."

Dale's goal is to live on earnings from his investments and stock trades, although this idea has been made more difficult by the market slide. Even though his 2001 stock sales shielded him from the market downturn, he didn't have sufficient money to retire in the style he wanted. Meanwhile Dale's looking for a job to recapture some of his lost funds.

Teaching as a Career Change

How many times have you said or heard a friend say, "I'd like to teach when I retire"? If you pursue it, you'll soon discover that colleges and universities are inundated with employment applications from would-be teachers in the 50-plus set. They, like the corporate world, have few openings as they reduce the size of their faculties. What about elementary and high schools? Perhaps they might be interested in a chemist as a science teacher or an editor to teach English composition? Practical as it sounds, the concept never flourished, and the U.S. Department of Education acknowledges a continuing teacher shortage. It projects a shortfall because of an increase in the school-age population and a corresponding rise in teacher retirement.

A few years ago, educational leaders reasoned that the entry of mid- to later-life career changers into education could offset that shortage of classroom teachers. A number of colleges developed teacher-training programs to attract to the classroom early military and corporate retirees, particularly those with engineering and scientific skills. And 45 states plus the District of Columbia have implemented alternative teacher-certification programs to quicken the transition. To date, more than 175,000 teachers have been licensed this way, says Emily Feistritzer, president of the National Center for Education Information (www.ncei.org). California, New Jersey and Texas lead the way with aggressive alternate certification programs.

Forty-five states plus the District of Columbia have implemented alternative teacher-certification programs to quicken the transition.

Dr. Feistritzer, who has surveyed what has taken place in alternative teacher certification since 1983, points out that, "Alternative teacher certification routes provide opportunities for people from various educational backgrounds and walks of life to become teachers. They open doors to teaching for persons from nontraditional backgrounds, including people transitioning from other careers or from the military, liberal arts graduates and early retirees."

Teaching opportunities are more readily available for the 50-plus set in independent schools, where state licensing and

---

POINTS TO REMEMBER

- **The business-as-usual concept no longer applies** to the job market.

- **Are you mentally, physically and financially ready** to start a business?

- **Franchising has its advantages,** as well as its pitfalls.

- **Thorough homework is important** for entrepreneurial hopefuls.

- **Running a successful consultancy** requires a different set of work skills, especially the ability to get out and hustle the work.

- **Operating from an at-home office** calls for different work habits.

- **Opportunities exist** by changing careers.

---

accreditation are not required, and prior work and professional credentials are accepted in lieu of teaching experience. What's more, the independents, unlike most public schools, can set salaries for entry-level teachers based on past work experience.

Some Who've Taken the Leap

Some of the victims of downsizing or forced early-retirement plans have been soured by their recent corporate experiences. Others in the 50-plus set are seeking a challenge commensurate with their age. As an alternative to uncertain corporate employment, they reenter the workplace on their own terms—as their own bosses. The profiles you are about to read illustrate a variety of ways to start all over again.

HE GOT A GOOD HEAD START

Mitch Badler

CORPORATE PUBLIC RELATIONS EXECUTIVE TURNED NEWSLETTER PUBLISHER

Long before the reality of downsizing dawned on most managers, Mitchell Badler was playing "what if" games. What would happen if he lost his job as a corporate public relations executive with Eastern Airlines or, later, with Amax, a mining and energy conglomerate? Mitch's newsletter-publishing sideline was his cushion. For nearly 20 years, he worked evenings and weekends on first one, then two newsletters dealing with imaging technology. How Mitch handled his dual careers could serve as a model for people age 50-plus who are anticipating the possibility of downsizing and plotting their next move.

"It began for several reasons," said Mitch. "To see if I could make money, to keep my hand in editorial work since my PR responsibilities were becoming increasingly more managerial, to have a possible fallback because I instinctively distrusted the corporate world, and for something to do if and when I ultimately 'retired' from the corporate world. Looking back, it worked on all four counts."

> For more than 20 years, Mitch combined days of corporate life with nights and weekends of self-employed publishing. All the effort paid off.

Mitch started to hedge as far back as 1969, when he launched the *Microfilm Newsletter* as a part-time activity. He learned about the microfilming industry earlier in his career as the editor of several photography trade magazines. At the time, Mitch was working as a public relations writer for Eastern Airlines.

Even though his career had proceeded steadily uphill, Mitch had good reason to distrust corporate employment. Prior to Eastern Airlines, he had worked four years for Citibank editing the bank's publications. "When I was at Citibank in the mid to late 1960s, I got caught in a power struggle between two executives competing to be CEO." His boss straddled the fence during this succession fight. Realizing that the new head of public relations would reorganize the department, Mitch left before it all happened. He joined Eastern Airlines and stayed with the company until it relocated to Miami.

Mitch was hired by Amax and a few years later was named its director of public relations. In the 1980s, Amax suffered a reversal in fortunes and lost $2 billion in three years. Heads rolled, but Mitch kept his. In 1991, he left Amax after it was acquired by another mining company. He retained a lawyer and negotiated a favorable severance package in the form of a one-time payout along with lifetime health care benefits.

Other executives might have looked for another corporate job, but not Mitch. "I decided that enough was enough. No more corporate jobs; I didn't need that anymore." Neither did Mitch need to retire. He held some valuable trump cards.

Throughout his corporate career, *Microfilm Newsletter* "went its merry way" as a sideline endeavor. In the early days, it was strictly part-time for Mitch and an assistant, another moonlighter, who handled circulation. After a few years, Mitch hired a full-time office administrator while he continued to write and edit the newsletter.

As a part-time editor and publisher for more than 20 years, Mitch's life was hectic. "My routine until I left Amax was to work on the newsletter at least one full day each weekend and most evenings." His one-newsletter company grew. He introduced a biannual industry directory. He started, then dropped, two other newsletters, and in the late 1980s,

he spun off *Imaging Technology Report,* previously a supplement in *Microfilm Newsletter,* as a separate monthly. The newsletters were Mitch's long-term security blanket, a way to control his destiny. It was employment that he totally controlled.

Newsletter publishing rarely conflicted with his corporate life. He spent vacations at microfilm industry trade shows. There were few problems with either Eastern Airlines or Amax because the subject of the newsletters did not conflict with his line of work at either company.

When he left Eastern Airlines, Mitch briefly considered becoming a full-time editor and publisher, but the income from newsletter publishing at that time wasn't sufficient to support his family. It did, however, produce enough supplementary money to send his children through college and graduate school.

Having left Amax and with the corporate workplace behind him, Mitch worked as an editor and publisher five days a week. His staff consisted of a full-time office manager, a part-time circulation manager and freelance editorial correspondents. Compared with his former schedule, Mitch notes, "it was like being on a part-time holiday.

> **"My employer never owned me on a full-time basis. Above all, publishing was something that did not depend on the whims of other people."**

I actually had time to watch TV at night. I'd get to work about 10 in the morning and home about 6." He supplemented his newsletter income by tapping his investment portfolio, so that his lifestyle didn't change after leaving Amax.

Looking back at his dual corporate and publishing careers, Mitch knows that the relationship, though complex, gave him career options. "My employer never owned me on a full-time basis. Above all, publishing was something that did not depend on the whims of other people."

As he got older, it furnished still another benefit. "I never considered retirement. I'm not a golfer. I wanted to keep my hands in something useful."

In 2000, Mitch began to back down a bit from work. "I decided that I no longer wanted the responsibility for day-to-day circulation drives, advertising sales and maintenance of subscriber lists."

By 2002, Mitch sold his *Micrographics & Hybrid Newsletter* to Micrographics Marketing, Ltd., in England. "To date, the sale has worked out very well. Besides paying me the sale price, the company retained me as the North American editor. I contribute a monthly recap of what's happening in the U.S. and cover two big trade shows a year. I'm only doing editorial work, spending about one-third to one-half the time I did before and getting what I feel is a fair fee."

THE EDUCATOR EDUCATES HIMSELF

Thomas Lutton
COAST GUARD CAPTAIN TURNED TEACHER

The day after Thomas Lutton retired from the Coast Guard, he started a new career in education. Tom's move was actually a pretty natural segue from his career. After 30 years as an officer, a role that required him to train personnel, he finds teaching to be an equally rewarding career. "You're on stage for 50 minutes at a time. You're the entertainer, and it takes a lot of preparation to be good. Since I'm a late starter, I'm also more enthusiastic than most teachers my age."

Growing up, Tom wanted to be an engineer. By chance, during his senior year in high school, he saw a Coast Guard Academy brochure, "Career for Tomorrow." It represented an opportunity to combine many interests in a single career.

While he spent many years working in line, staff and technical assignments, Tom was continually looking ahead, planning for the future and engaging in personal "what if" exercises. As a result, he earned a bachelor's degree in electronic engineering from the Naval Postgraduate School in Monterey,

> **Despite his training and technical skills, Tom encountered the usual impediments to this postretirement career change. Persistence paid off.**

California, and a master's degree in engineering administration from George Washington University, both of which were suitable for conversion to the corporate marketplace.

After 20 years of service, Tom was eligible to retire, but a number of assignments were too challenging to refuse. One was as the Coast Guard's chief of avionics, a job that requires a technical knowledge of both electronics and aviation. When he finally retired at age 50 as a captain, Tom was chief of staff for the Atlantic Area, based on Governor's Island in New York, a command responsible for all Coast Guard operations east of the Rocky Mountains.

A few years before his 30th anniversary, a normal time for many senior officers to retire from military service, Tom began to play "what if" again and considered future job opportunities. "Working within the military-industrial complex would have been the logical step, but I soon discovered that the jobs they offered were only a civilian counterpart of my

Coast Guard jobs. There were few new challenges.

"Above all in looking for work, I did not want to face the day and say, 'What's next?' I wanted to have a plan." Income wasn't an issue in Tom's decision-making because he had a full Coast Guard pension and investments, and his two sons were grown. He could afford to take an entry-level job.

Tom was interested in teaching. Besides having had some specific teaching assignments in the Coast Guard, he says, "It's part of an officer's life to teach because you're held responsible for training personnel in your command." In his last year in the Coast Guard, Tom attended a job fair conducted by the National Association of Independent Schools (see page 198). By then he had discovered that even with his technical background, it would be difficult to become certified to teach math or science in a public school. He encountered the kind of bottleneck in obtaining state teaching certification that too often foils otherwise capable applicants.

"My credentials were more readily accepted by independent schools where state licensing and accreditation are not required. What's more, independent schools are more flexible because they are not tied into the unions or large administrative systems. The pay is also based on academic skills

> *"...training should start before you retire. In fact, you can't get started early enough."*

and life experiences."

When he started in his new career in education, it wasn't in the way he had hoped. "I received several offers. I wanted to get going and do something." He took a job as business manager of Woodmere Academy, an independent school on Long Island. "While I wanted to teach science and math, Woodmere thought my past executive experiences were better suited to administration." A year later he got the chance to teach math, along with handling some administrative assignments, when he transferred to the Collegiate School in New York. Two years later he left Collegiate to become a full-time math teacher at the Buckley School, another New York City independent school.

To further increase his professional skills while teaching at Buckley, Tom enrolled in the doctoral program at Columbia University's Teachers College. He was part of the Operation Plowshare program, now ended, that was designed to help military retirees like Tom train for second careers in education.

For his doctoral thesis, Tom drew on his experiences as a Coast Guard officer. He surveyed more than 1,600 retired or eligible-to-retire senior-level Coast Guard officers regarding their interest in teaching math or science in the public schools. About half of the 1,000 officers who completed the survey said they would like to teach, preferably math or science. Tom's findings supported the popular view that qualified math and science teachers could be recruited from nontraditional sources such as the military and other industries.

The results of the survey paralleled Tom's own experiences. "Teaching is an excellent second career, whether you're in the military or industry. But training should start before you retire. In fact, you can't get started early enough. In anticipation of retirement, start taking education courses and complete your [state's] teaching requirements." While math and science teachers are usually in demand, he warns other early retirees that there is less interest in English and history teachers.

Tom's training did not stop with his doctorate. He subsequently received a second master's degree, in curriculum development, and pursued another in math education, both useful professional tools for someone who hopes to teach indefinitely.

Tom left Buckley nine months after his wife died. He moved to northern Florida, nearer to his two sons and their families. Tom did some substitute teaching, which left time for traveling with his second wife, Barbara Ann Nelson.

In 1999, Tom's teaching career took another turn. He and Barbara went to Kenya as Episcopal Church missionaries. Tom lectured in mathematics at Daystar University, while Barbara Ann worked in the university's public relations and communications department. Two years later, they returned to the U.S. "We are engaged in some domestic missionary work for the bishop of southeastern Virginia. I haven't been doing any direct classroom teaching, because I don't want to have a committed schedule."

TOOK THE OPPORTUNITY TO SERVE IN NONPROFIT

Leo Rogers, Jr.
BANK PRESIDENT TURNED COLLEGE ADMINISTRATOR

When Leo Rogers, Jr. found himself unemployed for the first time in 27 years, his career search was guided not by an outplacement firm but a passage from the New Testament: "From everyone to whom much has been given, much will be required; and from the one to whom much has been entrusted, even more will be demanded. For unto whomsoever much is given, of him shall be much required: and to whom men have committed much, of him they will ask more." This verse from the book of Luke inspired the search that led to Leo's job as a college administrator with Fairleigh Dickinson University.

> **Leo didn't just get a lucky break. He focused on his needs and desires, updated his computer skills, and got out there and hustled.**

Leo's résumé is impressive, summarizing a record of high achievement in business and community life. But at age 55, Leo's bubble was deflated. The bank where he was president fell victim to the collapsed metropolitan New York real estate market.

Leo's marketing know-how had helped to build the bank to a network of 74 branch offices. "I went into banking in 1965 as a marketer, and my job as president resulted largely from my work in marketing, advertising and public relations. I was part of the changeover when banks decided to alter their image and the ways they did business."

When the bank went into receivership, Leo's credentials attracted the interest of other banks, but he wanted to change fields and careers. Throughout his banking career, Leo also served on a number of boards of trustees, including a hospital, Rider University, and Blue Cross and Blue Shield of New Jersey. Those experiences later propelled him to look for a job in the nonprofit field. "I realized that nonprofit work is just as challenging as business, but there is more of an opportunity to serve others."

Fortunately, Leo qualified for early retirement from the bank, which gave him options in seeking a new job. "I didn't want a job just to say I got one. I wanted to be selective at this stage in my life," Leo says. "As a starter, I determined those things I like to do, do well and would like to continue doing in the future."

As an executive, Leo had been somewhat pampered by the corporate lifestyle. Without employment, these perks were no longer available. He had to learn some basic office skills just to hunt for a job. "I was computer-illiterate. Others had done that type of work for me." Carole, his wife, is a freelance writer who does her own word processing, and she encouraged him to develop computer skills and coached him. "I learned *WordPerfect* and *Lotus 1-2-3*. I did my own letters. This was important because I would most likely be joining an organization where these skills would be necessary. I had to learn how to make ordinary things happen because nobody else will do them for you."

Nearly eight months of networking and interviewing started to produce results. Leo was offered a job with one of the nation's larger outplacement firms to counsel other downsized senior-level executives. Though the business wasn't nonprofit, he liked outplacement because even there he would be involved in helping others. But after living and working in New Jersey most of his life, he was reluctant to commute to New York. "I took several practice commuting runs to the firm's offices. If they had offered me the same job in their New Jersey office, I would have taken it, but I had little interest in commuting three hours each day."

"I had to learn how to make ordinary things happen because nobody else will do them for you."

During the same time that he was negotiating with the outplacement firm, Leo received an offer from Fairleigh Dickinson University to be director of the George Rothman Institute of Entrepreneurial Studies.

"I had had my eye on this job ever since I left banking. I had heard about a possible opening from the university's president. When I learned officially that the institute's director was leaving, I called the university, received a job description and sent in a résumé along with a cover letter summarizing why I felt I was suited for the job. I was told that a search committee had been established, then I got a letter saying that I was among 75 very qualified candidates for the job. I said good-bye to this one. Then another letter told me that they had screened the résumés and that I was one of six selected to meet with the committee."

Leo met with the committee and soon afterward learned he was one of two finalists. "They invited me back to make a presentation. I worked on it for four days. The day after the outplacement firm's offer, I heard that the Fairleigh Dickinson job was mine."

Similar to his banking days, Leo serves as the institute's key representative in the New Jersey business community. Now, however, he's an advocate of entrepreneurship rather than banking services. Leo is also the institute's representative in the academic community. He finds that getting things done here differs greatly from business. "At the bank, we would meet, discuss an issue and reach a decision. In a university, one needs to be patient because decision-making is more collegial and takes much longer."

Leo, now in his tenth year as the Institute's director, has introduced a number of innovations to the curriculum, including these two: All undergraduate and graduate business school students are required to take a course in entrepreneurship, a

recognition of the growing interest on the campus in small-company management. The university also offers a certificate-of-entrepreneurship program for small businesses and entrepreneurs.

During the 2001–2002 academic year, Leo was named interim dean of the university's business school. Returning to the Rothman Institute afterward, he launched a drive to raise funds for an "incubator" to nurture students and adult nonstudents who want to start their own businesses.

Leo, who had longed to return to academia since he left it in his twenties, feels like he's home again.

DOES BUSINESS IN THE DESERT

Al Croft
PUBLIC RELATIONS EXECUTIVE TURNED INDUSTRY CONSULTANT

For decades, Al Croft read *Arizona Highways* and dreamed of someday living in the Southwest. The dream began to become reality when Al and his wife, Irene, bought a second home in Sedona, Arizona, about 110 miles north of Phoenix. Though they rented it out to start with, someday, Al mused, it would be their full-time residence and the site of an at-home office for Al. He put the next phase of his plan into effect, somewhat unexpectedly, the next year. At 61, he left his job as a senior executive in the Chicago offices of one of the nation's larger public relations firms following what Al describes as a "difference of opinion" with some of the firm's managers. A 25-year veteran of the public relations agency business, Al had already decided to use his agency management skills to start his own consultancy, one that focused on ways to better operate and manage public relations firms.

Al invested his severance package in office equipment and direct-mailing costs to launch his consultancy the day after he left his job. His objectives, then and now, were to offer a range of management services to public relations firms of all sizes, work at his own pace, and, above all, live and work in Sedona. Being familiar with PR agency management and marketing practices, he felt confident that there was a ready market for his niche specialty.

The Crofts waited four years, long enough for their daughter to graduate from college, before they moved to Sedona. By then Al's consultancy was well established. Sedona became their permanent residence and the headquarters of A. C. Croft & Associates.

> **A public relations veteran, Al took up counseling the counselors on better ways to operate and manage their firms.**

Sedona, a community of approximately 15,000 people, is a tourist haven, drawing more than four million visitors annually. The mountain landscape is the prime attraction. A number of other small consulting firms in other fields call Sedona home for reasons similar to the Crofts'. Most of these consultants find that they can carry on their work as easily in Arizona as in a metropolitan center.

The area is hardly isolated in the computer age. Computers and telecommunications have eliminated geographic isolation, and overnight delivery services are omnipresent. "On a trip to Flagstaff, 50 miles away, I counted nine United Parcel Service trucks making early-morning business deliveries along the route," says Al. His clients, scattered throughout the U.S. and Canada, can be readily serviced through personal visits, e-mail, fax and telephone. In reality, Al finds that e-mail has almost supplanted the telephone for much of his direct contact.

No formidable snags occurred in moving from Chicago to rural Arizona, and Al has found many pluses. "Clients like to take a few days off from their offices and meet with me in a leisurely fashion in Sedona. Some come from as far as Washington, D.C."

The nature of Al's work has changed dramatically from his days as a PR agency executive. "I don't do public relations for companies. I counsel the principals of public relations firms, write an occasional speech for an agency executive, represent a buyer or seller in an acquisition, conduct in-house account-management seminars and produce a monthly newsletter. Everything I do is geared to help agencies market their services and manage their operations more effectively."

Marketing is critical to building his client base. Toward that end, Al actively promotes his business with a newsletter on management strategies for PR firms. Al also sponsors the Sedona Roundtable, an annual two-day management workshop for the principals of public relations agencies. He has written a book, *Managing a Public Relations Firm for Growth and Profit.*

Being a niche specialist has certain advantages. He can bill clients up to $250 an hour. And, of course, because he is working at home his overhead is minimal. Irene, who has a sales and marketing background, handles the administration of the Sedona Roundtable.

Even with his good cash flow, Al had to make some adjustments when he became self-employed. "After 35 years of regular paychecks and several years as an independent consultant, I'm still not used to not knowing exactly what my income is going to be for the next month, or from year to year."

By corporate standards, Al might appear to be semiretired. "I work as hard as I want to, traveling outside the area two to three times a month. I make almost as much money as I did in the agency business but I also play tennis a few times a week. The most important thing is that it keeps my brain active. I couldn't imagine being retired, and I'm not the volunteer type. Why retire, when I like what I'm doing and I'm making money at it? At 76, I'm not ready to turn my brain off."

While Sedona has a reputation as a retirees' haven, Al points out that he's not alone in pursuing an active lifestyle. "One of my tennis partners is an 83-year-old plumber. After two hours of doubles, he goes back to work."

TEAM RETIREE

Erford Porter, II

PURCHASING EXECUTIVE TURNED INDUSTRY CONSULTANT

When Erford Porter II turned 50, he was tiring of corporate life. After 28 years with Union Carbide, Erf's career was anything but lackluster. But even with his corporate success, he felt that he had become a corporate nomad and in the process had made himself expendable. Erf took the bull by the horns. He opted for early retirement and set up Supply Planning Associates Inc., a nationwide consulting firm with a contemporary pitch. At the end of 2003, after a successful, 16-year run, SPA will cross its finish line and Erf will move on to the next thing. But the story of Erf and SPA demonstrates how a one-person consultancy can provide sophisticated services to major companies.

> **Erf is founder and the only full-time staffer among the some 50 consultants who work for Supply Planning. He runs his business informally from home.**

Besides personally handling consulting assignments, Erf is the firm's primary salesperson, traveling about 40% of the time, marketing SPAs' services to companies that purchase, market or transport raw materials, fuels and electricity. About 90% of the work is repeat business.

If SPA had an organizational chart, it would show that Erf is the only full-time employee. The balance of his staff consists of three part-timers—his wife, Jane, who is the bookkeeper; a secretary; and a computer analyst. Nearly all of SPAs' work is done at client sites. The "paperwork" and communications between the firm's offices and the consultants is handled by e-mail.

About 50 professionals a year work under SPAs' umbrella as independent contractors. Most are retired chemical engineers in their sixties (a few are in their seventies) who have escaped from retirement. Though they want to continue working to maintain their technical skills, many feel that social security income caps limit the amount of work they can do (see the discussion of earned-income limits, which are now somewhat less onerous, on page 265).

Erf stresses informality as a way to increase creativity. In a memo to associates, he said: "Supply Planning

Associates Inc. was started on a handshake understanding, based on trust, a pattern that has not changed over the years." Erf's philosophy may reflect a reaction to his many years of experience with big company administrative practices.

When Erf graduated from Alfred University with a degree in chemistry, he spent an obligatory two years in the Army to fulfill an ROTC commitment. He joined Union Carbide as a technical sales representative, and during the next 15 years he worked in field sales, sales management and corporate training.

In the mid 1970s, the company assigned him to the hydrocarbons purchasing group, where he was initially responsible for crude oil, offshore trading and shipping, and hydrocarbon planning and forecasting. Erf received successive promotions. In the early '80s, he coordinated Union Carbide's worldwide hydrocarbon needs and played an active part in assessing the feasibility of and developing the supply portfolio for numerous cogeneration power projects across the U.S. Little did Erf know then that a number of the suppliers and other companies he studied would someday become clients or associates of his consulting firm. Until he left

Union Carbide, Erf had never even considered going into his own business. "Why should I when I was doing challenging work?"

That changed when Union Carbide began downsizing and slated a 25% reduction in force in Erf's planning group. Erf and his cohorts acted first and planned their own departure; they all retired or left for jobs elsewhere. Erf's retirement offer did tack three years onto his age and service, but this didn't quite bring him up to full retirement benefits.

Once he made the decision to leave, Erf wasn't sure of the next step. "I knew I was good at keeping a number of balls in the air, and from what I knew about consulting that was an important criterion for success." Erf's marketing, corporate-planning and business-development positions gave him an edge, as did his corporate-training experience. Erf says the clincher in his decision-making was the support and encouragement of two of his former bosses. So, in 1987 Erf established SPA as a consulting firm. He recruited about eight other independent consultants to work with him on a project-by-project basis, and he went into business. He looked for work and found little interest. Nobody called.

Erf and his associates recognized the

> **"I knew I was good at keeping a number of balls in the air, and from what I knew about consulting that was an important criterion for success."**

need to differentiate themselves from other players in the consulting field. They studied market needs and changed their direction from general consulting to a specialty—the strategy and planning behind buying and selling of hydrocarbon raw materials, feedstocks and fuels. This is what Erf and his associates knew best, and the phone began ringing. "We were very fortunate to develop a unique group of clients with distinct interests. They don't compete, but their broad strategic interests are quite compatible with what we have to offer."

Using personal savings to capitalize the business, Erf started SPA in his home, then moved the following year to an outside office when he found the business was interfering with household routines. He moved to a new house where loft space was converted to an office over the garage. Erf and his wife moved in about the time that Greenwich, Connecticut, in recognition of the growing trend to home-based offices, changed its ordinances to permit consultancies and other small service businesses to operate from home.

SPA from its inception was, as Erf describes it a one-man consulting practice with ad-hoc associates and an office staff. During its peak years in the 1990s, the firm's annual billing rate was over $1 million. "Along the way, I had my share of health scares and setbacks. By 2001, it was time for me to disengage. The question was whether the practice had any residual value and if so, how to tap into it.

"Selling me along with the practice didn't offer any attraction to anyone unless I agreed to stay on for another two to three years. I was being offered an opportunity to work harder and use my reputation to bring in business for others to manage, on the assumption that I could make it all happen. I politely said, 'thanks, but no thanks.'"

Accordingly, SPA closes shop at the end of 2003, but Erf anticipates occasional consulting assignments that he'll handle personally.

TWICE DOWNSIZED, THEY TURNED TO SELF-EMPLOYMENT

Bill and Denise Gower
TELECOM COUPLE BECOME BED-AND-BREAKFAST OWNERS

At 50 and 49 respectively, Bill Gower, and his wife, Denise, were too young to retire. Because they were unable to find work in the already hard-hit telecommunications industry, their alternatives were limited. As a career alternative, they bought a bed-and-breakfast inn—a change of pace from their previous careers in corporate America.

In the late 1960s while a student at Pace University, Bill became a part-time New York Telephone Company (subsequently Nynex; now Verizon) worker. Over the next 25 years, Bill carried out numerous Nynex technical and management assignments. His last one involved the implementation of a private telecommunications service in New York City. By the mid 1990s, Nynex introduced a company-wide plan to reduce its staff. It offered Bill a package that increased his service from 25 to 30 years and correspondingly boosted the value of his pension. He took it.

Shortly thereafter, Denise, a Northern Telecom telecommunications manager for more than 15 years, was assigned for two years to Singapore.

> **This couple gave up the 9-to-5 corporate world to take on the 24-hour-a-day job of hosting their guests—on dry land and on the water.**

Based on his related communications experience, the company hired Bill for the same operation.

After completing their overseas commitment, the couple was rotated back to jobs in the metropolitan Washington, D.C., area. No sooner than they returned, the bubble started to burst throughout the telecommunications industry. By 2000, both Bill and Denise left Northern Telecom and found new jobs with different companies. One year later these jobs were also eliminated. Fortunately, decent buyout packages gave them a temporary financial cushion.

"We had given little thought of what we would do since we were both committed to the telcom field. But the industry collapsed so quickly. Few jobs were available, and September 11 made it even worse." The couple didn't consider the idea of retirement, but instead thought,"Why not self-employment? What about a bed-and-breakfast Inn?" Bill and Denise had stayed at inns while on vacations and had discussed what they liked about each one, never thinking that they would ever buy one.

The Gowers already owned the Elysium, a 44-foot yacht that they used for weekend and vacation cruises. Bill had obtained his captain's license, because he had planned to go on some longer cruises requiring additional boating skills. Little did the couple realize that they would integrate the Elysium into their upcoming career change.

"We sold our house in Leesburg [Virginia], moved temporarily onto the Elysium, and then hopped in our car and headed on an 1,800-mile trip that would take us from Maine to Florida. The goal was to create a short list of inns that were for sale, would fulfill our needs, and be the perfect home for our art and antique collection." Attending a workshop for prospective buyers, they were told that B&B ownership was not the typical 9-to-5 job, a point they came to appreciate as owners.

They narrowed the list of B&B candidates by eliminating seasonal New England inns and other northern vacation spots. They looked for an inn on the ocean or inland waterway in a warmer climate that would let them market the inn and their yacht year-round. The answer was the "1790 House," which is located in Georgetown, South Carolina, midway between Myrtle Beach and Charleston. Bought with the proceeds from the sale of their Virginia home, the 1790 House has six bedrooms and was built in the

year its name implies.

"Denise and I share in most phases of the Inn's operation, including cooking breakfast, something we both like to do. We have a big enough place to have someone come in to clean, but there are times when we have to pitch in. Denise does the marketing and I take care of housekeeping, but it ends up that we each do a little bit of everything. Our day starts at 7 A.M. when we wake up. The first thing to do is prepare coffee for our guests, followed by breakfast at 8. The schedule slows down during the mid part of the day and once again in the evening after guests have checked in."

"Business the first year was okay, but we didn't meet our marketing plan. We were hurt by September 11 and the slowdown in the economy. We also did about 30 intercoastal cruises that we call 'snooze and cruise.'"

After one year of keeping the inn, Bill also finds there is a slight seasonal influence. The spring and fall months are busy with a slowdown during the hot midsummer months. The slow period after Christmas enables the Gowers to take time off and visit family members in both New Jersey and Florida.

Because the Gowers live on the premises, the workday is rarely over. "My cell phone is always with me. When a guest needs help—and it can be at any hour—the innkeeper has to respond. That's why I have extra toilet parts available."

A NATURAL SEGUE

Susan Weinberger

MAKES TRANSITION FROM ADMINISTRATOR TO CONSULTANT

For Susan Weinberger, retiring was hardly a traumatic experience. She changed the locale of her office and continued to spend full time as a mentoring specialist. But, this time, instead of working as an administrator with the Norwalk, Connecticut, school system, Susan would head the Mentor Consulting Group. As an independent consultant building partnerships to support school mentoring programs, Susan could spread her enthusiasm and experience.

Susan's firm has received contracts from Allstate, the office of Juvenile Justice and Delinquency in the U.S. Justice Department, and the Ministry of Education in Bermuda, among others. One program brings together graduate students at Arizona State University in Tempe and kids on Indian reservations; another involves linking the Canon City, Colorado, district attorney's office with kids who are on probation.

Susan travels at least three days a week to train, consult and speak at conferences. She has spent a day training educators on mentoring techniques in the Houston (Texas) Independent School District and two weeks doing a media tour in support of the mentoring programs sponsored by Big Brothers/Sisters of Canada.

As an experienced classroom teacher, Susan still enjoys working one-on-one with children. Every Friday she mentors a student for one hour at the Silvermine Elementary School. He was in the second grade when Susan started with him two years ago. When away on a business trip, she faxes him things that he can consider. This work helps keep Susan on the cutting edge in mentoring by practicing what she preaches.

Raised in Brookline, Massachusetts, Susan majored in modern languages at Carnegie-Mellon University; met and married Norman, who was then a premed student; taught high school Spanish while Norman went to medical school; and moved to Norwalk when he completed pediatric training and went into private practice.

> **Susan's business, "The Mentoring Consulting Group," grew from a local effort that combined her interests with her teaching and administrative skills.**

Thirteen years and two children later, Susan went back into the classroom as a Spanish teacher, after which she became coordinator of bilingual and English as a Second Language programs in the Norwalk school system. "In 1983, I got interested in a new concept in school mentoring and the formation of partnerships to support it. The idea was to get local businesses to let employees spend one hour a week mentoring kids in the Norwalk schools."

Over the next 15 years, Susan who by now had received a master's in elementary and bilingual education from Manhattanville College and a doctorate in educational administration from the University of Bridgeport, had built a local network of businesses who provided mentors for Norwalk school children. Receiving national recognition, she was ready for the next step. "In 1995, I renegotiated my contract with the Norwalk schools so that I could spend about 25% of my time outside of Norwalk, instead of only 12%."

Three years later, Susan was ready to leave the Norwalk system and retire with a pension based on 23 years of service. Her objective as a consultant was to share her mentoring knowledge and know-how with other schools, companies and governmental agencies. "When I asked my husband whether I could go into business, he said 'seize the opportunity.'"

Connecticut's governor, John Roland, requested that Susan devote one-quarter of her time to the state's mentoring partnership and from that her business grew.

Consulting has paid off in many ways. In Susan's first year as a full-time consultant, she earned more money than she did as a school administrator. "Another advantage of being on my own is the freedom to take time off and go on vacation. Norman and I go to St. Bart's in the Caribbean in February. But there's a slight problem these days. I like to needlepoint, but I can't take the needles on the plane. To get around airport security, I send them ahead."

Susan's advocacy on behalf of mentoring is infectious. Her son, who she describes as an entrepreneur, and her daughter, a graphics designer, are mentors, too.

> **In Susan's first year as a full-time consultant, she earned more money than she did as a school administrator.**

WORKS SOLO IN FAMILY LAW

Daniel Hill
PROFESSOR GIVES UP TENURED POST FOR LAW SCHOOL

At 47, Daniel Hill had no plans to retire. A tenured professor in health administration at the University of Alabama's Birmingham's campus, Dan could have easily waited another ten years. By then, he would have accumulated a total of 27 years of college teaching in Alabama and previously at Pennsylvania State University.

Yet, Dan, who is married and has twin daughters, did not want to become a victim of what he calls academic malaise, a condition experienced by many professors who get in a rut years before they retire, but linger on solely to increase the size of their pensions. "I felt that I had gone as far I could go as a teacher. I wanted to be more productive." Dan decided to make his career change while age was still in his favor.

A sabbatical is the usual approach taken by academics who need to recharge their energies. This approach didn't meet Dan's need to do something different—now. He decided on law school—a new idea to him, not the fulfillment of a lifelong dream. "Looking back, I had negative feelings about being

> ## "I don't like to look back at things. I wanted a fresh start in a different field."

a lawyer when I was a youngster."

Up to then, Dan's academic career had been on course. After graduating from Ohio University, where his father was a professor, Dan got his doctorate from Purdue University in 1971. His dissertation was an economic analysis of health insurance with special reference to Blue Cross. The thesis formed the groundwork for his academic career at Penn State and Alabama and for his appointment to state, national and international health administration study groups.

Before deciding to switch careers, Dan talked with his wife, Ellen, who he says was nervous yet supportive; his sister, Charlotte, a former social worker who had already made a midlife career change into law; a number of lawyers; and his daughters. The twins were primarily concerned over whether the family would have sufficient money to pay for their college educations.

Dan decided against going to Alabama's law school, located about 50 miles from his home. "It would have been a much simpler decision and less costly, but I wasn't sure where I wanted to practice. I turned down a few scholarships, and went to the University of North Carolina's Law School, which had more of a national reputation than Alabama. Looking ahead, Chapel Hill was the type of place where Ellen and I wanted to live."

The Hills sold their house in Birmingham and used the proceeds to pay for their move and to help pay for law school. Ellen, who had already finished two-thirds of the requirements for an MBA degree, was hired by UNC Law School's career placement office, where she still works. Three years later, Dan, graduated with honors at age 50 as the oldest member of his class.

Dan was now looking for a job. Finding one would have been simpler if he had opted to fuse his knowledge of health care and law into a hybrid career. He could have followed a logical career path into health administrative law with a law firm or health care facility, but he decided against that. "I could have gone back to Birmingham and joined the largest law firm in the state, but it would have involved health law, which I felt was just another type of corporate law. Anyway, I don't like to look back at

> **As a teacher, Dan had enjoyed dealing with students, and that experience provided a natural bridge into family law, which requires similar people skills.**

things. I wanted a fresh start in a different field."

As a teacher, Dan had enjoyed dealing with students, and that experience provided a natural bridge into family law, which requires similar people skills. His alternative career path led him to a small Durham law firm, Hayes Hoffler & Associates where he was "of counsel." Six years later, he became a solo practitioner, although he kept his offices in the Hayes Hoffler suite. His specialty within family law is divorce, a practice that employs mediation rather than litigation skills.

In his early sixties, Dan, unlike many of his former faculty colleagues who are preparing for retirement, has no target date for retirement. Being self-employed, he can practice as long as he wants. Dan already receives a pension from the University of Alabama, and is covered by its medical plan.

"Because I was connected to the medical center at Alabama, I was paid more than professors on the main campus in Tuscaloosa. I didn't go to law school to make more money but to do something different and to avoid getting in a rut."

Escaping From Retirement

FOR SOME OF US, RETIREMENT CAN'T COME TOO soon—but when it does, it isn't what we expected. Consider my friend the manager, who retired at age 61 and moved to a rented apartment in Florida. Soon after, he went to the swimming pool and was greeted this way by one of his new neighbors: "Welcome to God's waiting room." That capped his impression of his new life. Disillusioned, he returned to New York the following day, and asked for and got his old job back. My friend escaped from retirement.

Early retirees and others who thought their working days were over are changing their tune. They are finding ways to go back to work, either as their sole pursuit or as one part of their retirement portfolio.

This is hardly a surprise to Dr. Letitia T. Chamberlain, who directs New York University's Center for Career, Education and Life Planning. She finds it normally takes people at least two to three years to settle down into a retirement lifestyle. They want to stay productive and above all be active. Some in the 50-plus set want to return to the workplace to fill an income shortfall between their cost of living and their retirement income. But many others miss the challenge of the workplace and its camaraderie, or they want to maintain technical and professional skills. As Dr. Chamberlain observes, there are many people who

---

BACK IN THE SADDLE WHEN?

There's a split of opinion on returning to the workplace after downsizing or retirement. Though your family's finances may influence the decision, take your choice:

- **Start the job search immediately.** Get to work just as quickly. You don't want to lose momentum and skills. Out of sight, out of mind rules the day for these folks.

- **Or take a break.** You might tell yourself: "I haven't had more than an annual ten-day vacation since I graduated from college 35 years ago. I'm going to take a few months off, enroll in a course in music theory and just relax. Then I'll start looking for a new job."

---

are not satisfied working as volunteers or hobbyists. Employment is what they knew and what they like. Paid work is their antidote to a "retirement lifestyle."

To the Parks—and Beyond

Most summers, Sandy and Joe Thompson play hooky by leaving Tucson, Arizona, to work as paid rangers with the National Park Service. While they enjoy the opportunity to live outdoors and escape Arizona's summer heat, it's just as important for them to make some additional money to supplement their retirement income.

The Thompsons retired young—54 for Sandy and two years younger for Joe. Living in Bethesda, Maryland, they started a voicemail and paging-service company in the early 1980s. "We had about 15 employees. We sold the company in 1993 when we got tired of running it and saw that it was becoming more difficult for a smaller company to compete. We got out when it was to our advantage to do so," Sandy says.

"When we sold Compuvoice, we had no master retirement plan, nor did we plan to move or work again." Instead, they bought an RV and for three years roamed the western U.S.,

Canada and Mexico. By 1999, they decided to sever their eastern ties. They sold their house and the RV, and became permanent residents of Tucson.

Though they now consider themselves retirees, the Thompsons have little desire to be sedentary. Long-time outdoor enthusiasts and hikers, they had volunteered for several summers with the National Park Service. Some ranger friends encouraged them to apply to become uniformed seasonal rangers, and they were assigned to Glacier National Park in Montana. "There are definite pluses and minuses to being a ranger versus a volunteer. A volunteer can come and go more freely than a ranger, whereas a ranger gets paid, puts in a minimum 40-hour workweek and gets a job evaluation," says Joe. "We're not the oldest couple. There are seasonal rangers who have been doing it for 35 to 40 years."

Joe and Sandy each have a different Park Service task. "I issue backcountry permits," Joe says. "I help operate a ranger station, and act as a resource counselor for visitors going into Glacier's backcountry." Sandy's job includes collecting fees, answering questions at the gate and patrolling the campgrounds. The couple earns between $15,000 to $20,000 for a season lasting up to five months. The income, though not large, has helped to offset the slump in the value of their investment portfolio.

The Thompsons hope that their outdoor adventures will take on an additional dimension. They've applied to the National Science Foundation for a five-to-six-month assignment in Antarctica, where they would do administrative and odd jobs. "Age is not a factor; we've had friends our age who've done it," says Sandy. "What's more, the pay is good."

The Sidelines Weren't for Him

Or, take Dr. Lawrence Walker, a downright miserable spectator. When Larry retired in 1991 as superintendent of schools in a rural North Carolina county, he learned some real-life lessons about early retirement. Following his retirement, he managed a statewide political campaign for a friend. His friend lost the election, and Larry was out of work.

Fortunately, Larry's expenses were pretty well controlled.

> ## RULES FOR GOING BACK
>
> - **Don't think like a "Pampered Corporate Baby"** (see Chapter 1).
>
> - **You will need to convince a company that it should hire a 62-year-old.**
>
> - **Don't expect to get a prestigious title.**
>
> - **Be prepared to do hands-on work, even in a manager's job.**
>
> - **Be prepared to accept less money than you are used to.**
>
> - **Above all, be flexible.**

He and his wife, Mary, a nurse, owned their home in Yanceyville, a town of 2,000 and the county seat of Caswell County. Too young to collect social security benefits, Larry had a pension, health care benefits and savings. He worked a few hours each day in a convenience store that he had acquired in 1987 as an investment, had had others manage and has subsequently sold. But Larry's retirement would soon turn into a litany of disappointments.

"I got tired of tending my garden. Working in the store fulltime was not for me. My golf is miserable, so it made me feel even more miserable.

"My hobbies, collecting antique fountain pens and old American coins, are not the type of activities that keep you too busy.

"Neighbors and friends hearing that I retired thought I left due to illness. Their concerns made me concerned. I'm an optimist but I got down.

"I missed the camaraderie of school work. I found that I was starting to lose education and government contacts. It doesn't take too long to be out of the loop, and once you are out of it it's hard to get back in.

"I also did some consulting, but it's not the same as a full-time job. I needed a more solid base of operation."

Larry attended a meeting of retired school superintendents

and returned home depressed. Mary said: "You don't belong in that group yet."

Less than two years after retiring and as a result of networking among his fellow educators and government officials, Larry was reactivated as executive director of the Central Carolina Consortium, one of seven regional groups established in the state to link schools at all levels with industry and business. To take the job, he had to temporarily forgo a pension based on 33 years of service as a North Carolina educator. The state forbids "double dipping" for state employees who take another state job (see the box on double dipping on page 192).

When the Consortium assignment ended in the late 1990s, Larry was named executive director of the Carolina Regional Education Service Alliance, which serves 290,000 students in 16 school systems and one institution for hearing-impaired children. He spends about 50% of his time with the Alliance and the balance with his educational consultancy, Technical Services Associates. And, most importantly, the double dipping restriction no longer applies, so he receives a state pension and health care coverage.

> **"I found that I was starting to lose education and government contacts. It doesn't take too long to be out of the loop, and once you are out of it it's hard to get back in."**

Everyone Can't Be a CEO

Paul Rizzo retired from IBM in 1987 at age 59. In 1985, he had been considered a prime candidate to become CEO. Passed over, he left two years later and was named dean of the business school at the University of North Carolina, where he had graduated and had been a football star 40 years earlier. In mid 1992, Rizzo retired from UNC. Within four months he was summoned back to a troubled IBM on a full-time basis to help run the company as a "counselor and adviser" to then-chairman John Akers. When Akers was ousted, Rizzo was promoted by the then new CEO, Louis Gerstener, to vice-chairman. Rizzo retired from IBM a second time at the end of 1994. And, even still, he didn't retire. Now, he's the board chairman and a partner in Franklin Street Partners, a North Carolina investment firm.

A RÉSUMÉ TELLS A STORY

The résumé for the 50-plus set is practically an art form.

- **The résumé is a selling document.** Tell the reader what makes you unique. Simply put, what assets do you bring to the party?

- **Above all, give readers a fast career overview.** Stress what happened over the past 20 years. The rest is ancient history, and chances are the earlier jobs were stepping stones anyway.

- **A similar rule applies to education.** List the college degrees, but you can omit the graduation year.

Stanley Gault's career has a similar ring. After he lost out to Jack Welch for General Electric's top job in 1980, Gault left the company at age 54 and joined Rubbermaid (now Newell Rubbermaid) in Wooster, Ohio, as its CEO. Eleven years later, he retired from Rubbermaid after building it into one of the nation's most admired and profitable companies. Like Rizzo, who could have spent his retirement years joining boards of directors, Gault wanted to stay active in business, but he had achieved all he had hoped for in corporate America. He intended instead to put his talents to use in a small venture-capital start-up. But after Goodyear approached him several times to take charge, Gault finally conceded because he wanted to see this troubled American tiremaker survive.

Unfortunately, the mobility that permits older, high-profile CEOs to slide into another corporate job does not readily apply to many 50-plus-set managers. Odds are stacked against their getting another high-paid job in corporate America.

There are some notable exceptions: As midlevel management jobs are abolished, it is ironic that hands-on technical, financial and salespeople are in far greater demand than their immediate supervisors. To confuse matters even more, it is easier to place a 54-year-old downsized executive who has worked for four different companies over 27 years than someone who has worked for a single employer during the same period. Compared with a decade ago, says executive recruiter Randall Bye, employers now seek managers who have worked for several companies and have proved that they have the flexibility to adapt to different types of corporate cultures.

A New Way of Doing Things

Bleak as the situation may appear, it does not mean there is a total absence of job opportunities. Rather, the rules have changed and early retirees need to acquire new habits. The job-search winners are those applicants who recognize the need for new tactics and have updated their game plan.

Outplacement consultant Temple Porter of the Raleigh Consulting Group advises clients to disregard old road maps in favor of nontraditional and alternative routes to the job market. "Clients need to show their 'unique leverage' in terms of reputation, special knowledge and professional skills. If a company is looking for a turnaround expert, IBM's former chairman Lou Gerstener assuredly doesn't need to revise his résumé to apply for the job."

Avoid shooting yourself in the foot when trying to get a new job, says James Challenger of the outplacement firm Challenger, Gray & Christmas (www.challengergray.com). He finds that job prospects for the 50-plus set rise when they follow a few simple rules:

- **Sell them on your expertise.**
- **Look and act young.**
- **Avoid looking dowdy at interviews.**
- **Address yourself to the employer's needs, not your own.**
- **Above all, do not announce personal timetables** such as a desire to work for only four more years before retiring.

Staying smart is the key. Executive recruiters and business professionals all agree that keeping yourself informed through educational courses and corporate training programs is a key factor in your business success after the age of 50. In its study, "The Untapped Resource," the Commonwealth Fund (www.cmwf.org) urges corporations to offer training to older workers so they can continue to make as great a contribution to the organization

CLUES TO WINNING INTERVIEWS

You're scheduled for a job interview. Now don't blow it.

- **Act your age but don't overdo it.** Start by leaving the grandchildren's pictures and similar bric-a-brac at home.

- **Watch the narrative.** Avoid talking about 1980 or even earlier business trends. The date might predate the interviewer's own date of birth.

- **This is not the time to tell "war stories"** about the old days.

- **Talk in the present and future tense.** Emphasize what you've done recently and what your goals are.

- **Above all, be yourself.** The interviewer is well aware that you didn't graduate from college in 1990.

in later years as they had in earlier ones. If your company doesn't offer training programs or have a tuition-reimbursement program, check with local universities to see if they offer courses at a reduced cost to seniors. For less expensive courses, check with your local public school system for information about its adult extension program and with community colleges in your area.

Susan Lawley, who downshifted from a $250,000 human-resources position on Wall Street to open the Camelot Group, a human-resources consulting firm in Fairfield, New Jersey, maintains that escapees from early retirement often find jobs if they are willing to take a significant pay cut, are flexible in geographic location and can offer a variety of skills. Money is always a bargaining tool, especially in negotiating with small- to midsize companies. While a controller for a billion-dollar company might easily have earned a six-figure salary, such a salary rarely exists in a $20 million to $40 million company. Compared with a younger person seeking the same job, the 50-plus-set applicant should expect to work for less money, should not require a full menu of fringe benefits and should not feel a loss of identity if the job does not carry a title. The bottom line for a midsize company? Getting a senior executive at a bargain price.

If you're still concerned about the loss of prestige in taking a new job, then the best suggestion is to start your own consultancy or other business (see Chapter 7). You become your own boss and can act accordingly.

Alternatives to Business as Usual

The National Executive Service Corps— Nice Work If You Can Get It

The National Executive Service Corps (www.nesc.org) deals with retirees every day who have had their retirement fling and want no more of it. They seek employment for different reasons. Money, though a factor, is usually not the driving force, although many retirees find they need additional income to maintain a desired lifestyle, which may have become more difficult to achieve with the decline in the stock market. One retiree noted that "after my retirement, I thought all of my knowledge would be locked up like concrete in the brain, never to be used again."

Like so many organizations dealing with retired executives and professionals who want to return to work, the NESC has a backlog of 3,000 résumés of applicants. Its focus is on filling nonprofit management positions. No different from corporate America, nonprofits are also pruning staffs, says Paul Barrett, a NESC senior vice president, and a former corporate marketing and turnaround specialist. NESC applicants who are hired for a nonprofit position typically earn 25% to 50% less than comparable jobs in the corporate sector. In return, what most nonprofits receive is a seasoned manager at an affordable price. What the retirees get is a chance to return to the workplace, where they find the excitement, challenge and sense of achievement that they miss in retirement. NESC receives 20% of the annual base salary, somewhat less than the 25%-to-33% placement fee charged by private search firms.

In preparing candidates for nonprofit job interviews, Paul encourages them to think like nonprofit rather than corporate executives, and he helps them to prepare résumés that show how their corporate financial, marketing or computer experiences are transferable to a nonprofit agency. He finds that applicants who have served on nonprofit boards or have been volunteers often have an advantage because of their exposure to nonprofit oper-

THE NEW NETWORKS

You might not have expected to find a job through a local church or synagogue, but several thousand congregations nationwide are holding networking meetings each week. These informal networks are great sources of leads, support and job-searching tips. Their success in helping people find new jobs has been remarkable, so check for such a group in your local area and join up.

ating procedures.

Jackie Reinhard lost her job as executive director of information technology for the College Board when it reorganized. At 53, she had no interest in retiring. "I went to search firms looking for a technology job, but I found very few openings, and the competition was fierce. While I wanted to make the transition into a director's position with a nonprofit, I didn't know how to go about it. I went to NESC, not to ask for a job, but to volunteer my time. Besides wanting to keep busy and gain exposure, I hoped at some point that it would lead to a job." The opportunity presented itself faster than she expected. Recognizing that Janet's skills were indeed transferable, NESC's Paul Barrett recommended her to the New York chapter of the Lateral Sclerosis Association (the Lou Gehrig disease). She was hired as executive director responsible for the New York chapter's day-to-day operations.

The Part-Time Alternative

Make sure you know the differences between part-time and temporary work. The part-timer is a company employee, while the temporary worker may be an employee of a temporary agency. Part-timers, depending on the number of hours worked, may receive fringe benefits and may be eligible for paid vacations.

Some employees, particularly those who are nearing retirement age and whose skills are in demand, are switching from full- to part-time employment as part of a phased retirement plan. Some part-timers are also working at home, participating in the trend toward telecommuting for workers of all ages. The best bet for part-time employment at your skill level is your present employer, but make sure that you make arrangements while you're still on the payroll. Chances of making as good a deal are lessened once you've retired.

VISIT A LIBRARY

Job seekers will find public and university libraries to be gold mines of employment-related information. You can expect to find plenty of how-to and self-help career books, as well as countless directories and even online information that may be of help. Don't hesitate to ask the reference librarians for help in locating the information you want. That's what they're there for.

The New York Public Library (www.nypl.org), for example, has taken an additional step to help patrons. It established Job Information Centers in a few branches with a collection of books, directories, pamphlets and periodicals covering such topics as career choice, the job search process, résumé writing and interviewing techniques. Job counseling is also offered at its branch in the Bronx.

Also make sure that you won't reduce your eventual pension payout by continuing to work part-time with your present employer. This might occur, for example, if your payout was based on your highest salary for three consecutive years within the last five years of your employment. If the years when you're working part-time count in the five-year period, you run the risk that your highest-paying years—presumably those when you were working full-time—will drop out of the equation.

If part-time employment is for you, decide what form will best suit your needs. Permanent part-time positions are a traditional option in which the employee spends something less than a full workweek at the job, however the employer defines that.

Job sharing allows you and another employee to split a full-time job. Perhaps you will work two days and your co-worker will put in three days, allowing for some overlap time so that you can communicate about details and divide projects.

With telecommuting, thanks to advances in communications, many people find it possible to perform the same tasks at home that they used to do in an office setting. You cut back not only on your hours but also on commuting time and daily expenses.

With each of these options there are disadvantages, so find out more about them and consider your choices carefully.

TEMPING FOR YOUR EMPLOYER OR A NEW ONE

Several years ago hospitals began building their own in-house lists of temporary workers to call on when they found themselves short-staffed. Some businesses followed suit. Check with your current or previous employer to see whether it offers a similar program or has a similar need that you could meet.

Home Depot, however, takes a different approach. It hires retired plumbers, carpenters and other craftspeople as sales personnel, usually part-time. Home Depot recognizes that these employees will have practical solutions to customers' household problems.

Once you know what sort of arrangement you think you want, you have to convince your boss that it's a good idea. Things you should consider include:

- **What are your unique talents or skills?** Why is the employer better off keeping you on part-time instead of hiring someone new full-time?
- **Can your job realistically be redesigned to fit a part-time schedule?** How often do you need to meet face-to-face with your employer, clients and others? What will you be giving up?
- **What is your employer's attitude toward part-time work?**
- **Is there a set policy regarding flexible work schedules?**
- **Are there other employees on the payroll who have worked out similar arrangements?** What sort of precedent for other employees would you be asking your employer to set?
- **If others have gone the part-time route before you, what happened to them?** What hurdles did they encounter? How are their arrangements working out?
- **What difficulties, if any, might you be imposing on your employer?**
- **What will happen to your salary and benefits?**
- **What do you need to know to be successful?**
- **Who makes the decisions?** Draw up a political game plan.
- **Who can you safely use as a sounding board for your idea?**
- **Who should you discuss it with first in earnest?** Who can you

appropriately and effectively enlist as an ally if you anticipate a touchy situation?

At age 63, Jane T. was more fortunate than many of her retired contemporaries. A year after she retired, Jane went back to work three days a week, earning proportionately what she had been paid as a full-time employee. She also continued to receive her pension payments. What made Jane so attractive to her employer, a communications conglomerate, was her specialty as a legal expert on rates and tariff law.

When she retired, Jane's job was eliminated, but her responsibilities were divided among other staff members. Then, due to changes in government regulations, there was an increase in the tariff-law workload. The company needed professional assistance. It viewed retaining a law firm to handle the work as too costly an alternative, and when it tried to hire a replacement for Jane, it found the candidates lacked expertise. When it approached Jane, the company found a perfect candidate who was "thrilled" to return to work as a part-timer on an assignment that lasted another 30 months.

You Don't Have to Be a Kelly Girl

When you think of a "temp," you probably remember those folks who came to your office to answer the phones, do copying or perform some other necessary but low-level chore when a regular staff member was ill or on vacation. The temp field has expanded, however. Now there are executive temporaries who are politely referred to as interim managers. Kelly Services, employer of the temps you used to know as Kelly Girls, has a professional and technical division.

Even with the growth in temporary employment services, temps account for less than 2% of the total workforce. The U.S. Labor Department's Bureau of Labor Statistics (www.bls.gov) reports that 12% of temporary and contract workers are age 55 plus, a 2% rise since 1997. The difference lies in the increase in the number of professional and management positions being filled by temps, many of whom are in the 50-plus set. The median weekly earnings for temporary help agency workers of all ages is $396; compare that with professional and technical work-

---

THE PROS AND CONS OF INTERIM MANAGEMENT JOBS

THE PROS

- **Provides income** during a job search

- **Allows for networking** while on the job

- **May be a good fit** with your lifestyle

- **May lead to** a permanent position

- **Could fill in** while doing own consulting or self-employment work

THE CONS

- **Can make it difficult** to actively search for a permanent position elsewhere while on the job

- **Odds are low** for placement

- **Income can be** uncertain

- **No benefits**

Source: Executive Recruitment News

---

ers provided by contract firms who make $790.

The temporary service field has benefited from downsizing, early retirement and the trend toward getting retirement-age employees off the corporate books. As staffs are thinned, though, the corporate appetite for skilled managers and professionals hardly diminishes, and thus the birth of interim-management firms that place managers, staffers and professionals in temporary jobs. These agencies supply the manpower and handle all the employment-related paperwork.

Kennedy Publications, which tracks corporate human-resources trends, notes that "candidates over age 55, who may have difficulty finding permanent posts, are, with their wealth of experience and expertise, ideal for executive temporary placement. As the demand for specialization increases along with the need for mentoring, their skills increase in value. Interim executives who are placed are often overqualified for the jobs they perform."

Still, finding an interim-management job is a long shot. The best candidate for a temporary job is the highly skilled professional in a niche that's in demand, but the chances of getting a job as an interim executive are slim at any age. The ratio of applicants to job openings on file for people of all ages at the 110 or so firms that specialize in placing management and professional personnel is staggering, sometimes as high as 1,000 to 1. Dahl-Morrow International (www.dahl-morrowintl.com), a suburban Washington, D.C., specialist in the information systems and communications fields, has little difficulty attracting candidates to add to its database of more than 12,000 names. At Dahl-Morrow and most other interim-management firms, temporary assignments range from three months to one year.

Even with the low odds of success, retirees should not overlook the interim-management market. If nothing else, you might find it more efficient having an employment firm market your talents than trying to reach out to corporate America yourself. If you get an assignment, you may find it gives you a leg up on a permanent job—if that's what you really want. At Dahl-Morrow, about one-half of the interim-management assignments turn into full-time jobs. Because it's such a good opportunity for the employer to get to know the worker's skills, there's a growing trend toward converting temporary positions to full-time. Age is less of a factor than in the past. It's being overshadowed by the need to have current security clearances, a mandatory requirement at companies with government contracts.

> **Because it's such a good opportunity for the employer to get to know the worker's skills, there's a growing trend toward converting temporary positions to full-time.**

Part-time employment is another option for the 50-plus set who want to return to the workplace. The National Association of Part-Time and Temporary Employees (http://members.tripod.com /~NAPTE/) indicates that there are about 12 million part-time workers in the U.S. This organization's primary focus is lobbying for health care and retirement benefits for its members.

How They Resurfaced

Some people retire eagerly, looking forward to a leisurely lifestyle. In a little while—a few weeks, maybe a few months later—boredom sets in. A lifestyle based on golf, volunteerism

SUGGESTED READING

- *Breaking Out of 9 to 5,* by Maria Laqueur and Donna Dickinson (Peterson's, 1994). If you are interested in redesigning your job, this book is full of useful information concerning job trends, proposal writing, negotiation tactics and locating a flexible job.

- *Occupational Handbook 2002–3,* from the U.S. Department of Labor (VGM Career Opportunities). Published in alternate years. Provides vital information on dozens of professional and management careers that you might never have thought of.

- *The Over-40 Job Market,* by Kathryn Petras and Ross Petras (Poseidon Press, 1993). Lots of good practical hints on the workplace.

- *Second Careers: New Ways to Work After 50,* by Caroline Bird (Little, Brown, 1992). This book was based on responses to an AARP survey.

- *Switching Careers,* by Robert Otterbourg (Kiplinger Books, 2001)

- *What Color is Your Parachute,* by Richard Bolles (Ten Speed Press, 2003). A perennial for job seekers of all ages.

and hobbies is not for them. They miss the competitiveness of the workplace or, frankly, the chance to make some more money. Whatever the reason, their solution is to return to work. They find a new job or opportunity by networking and by virtue of their proven skills. Opportunities exist for those willing to explore and take a chance, like the group of former retirees you'll meet on the following pages. These include a registered nurse, school teacher and corporate executive who missed the workplace after they retired and found their answer in full- or part-time jobs using their former workskills.

POINTS TO REMEMBER

- **Boredom is an important factor** that draws the 50-plus set back to work.

- **Many retirees miss the challenge, competition and collegiality** of the workplace.

- **There's stiff competition** to get part-time or interim management jobs.

- **Avoid obsolescence.** Upgrade your skills before looking for employment.

- **If you're willing to accept a lower salary,** you can use that as an advantage in the marketplace.

- **You need to learn new ways to "sell" yourself** to a prospective employer.

THE MAKING OF A COMMUNITY ACTIVIST

Gerard Stoddard

PUBLIC-RELATIONS EXECUTIVE TURNED HOMEOWNERS ASSOCIATION LEADER

When Gerard Stoddard walks down Fifth Avenue in New York, he could be easily tagged as a successful corporate executive. And, for many years, he was one. But a corporate merger and an abiding interest in his home-away-from-home put him on his present career path. Jerry made the transition from corporate executive to volunteer president of the Fire Island (New York) Association and most recently to paid president. Defying retirement, Jerry converted the position into a demanding career using much of his professional experience and skills.

For 20 years, Jerry's career was closely associated with SCM Corp., once the nation's premier typewriter manufacturer. When SCM was acquired by Hanson Trust, a British conglomerate, Jerry's job as vice-president for corporate communications became redundant.

Jerry was protected financially by a contract, a fully vested pension, and savings and investments resulting from an excellent salary. In addition, he executed his stock options at a very favorable price. What's more, his expenses were contained. The townhouse that he owned and lived in New York's Chelsea section also included some rented apartments.

In the public relations field, an occupation noted for high job turnover, Jerry had had only two employers over a 25-year span. When he graduated from Cornell University, he was interested in public affairs and public policy, and took a job with the American Petroleum Institute, the oil industry's prime lobbyist. While an API employee, he obtained a law degree at night from New York University and passed the state bar exam, but never practiced law. In future years, he was, however, able to leverage his legal education.

He joined SCM as director of shareholder relations and six years later was named a corporate vice-president. While responsible for the company's full range of public relations activities, Jerry personally handled its lobbying activities in Washington and New York, a job that required a knowledge of

> **Job-hunting didn't turn up much. Consulting for law firms didn't cut it. With the Fire Island Association, Jerry found his calling in "retirement."**

public relations and the law.

When he left SCM, Jerry was much too young to consider retiring. Until the acquisition, he felt he had a secure and satisfying job, so in many ways he was unprepared for his departure from SCM. Unemployed, he looked for jobs through traditional search methods and even received a few offers, including one that, in effect, represented a career demotion. "At the time, I realized that this might very well be my last job offer. I would most likely never find a job equal to the one I had at SCM."

Jerry was not idle professionally as he looked for a full-time job. He started a public relations consultancy firm in his home. Law firms were then just beginning to market their services, and as a lawyer and public relations practitioner, Jerry received assignments from several large New York law firms. But lawyers, he soon concluded, are fine if they work for you—and not so fine if you work for them.

In the meantime, Jerry and his family, like so many New Yorkers, had had two residences. During the school year, they lived in New York City. In the summer, the family moved to their cottage on Fire Island, 55 miles from midtown New York. Jerry spent weekends on Fire Island with his family.

As is typical of many resorts, Fire Island's population soars in the summer to 25,000 residents and declines in the

off-season to about 500 year-round occupants. The swing in seasonal population places pressure on the island's environment and its relaxed lifestyle. This has led to a division among residents— those who want to see more commercial development and those who are opposed to it. Automotive vehicles are banned from the island. Walking or biking are the only modes of transportation. "I began to get interested in community life when someone wanted to build a hotel, something I didn't feel was in keeping with community living," Jerry says. "This activated me, and I got the local property owners to buy the land and make it into a park."

About the time he was leaving SCM, Jerry was elected president of the Fire Island Association, which represents the island's 3,000 homeowners. "As a professional lobbyist, I knew that our association was too small to have any impact in either Washington or Albany." To build a bigger political power base, he helped to form the Long Island Coastal Alliance, consisting of similar beach communities on Long Island's South Shore. The alliance gave him the incentive to start *Coastal Reports,* a paid bimonthly subscription newsletter devoted to coastal property owners, as well as an annual conference on coastal matters. Jerry had taken another step away from retirement.

As the association's president, Jerry

> ## Lawyers, he soon concluded, are fine if they work for you—and not so fine if you work for them.

has a varied job description. He has been involved in a number of environmental issues, including finding ways to control the influx of deer and the Lyme disease they can bring. The association also faces other challenges as many of the island's residents near retirement age and opt for year-round residence. The growing year-round population needs better transportation facilities and ways to realistically extend the season beyond the normal five months from May to early October.

At first, Jerry served on a volunteer basis as the association's president, but growing responsibilities and the expanding time commitment led the association's board of directors to begin paying him a $25,000 honorarium. Since receiving the honorarium, Jerry has sidelined his public relations consultancy and instead concentrates on his paid work with the Fire Island Association and

> **"The issues are fascinating, so I guess I'll stay on as president until the board gets tired of me and kicks me out."**

on his volunteer leadership of the Long Island Coastal Alliance. The work uses his varied professional skills, including writing, knowledge of government operations and lobbying in Washington and Albany with the state legislature and executive offices.

"There are many psychic pleasures with my job. I testified a couple of times before the U.S. Senate on the need for greater shore protection on Long Island, helped win a major victory to enable coastal property owners to obtain flood insurance, and I constantly meet and work with important people."

Jerry finds his present work is a much better alternative than retirement, but there are still drawbacks. "Volunteer groups can be as demanding as any client—or corporate president, for that matter. But the issues are fascinating, so I guess I'll stay on as president until the board gets tired of me and kicks me out."

COMPUTERS—AN ALLY IN REAL ESTATE SALES

Dorothy Arnsten
SCHOOL PSYCHOLOGIST TURNED REAL ESTATE BROKER

"Larry [her husband] and I do not like to hang out. I don't like going to lunch with the girls and I don't like shopping. We have lots of interests, but other than work no other single activity can fill up a day," says Dorothy Arnsten.

When Dorothy retired several years ago as a psychologist with the New York City public school system, she took a retirement route normally not associated with someone with a doctorate degree and over 25 years of classroom and counseling experience. Like many retired psychologists, she could have concentrated on her private practice, and enjoyed the income from an ample New York pension. Dorothy, however, was looking for a different stimulant consistent with her attitude toward retirement.

Dorothy started to plan a career switch several years before she left the school system. Her husband, an accountant, also owns and manages some property. "Larry would give me papers to look at. He asked me to read and then sign them. I discovered that I was the general manager. When I asked

She segues into a new career that uses her psychological and teaching skills.

about the title, Larry said, 'I work for you, sweetheart.'" This whetted her appetite to learn more about real estate.

She subsequently met Ileen Schoenfeld at a party and learned that Ileen, also a one-time teacher, was selling New York City co-op and condo apartments. "The work interested me. Selling real estate would add something different in my life. I took a real estate course and was licensed by New York State." Real estate added a third dimension to an already busy lifestyle as a full-time school psychologist with a part-time private psychology practice.

Dorothy's big break came when Ileen had to go to Florida to visit an ailing mother. She asked Dorothy to be her proxy, and in her absence Dorothy sold two apartments. Eileen and Dorothy became partners. "It's a great relationship since I can work my own schedule and we can spell each other on weekends and vacations." She admits, however, that she'd like to reduce her current 40-hour workweek.

While many retirees would be satisfied with a single post-retirement job, Dorothy works as both a full-time real estate broker and as a part-time psychologist. She purposely limits her psychology practice to no more than eight patients, all in short-term relationships, six hours for six weeks. "I don't take on patients with deep emotional problems. They're mostly people who are going through bereavement, an affair or have problems at work." Interestingly, Dorothy finds that real-estate sales combines a number of different skills including psychology and teaching.

As a real estate broker, Dorothy brings strong research and computer skills to the workplace. She was introduced to computers in the early 1980s when she took several courses in conjunction with her doctorate studies. Computers provide a key research and marketing tool for real estate brokers. It didn't take much to convince her that in-depth research on behalf of clients helps to clinch a sale. Either from a home or office computer, Dorothy feeds information on clients' needs into the computer, which generates lists of apartments or townhouses that fit the client's specifications. Her computerized listings are read by potential buyers in places as diverse as New York, Hong Kong and London.

OUT OF THE FRYING PAN AND INTO THE FIRE

Thomas Roeser

CORPORATE VP TURNED COLUMNIST AND PUBLIC AFFAIRS ADVOCATE

Thomas Roeser, at 62, was the oldest executive in a senior management position at Quaker Oats' headquarters in Chicago. As its vice-president for government relations, Tom felt no pressure to retire. "For a while, I thought I would stay until I was 70 and really be the company's grand old man."

But the idea of retirement was accelerated when Tom was injured so seriously that he received the last rites of the Roman Catholic Church. He had fallen while getting out of a shower and a blood clot formed on his brain. He recovered rapidly and was back at work in ten weeks. "But it got me to think about the future and what I might do if I retired."

This was not the first time that Tom had thought of leaving Quaker Oats and perhaps going into business for himself. He knew instinctively that if he ever left he would use his skills in public affairs as the basis of any new career. "Quaker Oats' chairman gave me a long leash and let me say publicly what I wanted to on issues as long as I kept the company out of it. But I

> After years of speaking for Quaker Oats, Tom found his own voice. He writes and debates about the issues, and represents public affairs clients who appreciate his point of view.

still had to be careful. There's always a need as a company executive to be discreet. By comparison, I knew that the owner of the smallest business has the freedom to speak his mind."

Tom has been speaking his mind in a variety of ways since he left Quaker Oats. His public affairs work became the basis of his consultancy practice and a patchwork career. He flourishes in the limelight as a lobbyist, public affairs consultant, newspaper columnist and radio talk-show host.

Tom writes a weekly column on local and regional political issues for the *Chicago Sun-Times* while continuing to do radio talk show gigs on local public affairs. "If you're up to date on the issues there's little preparation that is needed, but it is still demanding. One of the shows involves a McLaughlin Group–like, no-holds-barred discussion of local and state politics."

Tom's writing and radio shows occupy more and more of his time, but this builds name recognition with future clients. Tom sees his specialty as publicaffairs consulting to midsize companies. When he went into business, he had already arranged to represent Quaker Oats as a public affairs consultant. It helped get him started and provided him with an immediate source of income and a major company to include on his client list. The arrangement lasted about two years. "By then my successor no longer needed my assistance. I don't blame her. I wouldn't like my former boss looking over my shoulder, either."

Tom's clients tend to be companies with specific equal-employment or environmental problems that need to be brought to the attention of a government agency or elected official. These firms normally are too small to have a public affairs manager on staff, and their lawyers are usually trained in corporate law, not public affairs. They're the ideal candidates to retain a consultant. "I try to solve their problems by making things happen in either Washington or Springfield (the capital of Illinois)."

Tom still commutes to work from the suburbs to a downtown Chicago office that he shares with several other corporate retirees. He subleases space with a one-time business colleague, who is also retired and a consultant. The arrangement gives him an office, use of photocopy equipment and a conference room, and the part-time use of a secretary. "I need the discipline of an office where there are no distractions, no grandchildren to play with or snow blower to use. Going downtown to the office every day charges me up, and I want to continue doing this as long as I remain in good health."

Tom admits to working as hard as he did in his peak years but enjoys the freedom of being his own boss. He attributes his drive to his being a Depression-generation child. "It's an attitude that's hard to shake loose and one of the reasons I'm a political conservative. I'm uncertain about the future. I always knew that I didn't want to follow in my father's footsteps. He died at 68, tired and under self-generated pressures."

Tom began his career after graduating from St. John's University in Collegeville, Minnesota. He started out as a political reporter in Minnesota but left soon afterward to become research director and publicist for the state's Republican party. "I enjoyed being a reporter, but it was like being a stenographer; I wanted to be a newsmaker and political insider." He became a speechwriter for two members of Congress, then was assistant to the governor of Minnesota before joining Quaker Oats as a public affairs specialist.

Tom took a sabbatical from Quaker

> **"I need the discipline of an office where there are no distractions, no grandchildren to play with or snow blower to use."**

Oats in 1969 to serve as an assistant to Maurice Stans, President Nixon's first secretary of commerce, and spent about two years in the government. "When I left Quaker Oats, my boss said that I would not like working in Washington and he told me that I could have my job back whenever I wanted." Tom spent the next 20 years, until he retired, as the company's senior lobbyist and public affairs officer.

While still a Quaker Oats employee, Tom was involved in a number of outside activities that eventually provided an ideal bridge into retirement and his patchwork career. As a conservative public affairs analyst, he wrote newspaper and magazine op-ed pieces and appeared on radio and television. He also became the first business lobbyist to be named a John F. Kennedy Fellow at Harvard.

"I went into business the day after I left Quaker Oats. I advise others to do the same thing. Don't even take a vacation. That way you have no time to feel sorry for yourself or become depressed. I find my friends who need to unwind before taking the next step never get back to peak efficiency again."

Tom left Quaker Oats with a pension, stock options and a good investment portfolio. To bring his monthly income up to a preretirement level, he supplements his pension payment with a fixed monthly withdrawal from his investment account. "But even with my good pension, I continue to worry about money. The Depression syndrome kicks in. When I'm overly concerned about needing more work, my wife, Lillian, counters by saying that it's time to forget about money and enjoy what I'm doing."

The income that Tom receives from writing, radio and consulting goes into a separate account to cover the costs of maintaining a downtown office and other business expenses. He reserves the remainder against downturns in business.

Even with Tom's busy daytime schedule, he has been a student during evenings at the University of Chicago, where he has taken a course in Western literature and philosophy. "It's fun reading Plato at my age. It leads to lively discussions with the younger students.

"I don't feel I'm ready in the slightest to retire," says Tom. "If I ever do, it will be for one purpose: to have more time to reflect and write some books.

"There are so many things I wanted to do and I've done them—visit Israel, get a dog because I never in my life had one, and write. Above all, I like actively debating the issues. It beats my retired friends who have nothing to do all day."

ONE YEAR OF RELAXATION WAS ENOUGH

Barbara Hallan
RETURNS PART-TIME TO HER NURSING JOB

From the get-go, retirement didn't turn out exactly the way Barbara Hallan had anticipated. "When I retired, I thought I would have a great life, with time for a cup of coffee and the crossword puzzle. I could do all the things I had put off when I worked— gardening, putting photos in albums, spending more time with my grandchildren, and going to the fitness center at Duke." Her plans went slightly awry when she was assigned to a fitness program that met early in the morning, requiring her to arise early. Though fitness was important to Barbara, having a chance to relax and not having to adhere to a schedule was even more important. She dropped the fitness center.

And after only a year of retirement, Barbara Hallan was ready to return to work.

Barbara was a Depression baby. The family lived in Newport News, Virginia, where her father worked in a shipbuilding yard and for the C&O Railroad. She recalls that money was short, and though she liked to draw, the family never had money

Duke made Barbara a retirement offer she couldn't refuse, then allowed her to work part-time and collect her pension, too. What more could she ask for?

for art lessons—a fact of her childhood that she still hopes to overcome.

After graduating from high school, Barbara attended a three-year nursing school program at a local hospital. After two years of work as a nurse, she attended an 18-month nurse anesthetist course at Washington University in St. Louis. As a nurse anesthetist, her salary would be two to three times more than that of the average floor nurse. Soon after completing that training and obtaining a job as a nurse anesthetist, Barbara married, moved to North Carolina, and worked in the field for three years.

But after bearing three children in four years, her nursing career became secondary in Barbara's life for the next 20 years. She returned to her profession in the early 1980s following the trauma of a divorce. "I took a 12-week, nursing-update program. I was too out-of-date to go back to work as a nurse anesthetist. I would have had to go through retraining since things had changed so much."

In her early 50s, Barbara became a floor nurse at the Duke Medical Center in

Durham. "It was the first time I had done this type of nursing since finishing nursing school. I felt very fortunate to have a profession that I could return to after all that time and still love it." She moved on to an assignment on the neurology floor, followed by one in the recovery room.

A family medical crisis forced Barbara to leave work in the recovery room and switch to another nursing specialty, the outpatient heart catheterization laboratory. Her mother had developed Alzheimer's, and Barbara's daughter, who had been living at home and helping with her grandmother, married and moved out. With no one available to care for Barbara's mother at night, she could no longer alternate between day and night shifts as usual. The heart catheterization lab met Barbara's need for a 9-to-5 job.

Barbara's decision to retire in 1995 was precipitated when Duke offered a package that would boost her 12 years of employment to more than 17 years for purposes of calculating her retirement benefits. "Except for this reason, I would not have left, but I decided it was a good idea, because I didn't know what my life would be like over the next five years. Would I stay well? I had my mother to take care of.

"I had to retire to take advantage of Duke's plan. Because I wasn't expecting to leave at that time, I did little planning when I retired. When I left, it was with a mixture of joy, relief and sadness, all at the same time."

One year later, Barbara relished returning to work in the catheterization lab. She had missed the discipline of nursing and medicine. While Barbara was at work, an attendant cared for her mother. The balance of the time, Barbara attended to her mother until her death in 1998. As a retiree, Barbara is limited in the number of hours she can work without affecting her Duke pension. "I can only work 19 hours a week, which is about 2½ days a week, or no more than 999 hours a year.

But working as a part-timer offers Barbara some needed tangible and personal benefits. She's paid at the top of the salary range, and she says that the "good pocket money" supplements her pension, social security and savings.

"I feel more fortunate than many of my friends. Some of them have to do menial work when they want to work because they don't have a skill. I'll do nursing as long as my mind and body hold out. When I leave, I want to go with a good record, so I won't work beyond that point. Then maybe I'll finally take art lessons. This was something I liked to do as a youngster."

> **"I'll do nursing as long as my mind and body hold out. When I leave, I want to go with a good record, so I won't work beyond that point."**

WORKS FOR INTEREST, NOT MONEY

Tom Young

HUMAN RESOURCES MANAGER BECOMES NONPROFIT BUSINESS CONSULTANT

Ever since Tom Young retired 13 years ago from GTE as a human resources manager and in every community in which he's lived since then, he has volunteered for the Executive Service Corps. When Tom returned to the workplace, ESC became his employer.

Tom, and his wife, Pat, graduated together from Dickinson College. After two years of military service, he accumulated a career argosy of 13 corporate moves in 35 years. Tom worked four years at Union Carbide, returned to Dickinson as the paid head of the alumni association, held several other corporate jobs, and in 1966 joined GTE. Though he remained with the same employer for nearly 25 years, he was regularly transferred to different GTE offices in the U.S. In short, he lived a peripatetic corporate lifestyle.

Tom's specialty was human resources. One of his last assignments focused on identifying up-and-comers within the company, whom he recommended for promotion to higher-level jobs. "By 1990, I decided to leave GTE; I was 58 and I felt that I had no more worlds to conquer. Frankly, the job wasn't fun anymore. To make things easier, college and marriage expenses for our four daughters were behind us.

"I told my boss that I wanted to leave. My boss accepted my decision, but he asked me to stay on for one more year to help in moving the corporate offices from Connecticut to Texas." Tom found that the extra year enabled him to better plan for a more orderly transition from workplace to retirement.

During his transitional year, Tom was introduced to the Executive Service Corps and, unlike nearly all other ESC consultants who typically are retired, Tom took on a volunteer assignment while he was still a corporate employee. This project began what has now become a nearly 14-year relationship with ESC. Over the next three years, Tom served in a volunteer capacity as an ESC vice president and resident manager in its Connecticut operation.

The first priority on Tom and Pat's retirement-planning list was deciding whether to remain in Westport, Connecticut, where they had lived for 15

> **Tom began his relationship with the Executive Service Corps before he retired. Two moves and 14 years later, he's still working with ESC—with no end in sight.**

years, or to relocate. Their daughters lived in four different parts of the U.S. The decision was to leave Westport. "We felt that we had outgrown the community, and that it had become too expensive a place to live, particularly on a retirement income." Pat, who had taught high school for many years, had been unable to accumulate a decent pension due to Tom's frequent moves. Planning for their retirement, Tom knew that they could count on income from his pension, Pat's small one, social security and savings.

The couple elected to relocate to Modesto, California, about 50 miles east of San Francisco. One of their daughters and her family lived there. No sooner than they settled in than Tom joined ESC's San Francisco operation, became an active consultant and was elected to its board. ESC wanted to expand its operation in the Bay area, and Tom became the unpaid director of ESC's newly opened office in Modesto.

"After five years, we decided to move back east. One daughter lived in Las Vegas, and another in New York City. As much as we like New York, we couldn't afford the cost. Our fourth daughter lived in Raleigh, and we decided to buy a house there." ESC soon returned as part of Tom's retirement lifestyle.

From his experience with ESC in New York and Connecticut, California and North Carolina, Tom knew many of the organization's national leaders. One of their priorities was to make NESCAN (National Executive Service Corps Affiliate Network), which consists of 24 of the ESC's 32 affiliates, a more viable group. They recruited Tom, this time for a paid management position. The only possible hitch was NESCAN's New York location. "I had no intention of moving to New York so the deal calls for me to be in New York one week a month.

"My assignment is for two years. I see it as a full-time job although I'm paid for a 30-hour workweek. But I really put in more time than that. Except for the monthly trip to New York, I spend the balance of my time in my office at home, where I do my work by phone and e-mail. My job is to formalize the network and to make it work. Fortunately, I don't have to do travel a lot.

"I'm paid more than an honorarium. It's a financial cushion on top of my other retirement income. I've even set up a 401(k) to capture some of it. I'm sure of one thing. I wouldn't have taken this job without the pay."

The question now is what happens in 2004 when Tom's two-year contract ends. Family members differ in their opinions of what Tom will do. "I say I'll quit, but Pat doubts I'll it give up."

A FREE AGENT AT 62

John Wyman
FINDS NEW LIFESTYLE AS EARLY RETIREE

"**M**y wife, Nancy, taught me that you do what you have fun doing," says John Wyman. John credits his wife for setting him in the right direction since he took early retirement from AT&T in 1990 at age 50.

AT&T's buyout program was in many ways too good to turn down. Following graduation from Bowdoin College and military service in Vietnam as a lieutenant in a tank platoon, John worked for AT&T for the next 28 years. As a retirement incentive, the company offered a lifetime health care package and added five years of service, including credit for military service, to the retiring employee's pension calculation.

The only hitch was that John had 30 days in which to make a decision. Even with the incentive to take early retirement, John's income would drop. He talked the matter over with Nancy and their two daughters, one an 18-year-old about to start college and the other a 14-year-old. "It was a tough decision to leave a secure job with a benevolent employer and start out on my own. My family supported me to the fullest, never asking 'did you get another job yet?'"

John was too young to sit on the

> **A buyout let John leave AT&T early. A consultancy allows him to continue working, but maintain his independence.**

sidelines. During his AT&T career, he had moved 12 times and had 22 different management assignments. He didn't want another corporate job with frequent relocations. As an alternative, John became a consultant specializing in what he describes as quality improvement techniques.

John set certain consulting goals. One was to serve no more than five clients at a time. Engelhard Industries, a worldwide precious metal fabricator, became his first and ultimately his only client. Engelhard offered him a deal, asking that John put his consulting business on hold and instead become a full-time contract consultant for the company. John could even have become a full-time Engelhard employee, but the consultancy arrangement would allow him to work independently from his home office and be free of corporate bureaucracy. What's more, John didn't need health care benefits, because they were already part of his AT&T retirement package.

The ensuing nine years of extensive U.S. and overseas business travel offered other advantages. "Nancy could come with me on trips if she wanted. When I visited jewelry manufacturers in Europe, she went along and we combined business with a vacation. However, if I went to grubby mines in Georgia, somehow she had something better to do."

But international business travel has its problems. "I am 6'4" and traveling in tourist class with my knees scrunched against my chin for up to 12 hours wasn't to my liking. I was supposed to be retired and here I was traveling five to six days a week. I had a good investment portfolio that was growing fast [circa 1999]." After moving from New Jersey to North Carolina, John severed his ties with Englehard and made the jump to Koz.Com, a North Carolina-based, dot.com start-up as head of its professional services division.

Two years later in 2001 Koz.com went bankrupt, taking with it John's job and the dream of cashing in on his stock options. This might have caused panic among other 60-year-olds. Not so with John. Being frugal, he was able to adjust to less income.

As an AT&T employee he had contributed the allotted amount to his pension fund, while personally saving an additional 10% of his salary. He doubled his savings to 20% of gross income when he became an Engelhard consultant. He and Nancy live on his AT&T pension, and as of early 2003, on their combined social security income. Touching savings is off limits. "Nancy and I live below our means.

We're cash poor, and we live on less. Nancy might have a new car, but I drive used ones. We take few vacations or expensive trips. A few years ago we traveled to the Amazon, but we don't expect to take another vacation like that one for a long while."

After Koz.com went bust, John found time to volunteer. Besides lecturing at local Small Business Centers and working with SCORE (the Service Corps of Retired Executives; see page 99), John converted an interest in water lilies into a volunteer project. He works about ten to 12 hours a week as an unpaid advisor to the Sarah P. Duke Gardens on the Duke University campus, where he plants lilies in a 55,000 gallon pond, is developing a Website, and lectures on lily ponds to the garden's visitors.

> "I don't have to do commercial work for the money anymore, but more importantly because I find the work interesting."

John now does a limited amount of paid consulting, such as one marketing assignment for a technology company that netted him only $2,000. At 62, he considers himself a free agent who's only looking for a few revenue-making opportunities. "I don't have to do commercial work for the money anymore, but more importantly because I find the work interesting. I want to earn some money to support Nancy and myself, but I only do what pleases me— nothing else. I also wish to follow Nancy's example of the past 15 years by donating time to help nonprofit groups survive."

LIVING HER DREAM—AGAIN

Jackie Wooten
RETIRED, THEN RETURNS TO WORK AS A CLASSROOM TEACHER

Jackie Wooten is an unusual person. Ever since she was a youngster, she wanted to be a teacher. And that's what she's done her entire adult life. No sooner had Jackie retired than she was ready to return to the classroom. Retirement was not to her liking.

"In the past, I was asked why I didn't become a principal, since I'm so well organized. But I have no desire. I get my energy from teaching; it electrifies me. All I ever wanted to be was a classroom teacher."

Eight years later after graduating from the University of North Carolina in Greensboro, Jackie got a master's degree in reading and language arts from East Carolina University. She was certified to teach kindergarten through the fifth grades as well as social studies through the ninth grade. Throughout her 32-year career (and prior to her undergraduate education), Jackie has lived within 30 miles of Greenville in the eastern part of the state. She's taught third and fourth grades in two rural Pitt County communities—24 years in Bethel

Following retirement, Jackie was called back to work due to a teacher shortage. Now, she can have her teaching, her income, and her pension, too.

(population 1,800) and eight years in Stokes (population less than 500).

Jackie's game plan was to retire in her early fifties, collect her pension, and teach part-time, because that would not affect her pension status. When she retired in June, 2002, Jackie was making nearly $50,000 a year, the top of the pay scale.

It was difficult for Jackie to retire. "I don't play bridge or do things like that. I've always worked. I'm happy when I'm busy. I hoped when I retired that I would teach part-time, but I was called back to teach full-time in Stokes."

A temporary change in state law serendipitously permitted Jackie to return to the classroom as a full-time teacher. North Carolina, like most states, has a teacher shortage, and it sweetened the pot to attract veteran teachers. Almost six months to the day after she retired and received her pension, Jackie was back in the classroom as a paid teacher.

"Sure, I'm double-dipping. I'm being paid to teach, and I also get my pension. But there's a shortage of teachers. I can double-dip for another year, and then I'll lose that eligibility. By then, I expect the state will change the ruling again due to the continuing lack of qualified teachers." Besides earning more than $85,000 in combined pension and teaching salary, Jackie is eligible for paid vacation, sick leave and a bonus.

Even before her current full-time teaching assignment started, Jackie, then retired, was working twice a week as a volunteer remediation teacher at Bethel Elementary School, helping below-level students improve their reading and math skills. She also taught without pay for a friend who was on leave from her classroom following her husband's death. "These were the best three weeks of teaching in my life. I had no meetings, no clubs or any other duties. Just teach the kids. That's why I went into teaching."

> "I get my energy from teaching. It electrifies me. All I ever wanted to be was a classroom teacher."

During the summers for the past eight years, Jackie was a teacher and site manager at the North Carolina Teacher Academy, which runs week-long training institutes. "I'm paid $200 a day and I do this for four weeks."

A North Carolina Education Association activist, Jackie has attended 25 National Education Association conventions, which gives her a chance to travel since her husband, Kenneth,

doesn't enjoy it. Jackie also conducts training sessions for other state NEA affiliates. "There's no pay, but I get reimbursed for expenses. It's a chance to interact with teachers from other states."

In 1992 and 1996, Jackie was a delegate to the Democratic national conventions, and early on in Jackie's "retirement," she considered running for the state House of Representatives. She decided against it after researching the amount of money needed to run for the position. "I was also concerned about the length of the legislative session and decided that I didn't want to commit that much time to politics." However, she has continued in her political and community involvement as Bethel's precinct chairman for the Democratic Party.

Jackie's enthusiasm for her profession seems to have influenced her twin sons, who have both set their post-college sights on teaching. One son intends to teach high school in Pitt County where the Wootens live. Jackie says that she can see her other son getting a doctorate and teaching at the college level. So, ultimately, Jackie's love of teaching will be carried on by one or both of her sons.

How Will You Foot the Bills?

T**HE PRIMARY THRUST OF THIS BOOK IS TO HELP** you answer the question, "What will I do if I retire?" Questions that may be looming equally large in your mind are, "How much money will I need to live in retirement?" "Do I have enough?" and "Where is it going to come from?" While whole books have been written on these subjects, this isn't one of them. This book would be the perfect companion to a book on financial planning for retirement and to one on managing your investments to meet your goals. We recommend some appropriate resources in the box on page 40. And, of course, you've gotten at least a glimpse of how each person profiled in this book is financing his or her "retirement."

That said, this section will help you begin to assess the current and future status of your nest egg and the income it will provide you in retirement. You may realize that the funds you've accumulated for retirement are, in fact, enough and you can devote your energies to developing your new life in "retirement." Maybe you can afford to retire early and devote yourself to an unpaid labor of love or to work for the sheer joy of it, without regard to income. Perhaps accepting a buyout offer will provide the funds necessary to supercharge your retirement nest egg, allowing you ultimately to retire early, if not immediately. You may realize that if you just hang on for another few years and increase your rate of saving and investing, you can afford the travel you had always hoped for. You may learn that you're going to need to work after you retire, but maybe not the 50-hour weeks you've been putting in for the past 15 or 20 years.

The Income You Will Need

No two individual or family budgets are the same. What one family calls "just getting by" is luxurious living for someone else. However, one common rule of thumb is that you will need 80% of your preretirement income to maintain your "standard of living" after your regular paychecks stop. Some people may be able to do what they want on 70% or 75%, but unless you're looking forward to a more Spartan life than before, aim for the higher figure to help ensure that you'll achieve your retirement lifestyle dream.

Accounting for Future Dollars

The 80% of your income that you will need annually in the future isn't 80% of your income today. It's 80% of your income at the point when you are ready to retire, whether that's a year away, or five, ten or 15 years from now. The further out you're looking, the more your income is likely to grow due to raises and cost-of-living increases, and the less your purchasing power will be, due to inflation. All of this adds up to the need for a bigger nest egg than you might think. But you don't have to panic. The same forces that make your needs grow will help your nest egg grow, too.

How Long Will You Live?

Knowing how much money you will need in retirement also depends on how long you're going to need it—ten years, 20, 30 or even 40? Life expectancy is on the rise; the average woman retiring today at age 65 is expected to live another 19 years, and the average man can look forward to another 16 years. Those who have just entered the 50-plus crowd can expect to live even longer.

Assessing Your Resources

The cornerstone of your retirement nest egg is likely to be your pension (or other employer-provided defined-*benefit* plan) or a 401(k) or 403(b) (or other defined-*contribution* plan), together with social security. The rest of the gap between preretirement and postretirement income will be filled in by your own savings and investments, and from other resources such as profit from the sale of your home. If you're close to normal retirement age, you've probably accumulated a substantial chunk of your retirement savings. You may know precisely what you can expect from your pension and social security, but you may not be fully aware of all the resources available to you, or even how to figure out how long you can expect your nest egg to last. If you're just 50-plus, you've probably got a retirement savings plan under way and you just need time as your ally to fill it up and out. This section will show you what a difference you can make.

AVERAGE REMAINING LIFETIME

Average Number of Years of Life Remaining

Age	Male	Female
40	36.7	41.0
45	32.2	36.3
50	27.9	31.8
55	23.8	27.4
60	19.9	23.1
65	16.3	19.2
70	13.0	15.5
75	10.1	12.1
80	7.6	9.1
85	5.6	6.7

Source: *National Vital Statistics Reports*, Volume 51, Number 3; December 19, 2002; from the Centers for Disease Control and Prevention/Division of Vital Statistics. Based on 1990 U.S. Census data, year 2000 final mortality statistics, and data from the Medicare program.

Your Pension

The traditional defined-benefit pension plan is becoming increasingly rare. Many companies have switched to cash balance plans, which combine the protections of a traditional pension with the portability of a 401(k) plan. Under such plans, each year an amount equal to a percentage of your salary—say 5%—goes into the account. The money is guaranteed to earn a predetermined interest rate, usually tied to an index such as the consumer-price index or the Treasury-bill rate. If plan investments earn less than the promised interest rate, the employer must make up the difference. If they earn more, the excess counts toward the next year's contribution and reduces the employer's out-of-pocket cost.

Because the employer's contribution is based on a percentage of your current salary, benefits in a cash-balance plan grow more evenly over the years than those in a traditional pension plan, in which benefits are weighted more heavily toward your last years on the job. When employees leave the job, they can take a lump-sum payout of the account balance and roll it into an IRA. If they are of retirement age, it can be made into an annuity.

Traditional defined-benefit plans guarantee to pay you a specified amount when you retire based on your salary, age and years of service. Chances are that if your company still has a traditional defined-benefit plan or you've been contemplating leaving early, you've already received an estimate of your monthly pension benefit from your company's pension administrator. If you haven't yet received this information, you might be interested in knowing how a traditional defined-benefit pension is typically calculated. The formula looks like this:

final average monthly earnings x 1.5% x years of service (the benefit accrual rate) = monthly benefit due

Final average monthly earnings might be the average of the five consecutive years you earned the most—that will probably be your last five (add income for each of the five years and divide by 60 months).

So, for example, if you have worked for 30 years, your benefit accrual rate is 45%. If your final average monthly earnings is $5,000, then you would get $2,250 per month.

What percentage of your preretirement income will your pension likely replace? The answer varies greatly by employer, but a typical benefit is 50% of income at retirement minus 50% of social security, which works out to 37% of income for a 30-year worker retiring at a salary level of $50,000. Usually the longer you stay on at work, the greater the percentage of replacement, though there is usually a maximum period of service allowed for the computation.

To receive the maximum pension, most plans require that you work at the company for 30 years and wait until "full retirement age," which is usually 62 or 65. (Note that your company's definition of "full retirement age" may differ from social

WHEN YOU CAN RECEIVE FULL BENEFITS

Year of Birth	Age Years	Plus Months
pre–1938	65	0
1938	65	2
1939	65	4
1940	65	6
1941	65	8
1942	65	10
1943–54	66	0
1955	66	2
1956	66	4
1957	66	6
1958	66	8
1959	66	10
1960 and later	67	0

security's.) Some companies use a point system that lets you retire at full benefits once your age plus years of service total a certain number of points. An early retiree would probably see benefits reduced, depending on his or her age.

Social Security

In 2003 you can begin collecting your full social security benefits at age 65 and 2 months. Full retirement age will continue to increase until it reaches 67 in 2027 (see the table above). For an estimate of your social security benefit based on your earnings history, request a personalized benefits estimate from the Social Security Administration. Call 800-772-1213 and ask for Form SSA-7004, "Request for Social Security Statement." You should receive your estimate in about two to four weeks. The estimate you receive will be based on your retiring at age 62, retiring at full retirement age, and waiting to retire at age 70. (The SSA has begun automatically sending the benefits estimate annually to everyone age 25 and over.) You may also log onto www.ssa.gov and use online tools to create estimates based on your earnings.

The soonest you can begin collecting monthly social security checks is age 62, but if you do, your benefits will be reduced by as much as 30% for life. Using the table below, you can calculate your reduced benefit. Multiply your estimated benefit at full retirement age by the reduction percentage for the number of months early that you plan to retire. (On the other hand, if you expect to delay retirement, see the discussion on page 266–267.)

Once you begin receiving social security benefits, your spouse can also receive benefits based on your record, even if he or she never worked in a job covered by social security. A nonworking spouse is eligible to begin receiving benefits at age 62. At your full retirement age, you will together receive 150% of what you would receive on your own.

If your spouse works, he or she will receive a benefit based on his or her actual earnings or 50% of your benefit, whichever is more, assuming that you're the first one to retire.

Other Current Savings

Add up what you've got socked away in any of the following, whether yours or your spouse's:

HOW EARLY RETIREMENT WILL REDUCE YOUR BENEFITS

Months Early	% of Full Benefit	Months Early	% of Full Benefit
2	98.9%	32	82.2%
4	97.8	34	81.1
6	96.7	36	80.0
8	95.6	38*	79.2
10	94.4	40*	78.3
12	93.3	42*	77.5
14	92.2	44*	76.7
16	91.1	46*	75.8
18	90.0	48*	75.0
20	88.9	50*	74.2
22	87.8	52*	73.3
24	86.7	54*	72.5
26	85.6	56*	71.7
28	84.4	58*	70.8
30	83.3	60*	70.0

* As full retirement age rises to age 67, these early retirement percentages will apply.

- **profit-sharing or any other company-sponsored defined-benefit plans**
- **401(k) or 403(b) plans**
- **individual retirement accounts (IRAs)**
- **Keogh plans**
- **other retirement savings**

Your Home

And don't forget the house. If you own a house and plan to use the equity in it to help finance your retirement, you're further along to your goal. Of course, for a realistic picture, you'll need to subtract from your home's market value any mortgage you expect to still owe at retirement, sales commissions and closing costs, and any part of proceeds of the sale of the home you'll use for the down payment on a retirement home. Thanks to a provision in the Tax Act of 1997, chances are you won't have to pay a dime in taxes on the profit when you sell (see page 264), so anything remaining can be added to your nest egg.

Figuring the Gap

Let's say that you're age 62 in 2003 and you plan to retire from your employer of 32 years at age 65. Your spouse, a late-blooming professional five years younger than you, expects to continue working for four years after that.

Your current salary is $60,000, and you expect a 4% cost-of-living increase for each of the next three years ($2,400 in year one, $2,496 in year two, and $2,596 in year three), putting your preretirement income at $67,492.

Your spouse's current income is $40,000 per year. Between merit raises and cost-of-living increases, you think that he or she can reasonably expect an average income increase of 7% for each of the eight years until he or she reaches retirement, setting his or her preretirement income at $68,800. For the first five years of your retirement, you will need to replace 80% of your annual preretirement income, or $53,994 per year ($67,492 x .80) and in the following 20 years, 80% of your and your wife's preretirement income, or $109,034 per year ([$67,492 + $68,800] x .80).

Now, where's that money going to come from?

Social Security and Pension Benefits

THE FIRST FIVE YEARS. Per our calculations using the quick estimate feature at the social security Website, your annual social security benefit will be $18,072 ($1,506 a month x 12; for the purposes
of this example only, the monthly figure is based on estimated
social security benefits for the year 2003).

You know that your annual pension benefit will come to
$24,710 (50% of preretirement income minus 50% of social secu-
rity; [.50 x $67,492] – [.50 x $18,702]).

HOW A LUMP SUM WILL GROW

This table is useful for anticipating how money you've already accumulated
will grow over various lengths of time at various rates of return, compounded annually. Choose the appropriate number of years from the left-
hand column and the assumed rate of return from across the top,
and multiply the starting amount by the factor that's shown where the two
columns intersect. For example, say that you have $20,000 in a mutual fund that
you expect will pay 12% per year for the next 8 years. At the end of that time,
you'll have $49,600 ($20,000 x 2.48).

Future Growth Factor

Year	3%	4%	5%	6%	7%	8%	9%	10%	11%	12%	13%	14%	15%
1	1.03	1.04	1.05	1.06	1.07	1.08	1.09	1.10	1.11	1.12	1.13	1.14	1.15
2	1.06	1.08	1.10	1.12	1.14	1.17	1.19	1.21	1.23	1.25	1.28	1.30	1.32
3	1.09	1.12	1.16	1.19	1.22	1.26	1.29	1.33	1.37	1.40	1.44	1.48	1.52
4	1.12	1.17	1.22	1.26	1.31	1.36	1.41	1.46	1.52	1.57	1.63	1.69	1.75
5	1.16	1.22	1.28	1.34	1.40	1.47	1.54	1.61	1.69	1.76	1.84	1.93	2.01
6	1.19	1.26	1.34	1.42	1.50	1.59	1.68	1.77	1.87	1.97	2.08	2.19	2.31
7	1.23	1.32	1.41	1.50	1.61	1.71	1.83	1.95	2.08	2.21	2.35	2.50	2.66
8	1.27	1.37	1.48	1.59	1.72	1.85	1.99	2.14	2.30	2.48	2.66	2.85	3.06
9	1.30	1.42	1.55	1.69	1.84	2.00	2.17	2.36	2.56	2.77	3.00	3.25	3.52
10	1.34	1.48	1.63	1.79	1.97	2.16	2.37	2.59	2.84	3.11	3.39	3.71	4.05
15	1.56	1.80	2.08	2.40	2.76	3.17	3.64	4.18	4.78	5.40	6.25	7.14	8.14
20	1.81	2.19	2.65	3.21	3.87	4.66	5.60	6.73	8.06	9.65	11.52	13.74	16.37
25	2.09	2.66	3.39	4.29	5.43	6.85	8.62	10.83	13.59	17.00	21.23	26.46	32.92
30	2.43	3.24	4.32	5.74	7.61	10.06	13.27	17.45	22.89	29.96	39.12	50.95	66.21

Between what you will get from your pension and social security, you will have accounted for $42,782 per year, which is short by $11,212 of your estimated need of $53,994.

THE NEXT 20 YEARS. Now your spouse retires and claims his or her social security benefit; he or she doesn't have a traditional defined-benefit plan, but we'll account for the value of his or her deferred profit-sharing later.

When your spouse retires, he or she will also be considered a higher-than-average wage earner and qualifies for an annual benefit of $19,812 ($1,651 x 12).

You and your spouse's combined annual income from social security and your pension benefit thereafter will be $62,594 ($18,072 + $24,710 + 19,812). That leaves you with a $46,440 gap between your needs and what your defined benefits will provide ($109,034 − $62,594).

Your Retirement Savings and Investments

How will you fill that gap? Let's look at the retirement savings and investments that will be available following your retirement:

- **Deferred profit sharing.** You estimate that account at retirement will hold $256,448. You plan to take the money and reinvest it.
- **Your individual retirement account.** By the time you retire, your IRA will be worth $26,000.
- **Investment portfolio.** Over the years you've invested in blue-chip stocks and bonds currently valued at $250,000. At an 8% rate of growth, you estimate that your portfolio will be worth $315,000 in three years ($250,000 x 1.26; see the table at left for an explanation of how to figure money growth).

That gives you a lump sum of $597,448. Off the top you draw about $60,000 to cover the annual income gap of $11,212 you'll have the first five years and put it in a money-market IRA. You leave the rest to cook until your spouse's retirement; at 8% per year for five years, you'll end up with $790,049 ($537,448 x 1.47).

THE NEXT 20 YEARS. You estimate that when your spouse retires, he or she will have $125,592 in his or her 401(k) plan and

$36,000 in an IRA, making your total assets $951,641.

Your Home

Finally, let's consider one more resource: your home. When your spouse retires, you are planning to sell your suburban home and move back to your hometown. Your home's current value is $358,500, and you believe you can expect a 3% average rate of appreciation each of the next eight years. By the time you're ready to sell, the house should be worth about $455,000 ($358,500 x 1.27 [for money-growth factors, see the table on page 262]). Your mortgage is paid off. Thanks to the 1997 tax act, which exempts from taxation $500,000 in profit from the sale of a home for those filing joint returns ($250,000 is tax-free for those who file single returns), you'll pocket the whole sales price, except for commissions and other sales expenses. That's $416,637 ($455,000 sales price minus $38,363 for commissions and other expenses). You know that you can purchase the home you want in your hometown for $160,000 in cash. That leaves you $256,637 to pad your investment portfolio.

The Final Tally: How Long Will It Last?

You now have a grand total of $1,208,278. Will it generate the income that isn't covered by social security and your pension? And how long will it last? You can use the table on page 266 to figure that out.

You know that you need to come up with $46,440 a year ($3,870 per month) for 20 years. You expect that your nest egg will continue to earn 8% annually. The point where 20 years and 8% intersects is $119,550. That's the amount needed to produce $1,000 in income per month for 20 years. (The $1,000 will be exhausted at the end of the period.) Because your monthly requirement is 3.87 times that amount ($3,870 ÷ $1,000), multiply $119,550 by 3.87 and you get a total nest-egg requirement of $462,658. You have more than twice that!

But wait: Before you assume that you're on easy street, keep in mind that you need to account for what inflation will do to your nest egg over those 20 years. A safe rule of thumb is to add 25% to 40% to your total nest egg as an inflation cushion. In this example, that would bring the total required nest egg to between $578,323 and $647,721 [$462,658 x 1.25=$578,323); $462,658 x 1.40 = $647,721]. So, even with inflation, your nest egg is more than sufficient.

Taxes will also take a bite out of your retirement income. The taxes you pay will depend upon many variables including: your tax bracket in retirement; the extent to which your social security benefits will be subject to income tax; the share of your income that comes from savings that have already been taxed; and how long you postpone withdrawing funds from tax-deferred accounts, such as 401(k)s and IRAs. In the early part of your retirement, you and your spouse might depend on your investment portfolio, on which you've paid income tax right along. If you delay tapping your IRAs and deferred profit-sharing for as long as possible—or until age 70½, when you must begin to withdraw the money—those accounts can continue growing tax-deferred, and you put off the inevitable tax bill. (If you start a Roth IRA, or convert a traditional IRA to a Roth, you avoid the tax bill altogether, and there is no requirement to begin withdrawals at age 70½.)

Regardless, you're lucky. You've got some options. Maybe you would like to retire now, rather than later. Maybe your spouse would like to retire earlier than planned. Maybe you'll be able to do things in retirement that you hadn't imagined. You could give more to your favorite charities or leave more to the kids. Bottom line, you don't have to worry if you live longer than expected.

Ways to Fill in a Gap

Well, nice for the guy in our example, but what if you end up with a gap that you must fill?

YOU CAN RETIRE ANYWAY AND SEEK OUT A NEW WORK ARRANGEMENT. Look for a situation that offers some of the satisfactions of retirement—say, a more flexible schedule—as well as income. This book is filled with examples of people happily pursuing this strategy, whether they have started a business,

HOW BIG A NEST EGG YOU NEED TO COVER AN INCOME GAP

Years in Retirement	Savings Needed to Permit Monthly Withdrawals of $1,000 at Each Rate of Return							
	5%	6%	7%	8%	9%	10%	12%	14%
5	$52,990	$51,730	$50,500	$49,320	$48,170	$47,060	$44,960	$42,980
10	94,280	90,070	86,130	82,420	78,940	75,670	69,700	64,410
15	126,460	118,500	111,250	104,640	98,590	93,060	83,320	75,090
20	151,530	139,580	128,980	119,550	111,140	103,620	90,820	80,420
25	171,060	155,210	141,490	129,560	119,160	110,050	94,950	83,070
30	186,280	166,790	150,310	136,280	124,280	113,950	97,220	84,400

become consultants (in some cases selling their services back to their former employer), chosen to work part-time, turned volunteer interests into paid positions or created other options.

You can postpone leaving your current employer beyond your hoped-for retirement age. This option will allow you to contribute more to your savings and investments for as long as necessary, and while you're at it, be thinking about and planning for what you will do next.

YOU CAN RETIRE ANYWAY AND LOWER YOUR POSTRETIREMENT STANDARD OF LIVING. Some 50-plusers may take certain steps in this direction anyway, by simplifying their lives. For example, some 50-plusers whose kids are out of the house may trade in their larger, high-maintenance home for a smaller, lower-maintenance one. From their point of view, they're not lowering their standard of living, but improving it.

YOU CAN GAMBLE THAT HIGHER-RISK INVESTMENTS WILL PROVIDE YOU WITH HIGHER RETURNS, NOT LOSSES. This isn't a smart idea if you don't have plenty of time to recoup a loss. This advice applies to business start-ups, too (see Chapter 7).

YOU CAN WAIT TO CASH IN ON SOCIAL SECURITY. Social security now offers a bonus, the delayed-retirement credit (shown in the table on the next page), for each year that you continue working or delay applying for social security past your full retirement age. This can mean significantly larger monthly checks when you do decide to call it quits or cash in. Of course, the longer you work, the larger the wage base that your benefit will be calculated on to begin with. Plus, for every year you wait to collect your benefit, the bonus is compounded; that is, each year's bonus percentage is applied to the base benefit plus any previous years' bonuses that you've already earned. And that's on top of cost-of-living increases in social security, if any. A financial planner, accountant or the Social Security Administration can help you figure out how waiting will boost the size of your nest egg.

If You Work and Collect Social Security

Until you reach full retirement age (65 and 2 months in 2003), if you work and collect social security, the government takes away some of your social security benefits if your earned income exceeds certain limits. In 2003, if you're age 62 through the year before you reach full retirement age, the government reclaims $1 of benefits for every $2 you earn over $11,520; if you reach full retirement age in 2003, the limit is $30,720. In the year up to the month in which you reach full retirement age, the government deducts $1 of every $3 you earn. In the month that you reach full retirement age you will receive full benefits no matter how much you earn.

THE LATE-RETIREMENT BONUS	
Year You Were Born	**Annual Bonus for Working Beyond Full Retirement Age**
1929–30	4.5%
1931–32	5.0
1933–34	5.5
1935–36	6.0
1937–38	6.5
1939–40	7.0
1941–42	7.5
1943 or later	8.0

If you are collecting social security, or soon will be, you won't be alone if you view that as an unfair "tax" on top of your regular income taxes. You'll find that many social security beneficiaries profiled in this book have limited their paid work to avoid being "shorted" on the money they're due. But believe it or not, the final effect of the earnings limit isn't as bad as most people think it is. That's because it's offset by the delayed-retirement credit, described above, and something called automatic benefit recomputation.

Let's say you're 63 and you earned $50,000 in 2003 from a

THINKING OF RELOCATING?

A common consideration in planning for retirement is whether to move to a new location. The motivation may be to live closer to family members, to achieve a new lifestyle, to return to a home from years past, or to live someplace that's always been a dream. Whatever your reason, ask yourself these questions while making the decision.

- **Most important, why are you moving?** Moving under any circumstances is wrenching and a lot of work. Moving for less than well-considered reasons may be an expensive boondoggle.

- **Is the climate comfortable** for you on a year-round basis?

- **Will this be your only residence,** or will you maintain another?

- **Are any members of your immediate family nearby?** (That could be a plus or a minus, depending on how you feel about your family members.)

- **Do you make friends easily?**

- **How many miles from where you're now living** is the new location? Does that matter?

- **Is the area served by a major airline,** not only for your convenience but for that of family and friends who want to visit?

- **How do you rate the area's health care facilities?** Do you have any special needs they can't provide for?

- **Are cultural and sports facilities available** for those activities you enjoy?

- **Are there opportunities for part-time and volunteer work** of the sort you desire?

- **Have you already spent some time in the area**—preferably during different times of the year? It's not smart to invest in an unknown quantity.

consulting job. That's enough to eliminate all $14,000 of your social security benefits ($50,000 − $14,000 = $36,000; $36,000 ÷ 2 = $18,000). But because you didn't get any benefits, the government treats you as if you had delayed applying for social security by one year, and your future benefits will be hiked by 5% (see the table on page 267). That would add about $700 a year

($14,000 x .05)—plus future cost-of-living increases on that amount—to your benefits for the rest of your life. This will apply each year that your benefits are withheld before you reach age 70.

Even so, this bonus doesn't entirely make up for the loss of benefits you'll incur. Assuming an average lifespan, the higher benefits resulting from the credit will pay back just over half of what you lose to the earnings test. As you can see from the table, the situation will improve over the years for younger 50-plusers, with the credit rising to 8% for those retiring in 2008.

The practice of automatic benefit recomputation helps if, in a year when you lose benefits, your annual earnings exceed the lowest yearly income (adjusted for inflation) originally used to figure your monthly benefit. Plugging a higher number into the formula pays off in a higher level of benefits. That can be particularly valuable if you have fewer than 35 years of employment. In that case, your earnings after retirement would replace a year without earnings earlier in your life.

While you may want to review your income-producing plans with a financial adviser, your choice on this issue may ultimately come down to principle: You'll have to decide which means more to you—working for pay or collecting the full amount of the social security you're due. It's up to you.

Using the Equity in Your Home

The Tax Act of 1997 included a wonderful break for home owners. It excludes up to $500,000 of profit on the sale of every principal residence you own—provided you've occupied it for at least two of the last five years prior to the sale—if you file a joint return ($250,000 is tax-free if you file a single return). Until that new law was enacted, those over age 55 had a one-time opportunity to take the first $125,000 of profit on the sale tax-free. And there were other restrictions, as well.

If you own your home outright, another way to get at your equity in it is a reverse mortgage. A lending institution sends you a monthly check against the equity in your home. The older you are when you apply for a reverse mortgage, the more money you're likely to get, because you won't be around as long to collect the monthly checks. When you sell, move or die, the loan

AN EARLY-RETIREMENT WORKSHEET

I f you want to retire early, as many of the people profiled in this book did, you'll have to figure out not only how much of a nest egg you will have by the time you want to leave but also how much of it will be available to you then. The worksheet on these pages will help you with your planning.

HOW MUCH INCOME WILL YOU NEED?

First calculate your income goal at retirement. Multiply your current salary by a future-growth factor from the table on page 262. For example, use 4% estimated annual inflation and add that to the amount you expect your salary to rise each year, say 3%, for a total of 7%. If you want to retire early in 10 years, look where 7% intersects 10 years and you find the multiplier 1.97.

Multiplying that by your current salary—say, $50,000—tells you what you'll be earning ($98,500 in this example) at the point you want to retire. Figure on needing 80% of that once you retire, and you arrive at an annual income goal after early retirement of $78,800.

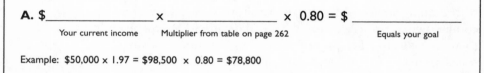

A. $_____ × _____ × 0.80 = $ _____

   Your current income   Multiplier from table on page 262   Equals your goal

Example: $50,000 × 1.97 = $98,500 × 0.80 = $78,800

---

comes due. The lender repays itself the balance of your loan plus interest from the proceeds of the sale of your home. The disadvantages of reverse mortgages are the costs associated with getting one and the relatively high interest rate. That's why it's wise to compare the pros and cons of a reverse mortgage with those of a home-equity loan or a second mortgage. However, it can be a good alternative for people with little monthly income who would probably not qualify for a home-equity loan. And, if you do get a reverse mortgage, you'll want to make use of it for long enough (say, not less than five years) to lessen the impact of its costs and maximize its benefits. For more information, contact the National Center for Home Equity Conversion (360 N. Robert, #403, Saint Paul MN 55101; www.reverse.org) or AARP's Home Equity Information Center (601 E St., N.W., Washington, DC 20049; www.aarp.org/revmort).

AN EARLY-RETIREMENT WORKSHEET

ANTICIPATED RESOURCES AT CRUCIAL AGES

One of the obstacles to early retirement is that you can't count on all your long-term savings and investments to kick in with income right from the start. You also won't be eligible for medicare until 65 and will have to find some way to cover your health insurance needs until then.

The worksheet below reflects the fact that employer pension benefits are rarely available before age 55, that social security benefits can't start before age 62 and that IRA funds, except contributions made to a Roth IRA, are generally tied up until age 59½. (Regular IRA funds can be tapped earlier if the money is taken via roughly equal installments based on your life expectancy. To use this loophole, you must stick with the lifetime payout schedule for at least five consecutive years and until you're at least 59½. For more information, consult IRS publications #590, *Individual Retirement Accounts,* and #575, *Pension and Annuity Income.*)

To determine whether you can live on the investment income (before pension and social-security payments and certain retirement-fund money become available) without depleting capital, multiply your assets by the percent you believe they can earn each year—the example below assumes an 8% earnings rate.

			Target Age			
			50-54	55-59	60-62	62-plus
1. Savings	\$_____	X 0.08 = \$_____	\$_____	\$_____	\$_____	
2. Home equity	\$_____	X 0.08 = \$_____	\$_____	\$_____	\$_____	
3. IRAs*	\$_____	X 0.08 = \$___NA___	\$___NA___	\$_____	\$_____	
4. Keoghs	\$_____	X 0.08 = \$___NA___	\$_____	\$_____	\$_____	
5. 401(k)s	\$_____	X 0.08 = \$___NA___	\$_____	\$_____	\$_____	
6. Pension**	\$_____	= \$___NA___	\$_____	\$_____	\$_____	
7. Soc. security**	\$_____	= \$___NA___	\$___NA___	\$___NA___	\$_____	
B. Column totals		\$_____	\$_____	\$_____	\$_____	
C. Shortfall (A minus B)		\$_____	\$_____	\$_____	\$_____	

*You can withdraw your own contributions to the new Roth IRA penalty-free anytime before age 59½.
**When they become available, your pension and social security benefits form the cornerstone of your retirement income. It's assumed you will not be investing them.